¡No Se Vende!
Water as a Right of the Commons

¡No Se Vende!
Water as a Right of the Commons

By Kay Matthews

ACEQUIA MADRE

P•R•E•S•S

First Edition 2018

ISBN 978-0-940875-11-1

Library of Congress Control Number: 2018905868

Printed in the United States

Photographs by Kay Matthews unless otherwise attributed

Cover and Design by Kay Matthews

ACEQUIA MADRE P•R•E•S•S
162 El Valle Road
Chamisal, New Mexico

Dedicated to the memory of Tomás, Arsenio, Orlando Montoya and Mark Schiller (all pictured on the cover).

CONTENTS

Prologue/11

Preface/13

Introduction: Managing the Commons/17

One
From the Commons to the State/23

Two
Becoming a Parciante/28

Three
Acequias—Organize!/33

Four
Filing a Water Transfer Protest/40

Five
We First Find Out About Top of the World/46

Six
Instream Flow/50

Seven
Protecting Acequia Pre-existing Rights on Federal Land/56

Eight
San Luis Valley Water Wars/63

Nine
Lomos Altos Water Transfer Protest/67

Ten
With Dedication *and* Dysfunction, the Acequias Persevere/75

Eleven
Will Top of the World Water Get a New Destination?/79

Twelve
2003 State Statute Gives Acequias More Power to Protect Water Rights/84

Thirteen
State Water Plan/92

Fourteen
State Engineer's "Proposed Active Water Resource Management
Regulations"/97

Fifteen
Pueblo Water Rights Doctrine/102

Sixteen
Women of El Norte/107

Seventeen
Taos County Regional Water Plan and Public Welfare/112

Eighteen
Abeyta, or Taos Pueblo Adjudication/118

Nineteen
"Taking On" Los Alamos National Laboratory/126

Twenty
Aamodt Adjudication and Top of the World Saga Continues/132

Twenty-one
Acequias Once Again Confront Forest Service Over Access Rights/139

Twenty-two
Acequias de la Sierra/144

Twenty-three
The Pueblo of Picuris/150

Twenty-four
Take Me For a Walk in El Valle/157

Twenty-five
Aamodt Again/164

Twenty-six
Ski Area Expansions in the Southwest/168

Twenty-seven
The Mother of All Water Rights Adjudications?/178

Twenty-eight
The Drought Hits Home in El Valle/186

Twenty-nine
How Not to Manage Water in a Drought/191

Thirty
Taos County Public Welfare Advisory Committee:
Abeyta Movidas Revealed/198

Thirty-one
Backlash/206

Thirty-two
How Far Can a Lawyerless Protestant Get?/209

Thirty-three
Dam the Gila River?/215

Thirty-four
Acequia Madre Objects to Terms of the Abeyta Settlement/218

Thirty-five
Top of World Transfer Application Finally Filed/224

Thirty-six
San Augustin Plains Water Grab/229

Thirty-seven
Maintaining Traditional Acequia Systems in a World of Technological
Fixes/232

Thirty-eight
TOW Water Transfer Goes to a Hearing/238

Thirty-nine
Deadline Looms: Will the Aamodt Meet the Terms?/243

Forty
The Abeyta Settlement Gets Even More Contentious/249

Conclusion/255

Prologue

Thirty years before I moved to El Valle, a small village in the southeast corner of Taos County, the people of Taos rose up to defend themselves against the development of the Indian Camp Dam and the establishment of a conservancy district that was conceived to impound the dam waters from a river southeast of the town in the Pot Creek area. These folks did their homework and knew the history of conservancy districts in New Mexico in both the middle and lower Rio Grande basins: control of the water passes from communities and acequias to often politically appointed boards that end up disenfranchising small farmers and underwriting development. The Tres Ríos Association fought the conservancy—pushed by then State Engineer Steve Reynolds, the Bureau of Reclamation (the agency that would build the dam), and Taos bankers, lawyers, and developers—for nine years.

John Nichols, well-known Taoseño writer, was an active conservancy opponent and wrote numerous articles in the muckraking Santa Fe newspaper *The New Mexico Review*. In the July 1972 issue he said:

"The fact is, the history of Conservancy disasters in New Mexico, in which the small Chicano farmer has always been the fall guy, is lengthy and depressing. It can be summed up in these words from noted sociologist Dr. Clark Knowlton: 'Every major irrigation or water conservation project along the Rio Grande River, from Elephant Butte Dam to the Middle Rio Grande Conservancy district, has been responsible for land alienation on an extensive scale. The Spanish-Americans have been replaced by Anglo-American farmers. Their subsistence agriculture has made way for a highly commercial, partially subsidized, and basically insecure agriculture made possible by government programs. Little thought has ever been given to the rights and land use patterns of the Spanish-Americans in planning water projects in New Mexico and in neighboring states.' "[1]

The proposed Rancho del Rio Grande Conservancy District in Taos was rather ridiculous if the goal was to turn more land into agricultural production. A large area slated for "new water," what is now the subdivided Weimer Estates of Taos, was already mostly owned by developers, businesses, real estate companies, and bankers who had no interest in turning over their properties to agriculture.

Eventually the district court approved the Rancho del Rio Grande Conservancy District but the New Mexico Supreme Court overturned that decision on a technicality. After the La Serna Land Grant voted to be excluded from the district, the conservancy proponents found additional lands to replace those of the grant, but the law required that if there was a change in the make-up of the district it had to be dissolved first and than reconstituted. While the decision wasn't a validation of the argument against the conservancy, it did plant a seed in John Nichols' creative brain and we got *The Milagro Beanfield War*, where Joe Mondragón fights the conservancy dam by planting a beanfield. Twenty years later there are other Joe Mondragóns out there planting many more beanfields as I hope this book will demonstrate.

Preface

"As April slides into May in the upper Sangre de Cristo watershed I'm thankful for whatever green I get: the pasture grass first, emerging almost overnight into clumps of mixed brome, rye, timothy, and various unidentified shoots. The apricot trees in the orchard are just breaking into bloom, with an intrinsic knowledge that any flower display before the end of April is a fool's game (and they were indeed zapped last Thursday night). The ornamental forsythia at the front door flaunts this rule but unlike the apricot doesn't have to prove its worth in fruit; its justification is its persistent yellow beauty. The unrelenting wind makes Eliot's declaration of April being the cruelest month manifest by threatening to rip the hoop house plastic from its tenuous hold on its PVC frame.

Hoop house in early May snowstorm

The irrigation water in my first-in-line village starts flowing around the same time, depending on the commissioners' adherence to formal tradition—the water isn't released until the acequia is cleaned—or informal tradition—whoever has a direct line to the commissioners gets the water whenever they don't have it.

Although my village lies only a few miles away from Picuris Pueblo, whose priority date is 'time immemorial,' there is no question that we are literally 'first in use' in my valley, as the New Mexico Water Code defines priority administration of water rights. With a priority date in the 1700s this village on the Rio de las Trampas gets the water first as it flows from the high Pecos peaks directly through the pastures and gardens of the village parciantes. We are allotted a certain amount for irrigation, although no meters, only gauges measure the surcos that traditionally correspond to shovel widths of water flowing through our three presas, or diversion dams, on the river.

Yet the concept of 'priority date' implies that the water we use we own, which is contrary to the way the acequia communities throughout northern New Mexico have always managed their water. José Rivera, in his book *Acequia Culture, Water, Land, & Community in the Southwest*,[2] quotes from an affidavit submitted by acequia commissioners in the early years of the Taos Valley Adjudication to determine priority dates and ownership of water:

'the aforesaid acequias by and through their fully elected commissioners agree that they will continue to follow and be bound by their customary divisions and allocations of water and agree that they will not make calls or demands for water between and among themselves based upon priority dates.'

In accordance with the traditional practice of repartimiento, or water sharing, the acequias did not want to establish a practice whereby a priority call could shut off water to 'junior' water rights holders in times of drought.

The Office of the State Engineer (OSE), the agency that administers water in New Mexico, has also been reluctant to issue priority calls to junior users but not with such altruistic motives: junior water rights largely belong to urban areas developed after the establishment of Pueblo and Hispano acequia communities and a priority call would generate a political nightmare."

This is from an April 23, 2013 article I wrote for *La Jicarita*,[3] the online journal of environmental politics that I have edited since 2012. It went on to discuss in more detail a priority call that was made on the Pecos River in southern New Mexico, which I will discuss in a later chapter. But I wanted to use the first part of the article to illuminate one of the basic themes of this book: that despite state water policies, water law, the economic pressures of neoliberalism, and changing demographics, the concept of water as a right of the commons, for all to use and share but not own, remains alive and well within the land based communities of New Mexico.

Custom and tradition within acequia communities, despite New Mexico law that assigns a priority date and implies ownership of water, still govern the use of the water by mayordomos and commissions, and repartimiento, or water distribution and sharing, is worked out among communities without state oversight. New Mexico communities have maintained—not preserved—their commons in ways that remain part of our everyday lives: parciantes irrigating crops and fields with acequias; extant land grants managing their forest resources communally; grazing associations forming to collectively raise cattle on private and public lands; and pueblo farmers saving seed to reproduce crops regionally grown for hundreds of years. As an editor of *La Jicarita* I've often referenced the work of economist Elinor Ostrom, a proponent of the philosophy that people can create rules to manage shared resources, without the interference of the state or marketplace.

But, as contributing *La Jicarita* writer Suzy Kane titled a 2013 article, "Water is Complicated."[4] What she was referring to were the changing demographics of an acequia community near Taos, where folks wanted to transfer acequia water rights from pastures no longer being irrigated to the local domestic water association that needed them to meet household growth. In 1996, when *La Jicarita News*, the predecessor of the online *La Jicarita*, published its first hard copy newspaper in the Peñasco Valley of el norte, we entered that complicated water world with a story about the Sipapu Ski Area that wanted to use its water rights to make more snow to expand its skiable acres. That elicited a storm of controversy, which I wrote about in another book, *Culture Clash: Environmental Politics in New Mexico Forest Communities*, and which I will again address in a chapter on ski area development.

In the 22 years since that first issue of *La Jicarita News* and its transition to its online version in 2012 we've covered all the water stories that both challenge and complicate the idea of the commons: priority administration; state and federal adjudications; pre-existing rights on federal lands; regional water planning; ski area development; changing demographics; drought and climate change; and much, much more. This book will guide the reader through that history with stops along the way to tell the stories of those trying to "keep their eye on the prize," i.e., water as a right of the commons.

Introduction: Managing the Commons

As I write this introduction in the spring of 2015, the acequias in northern New Mexico are full and the tributaries are running rapidly to the Rio Grande during this unusually wet month of May. At least for now, parciantes have enough water for their fields, orchards, and gardens, and Rio Grande releases are supplying middle and lower basin irrigators.

The fact that we have the ability to water our agricultural lands is because indigenous ancestors built these irrigation ditches when they first settled the river valleys of el norte and along the Rio Grande corridor, without sophisticated tools or implements to measure grade and elevation. They matched their wits with nature's elements to create a system that sup-

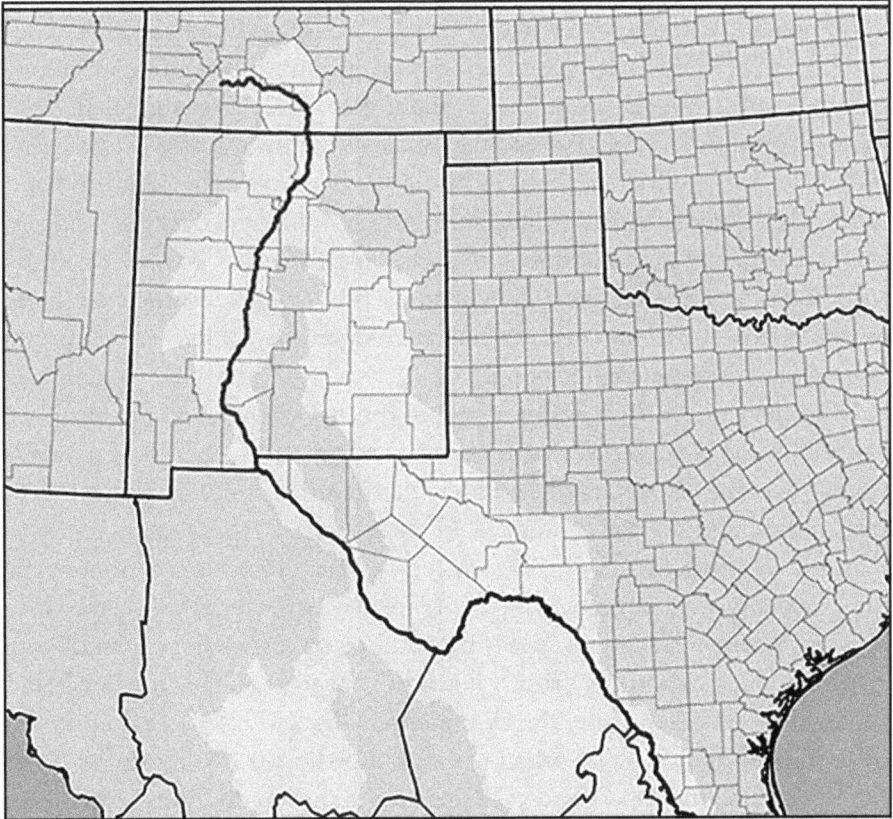

Rio Grande corridor from southern Colorado to Mexico

ported both themselves and the ecological integrity of the river valleys. In other words, they "managed" nature in a mutually beneficial way.

The concept of "managed" nature remains an anathema to certain mainstream environmentalists and deep ecology advocates who see nature as the pristine "other" and humans as the invaders. *La Jicarita* was witness to the damage this kind of thinking caused in the forests of northern New Mexico in the 1990s and early 2000s. Movements like "Zero Cut"—no logging on public lands—and "Cattle Free"—no cattle on public lands—sought to disrupt land-based communities access to national forest resources and replace a traditionally work-based ethic with that of a visitor-only one. Again, man the intruder, nature best left alone.

Community based foresters, ranchers, and acequia parciantes fought back, along with groups like the Quivira Coalition, which worked to restore ranch lands and watersheds through land-based partnerships. They won a few battles and changed a few perceptions, but many community people lost their livelihoods. Demographics continue to marginalize land-based economies as the traditional caretakers of the acequias are growing older and our children are leaving home for better employment opportunities elsewhere. It remains to be seen if they will come back, as many of their parents and grandparents did after being forced to leave temporarily to find work. The querencia that inhabits their souls kept their land and traditions intact. Resurgence in small farming and ranching among young people of all stripes creates hope.

The management of water remains the key. Because every drop of water in New Mexico has already been apportioned—surface or groundwater—whether by interstate compact, by court decree, by projects and settlements, and no new water can be appropriated, the human ability to manage—or should I say "manipulate"—water has grown exponentially more sophisticated and problematic. Instead of gravity-based acequias we now have dams and pumps and canals and reservoirs to harvest and store water supplies that come from inter-basin diversions like the San Juan/Chama Project that crosses the Continental Divide. This water is contracted to both agricultural and urban use from northern Taos County south to the cities along the Rio Grande. The parties to the adjudication settlements in the northern part of the state—the Aamodt and the Abeyta—haggled

Lake Mead

over which settlement would get the available water rights from the Project.[5]

Apportionment on the Colorado River is unbelievably complicated. The states dependent on the Lower Colorado Basin—Arizona, Nevada, and California—are watching what's going to happen with the water depths at Lake Mead, which was at its lowest point ever, at 1, 077 feet in 2015, as managers held back more water in Lake Powell, which is the reservoir for the Upper Colorado Basin. At that time, the Bureau of Reclamation released these projections: observed unregulated inflow into Lake Powell for the month of April was 61 percent of the 30-year average from 1981 to 2010; the forecast for May unregulated inflow into Lake Powell was 43 percent of the 30 year average; and the forecasted 2015 April through July unregulated inflow was 41 percent of average.[6] As Lake Mead diminishes, the city of Las Vegas, which gets the majority of its water from the lake, is locked in battle with ranchers in northern Nevada over groundwater supplies the city wants to acquire.[7] Projections from the U.S. Bureau of Reclamation indicated Lake Mead could fall low enough in 2016 to reduce power generation and shut down one of the intake pipes used to supply the Las Vegas Valley with water. (Steve Andrascik/*Las Vegas Review Journal*)

In California, the huge farms of the Central Valley and the sprawling urban cities of Los Angeles and San Diego get their water from two man-made water projects, the Central Valley Project and the State Water Project, built in the 1930s through the 60s. Both projects take water from the rivers of the north and deliver it via dams, pumps, aqueducts, canals, and ditches to the valley farm lands and "spouts" of the cities. In an interview on NPR's Fresh Air (Thursday, April 30, 2015), journalist Mark Arax discussed the drought in California that was forcing farmers to revert to the groundwater supplies they previously used to water their fields before the "managed" surface water supplies were created.

Only they are pumping so much more and so much deeper that the ground is sinking. The wells are accessing aquifers that are thousands of years old. Listening to Arax talk, I was reminded of the plan to pump 1,000-foot deep wells in the Taos Valley Abeyta Adjudication Settlement (more on this later); aquifer water that is probably just as old and that will take decades to replenish.

Arax also discussed how the water crisis has devolved into a fight of the "urbanite against the almond." The largest and highest value crop in California these days is the nut crop, primarily almonds and pistachios. Many of these farmers, years ago, switched from cotton, which uses significantly more water than the higher value almond, which itself uses 10 percent of the allotted water in the state. Corporate farmers are planting tens of thousands of more "permanent" almond orchards, which unlike fields that can be left fallow to periodically conserve water, have to be watered every year to sustain the trees. But as Arax points out, the orchards are "not as permanent as the suburbs we're planting" as farmers in the Central Valley start selling off their lands to developers: "Slowly the rivers are becoming rivers of suburbia."

New Mexico's drought continues despite a wetter spring and an almost-average snowfall over the winters of 2015 and 2016. The San Juan/Chama Project has several times failed to deliver the full amount of contracted water. Snowpack in the Colorado River headwaters that feed the San Juan/Chama Project was 35 percent of average in 2012. In 2002, only 6,000 acre feet of project water came through the Azotea Tunnel under the Continental Divide into Heron Lake. Yet the Office of the State Engineer, the Interstate Stream Commission, and the Department of the Interior continue to approve adjudication settlements based on fully allotted San Juan/Chama water rights as well as intrastate cross-basin transfers and deep wells to meet projected future water demands.

Which brings us to the question: How do we decide what kind of management is good management? A book about Western water management would be remiss without a reference to John Wesley Powell, who his biographer Wallace Stegner described in his book *Beyond The Hundredth Meridian* resisted "with all his energy the tide of unreasoning, fantasy-drawn settlement and uncontrolled exploitation" of the arid West. Instead, he promoted watershed basin management recognizing that local resources—metals, water, timber, land, and grass—should determine settlement practices.

The engineering feat of the acequias was extraordinary. The building of dams and aqueducts and canals and ditches in California's Central Valley turned it into the breadbasket of the country. But as we face continuing drought and climate change catastrophe, limits must be recognized and critical management decisions must be made. Unfortunately, that insidious "highest and best" use principle that is a euphemism for growth and development rears its ugly head over and over again in as diverse locales as New Mexico's basin adjudications, California's Central Valley, and Las Vegas's water grab.

Closely related to this principle is the rationale that if we rigorously conserve water in these locales we'll be able to continue with business as usual: moving water to money. In the Aamodt Adjudication, well users are urged to turn over their water rights to Santa Fe County for a water delivery system; those who retain their wells must abide by new, much more restrictive regulations. Yet thousands of acre feet of water are being moved to the Valley to facilitate future use. In the Central Valley, corporate almond farmers are planting new orchards while hundreds of thousands of acres of farmland are being left fallow as houses creep to their borders. In Las Vegas, the city has implemented water conservation measures but continues to insist on the insurance of its now projected $15.5 billion dollar water transfer project. (Taos attorney Simeon Herskovits is one of the lawyers working with the ranchers protesting the transfer.)

This is what historian Richard White says about the Columbia River, but it could be said of the Rio Grande or the Colorado or any river in the West: "If the conversation is not about fish and justice, about . . . ways of life, about production and nature, about beauty as well as efficiency, and about how these things are inseparable in our own tangled lives, then we have not come to terms with our history on this river."[8] What White, author of *The Organic Machine: The Remaking of the Columbia River* is talking about is that humans are capable of managing resources in a way that improves and protects human society and biodiversity. If free market forces continue to determine who's going to get the water, then there's not much hope for mutually beneficial management based on fish, justice, ways of life, production, and beauty.

One

From the Commons to the State

The Rio Grande Compact, which governs the distribution of water from the river within Colorado, New Mexico, and Texas, divides New Mexico into three sections and has served as a de facto barrier to the transfer of water from one section to another. The three sections comprise the area from the Colorado state line to the Otowi Gauge (where the Otowi Bridge crosses the Rio Grande between Pojoaque and Los Alamos), from the Otowi Gauge to Elephant Butte Reservoir, and from the Elephant Butte Reservoir to the Texas state line. The Otowi Gauge is so named because it is the location of the gauge indexing the river flow and determining how much water must be delivered to Elephant Butte Reservoir.

In 1997 the city and county of Santa Fe were finalizing plans to transfer 588 acre feet per year (afy) of water rights from Top of the World Farms, a vast area of land in Sunshine Valley, near the Colorado border, that the county had recently acquired. It planned to build an "infiltration gallery" (takeout) on San Ildefonso Pueblo land to divert this water from the Rio Grande above the Otowi Gauge and pipe it below the gauge to the Buckman Well Field, Santa Fe's main source of water. This plan, once discovered by the acequia community of northern New Mexico, set off a firestorm of concern about what it perceived as a raid on norteño water by downstream urban users. This project was seen as an attempt to circumvent the rules of the Rio Grande Compact by diverting water above the Otowi Gauge and piping it to an area south of the gauge. If this project were successful, it could set a precedent for other municipalities and developers to acquire water rights in northern New Mexico and transfer them to other locations throughout the state.

In the mid-2000s, Santa Fe County had a change of heart (with pressure from some federal bureaucrats) and decided that these proposed water rights could be better used to help meet the needs of the Aamodt Adjudication, the longstanding federal adjudication of the water rights of four pueblos and non-native residents in the Pojoaque Valley, north of Santa Fe (and above the Otowi Gauge).

In 2016 this proposed transfer of water rights from Top of the World Farm was protested (an administrative process I will describe later) by the County of Taos, 19 years after the project was first put forth, when it was protested by a group of acequias and acequia parciantes (including my *La Jicarita* co-editor and partner Mark Schiller and me). The Aamodt Adjudication, which was initiated in 1966 (that's over 50 years ago), had until September of 2017 to finalize those water rights from Top of the World and to reserve them for the water delivery system for the people of the Pojoaque Valley.

I will discuss both the history of the Top of the World proposed transfer and the Aamodt Adjudication in much more detail in later chapters. I use them now to demonstrate how excruciatingly complex and laborious the management of water under New Mexico state statute and federal oversight became after the Spanish and Mexican administration of acequia culture that flourished in the seventeenth, eighteenth, and nineteenth centuries. Many books by academics and historians tell the colorful stories of the social and legal history of water in pre-statehood New Mexico when the acequia system, built upon water systems developed by Native Americans, expanded under the Spanish colonial, Mexican, and territorial settlements throughout the southwest. I mentioned José Rivera's book in the Preface, *Acequia Culture, Water, Land, & Community in the Southwest*, which delineates the legal and administrative nature of pre-statehood acequia culture. Michael Meyer's book, *Water in the Hispanic Southwest*, is a social and legal history of water from 1550 to 1850. John O. Baxter's book, *Dividing New Mexico's Waters*, discusses the evolution of water administration from the colonial era to New Mexico statehood in 1912.

Water rights were then considered community property, tied to the land. The Treaty of Guadalupe Hidalgo, which ended the Mexican-American War, was supposed to have preserved these rights as "inviolable," but after the United States acquired the northern half of Mexico in 1848 this concept of community property began to be eroded as the Anglo-European concept of private ownership of the water and its severance from the land began an inexorable march towards New Mexico statehood. In 1907 the Territorial Water Code was instituted and became the basis of state water law, which included the Doctrine of Prior Appropriation in Article 16 of the New Mexico State Constitution. This is the now familiar "first in time first in line" concept whereby in times of shortage those with first in time, or senior water rights, can claim their water before junior water rights holders can use any. Those who can establish that their water use was established before 1907—Pueblos and acequias, primarily—are the owners of senior water rights, while those established after 1907 are junior rights.

Water rights adjudication is the process by which the New Mexico Office of the State Engineer (OSE) determines the extent, ownership, and priority of water rights in a specific geographic area of the state. It is similar to a quiet title suit that establishes ownership of property. The adjudication process involves two phases. First, the OSE conducts a hydrographic survey that determines ownership of the water right, purpose of water use, priority (the date at which the water was first put to beneficial use on that property), point of diversion, place of use, amount of acreage irrigated, and the amount of water required. Second, the state or federal government file a lawsuit through which court orders are issued, stating how much water each user is entitled to and the use to which it can be put. State law requires that adjudications be conducted as a lawsuit and all water rights users are joined in this suit. When this has been completed, the OSE sends an offer of judgment to each water right owner. The owner may accept or reject this offer. Objections are resolved through further investigation by the OSE or a court hearing. When an offer is signed by both the state and water rights holder, the court enters an order confirming the agreement. When all rights have been settled in a given stream system, an individual or group of individuals can challenge the water rights judgment of others in that stream system if they feel that those rights have been unfairly adjudicated. The OSE then conducts hearings on these challenges. When they are resolved, the court enters a final decree that specifies the rights of every water right owner within that system.

Thus, establishing a priority date became *de rigueur* and the adjudication process pitted not only Anglo-European society against the Indigenous, but also the Pueblo and Hispano communities against each other at the expense of both. So much of what transpired during the water wars of the1990s to the present is the direct result of this priority administration concept, particularly the attempt to assign an economic definition of "high value" to water, resulting in the increased movement of water rights from agricultural to urban, industrial, and recreational use.

In 1997 a report called the "Water Management Study: Upper Rio Grande River Basin" succinctly set the agenda for the ensuing years battles over what defines the value of water. Commissioned by the Western Water Policy Review Advisory Commission, it was mandated to define the federal role in water policy for the west. The report, among other things, stated that "We recommend federal agencies in the [Rio Grande] Basin do more to mitigate the constraints to competition that keep water and other resources in low-value uses while high value demands go unmet." In other words, high-value water uses, such as urban, industrial and recreational, rather than low-value agricultural uses, should dictate how water will be allocated in the future. It went on to say that acequia associations and irrigation and conservancy districts had exercised undue influence on legislation pertaining to water distribution in the state and that the Rio Grande Compact governing distribution on the Rio Grande between Texas, New Mexico, and Colorado ". . . reflects the agrarian economy . . . that existed at the end of the 1920s, not today's highly urbanized economy."

Since the issuance of this report there's been enormous pressure to transfer agricultural water rights to urban and suburban areas using this rational. *La Jicarita* wrote a response to the report, challenging the economic lens through which the report sees water and also rebutting the report's claim that agriculture accounts for 80 percent of water consumption in the Rio Grande basin with Bureau of Reclamation statistics that show half of this use is actually consumptive use by the riparian corridor, i.e., cottonwoods, willows, and other flora. Both of these claims of "high-value" water use and agricultural over-consumption would be used repeatedly throughout the years to rationalize the movement of water out of its area of origin.

While acequias are classified as subdivisions of the state of New Mexico, with practices protected by state statute, they represent the contested terrain between the commons and free market capitalism. Those who believe in the integrity of the commons work to keep water in its area of origin, where its ecological integrity is maintained by its connection to geography, climate, and relationship to those who value it as a resource, not a property right. Those who believe that market forces should dictate the movement of water, which has been defined by the state as private property, don't want any regulatory or public oversight to get in the way of development. Allowing natural resources to help determine sustainable growth and development patterns is not the way things work in a market economy.

There is a profound difference between economic growth and economic development. Elinor Ostrom, the much admired professor of economics at Indiana University who I mentioned in the Preface, was an influential voice who explicated this difference in the language of the commons: shared resources can be managed by the people whose lives are directly affected at the local level by the management of our land and water with sustainable economic development, not the unrestricted growth dictated by the state or the market.

Two

Becoming a Parciante

When Mark and I and our two kids left the newly gentrified village of Placitas, in the Sandia Mountains near Albuquerque, and moved to the more remote village of El Valle in 1992, I was amazed by the extent of the acequia system that watered the fields, orchards, and gardens of this 20-family community. While I had access to acequia water while living in the Placitas village proper—and participated in the annual limpieza, or ditch cleaning—after Mark and I built a house out on a nearby mesa we got our domestic and irrigation water from a well. That severely limited our agricultural endeavors to a kitchen garden, a few fruit trees, and a native grass yard. Wells in the Placitas area draw water from the many fractured aquifers fed by snowmelt in the Sandia Mountains, with varied depths of anywhere from 100 to 500 feet. At my home in El Valle I have 10 acres of hay fields, an orchard, a huge vegetable garden, a hoop house full of raspberry bushes, and, indulgently, a small Kentucky bluegrass lawn, all watered by two acequias. The acequias run all summer long, with enough water to flood irrigate the hay fields and orchards on a rotational basis based on the number of parciantes, or irrigators, in the village.

Of course, how and by whom that rotation is managed is a complicated story. El Valle has three acequias that are diverted from the Rio de las Trampas, whose headwaters lie deep in the Pecos Wilderness at the Trampas Lakes. The county/forest road that leads through the village terminates at the trailhead leading six miles to the lakes at 11,000 feet in elevation. The presas, or diversion dams, for the three acequias are located in the narrow canyon above the village and in the village itself; originally constructed of logs and rocks, serving this village that dates back to the 1700s, they've now been rebuilt with concrete and gabion rock, paid for with monies allocated through state-funded acequia programs, private foundations, and the parciantes themselves. Two of the acequias are on the north side of the river, where most of the people live, and one, Acequia del Llano, is on the south side where folks have fields but few still live.

The three acequias irrigate the lands of approximately 25 parciantes, whose water rights, or derechos, vary from less than one to four. A derecho, or the amount of water each parciante gets in the rotation, is based on how much land he or she owns. Through the years, as land parcels have been divided up among family members, or have been sold to newcomers, the number of water rights has increased. The amount of water that is divided among all these rights remains the same, however; each acequia is allotted a certain amount of water that is measured by several gauges set along the river.

How often a parciante gets the water is determined by how long it takes to get the water from the lowest parciante's property on the river to the highest. In El Valle, it takes about 10 days to two weeks to get from Bill deBuys property (his book *River of Traps, Life in a Mountain Village*,[9] describes his learning curve figuring out the system) up to Larry Velasquez's fields, the last irrigated property before the village road enters the national forest. Those parciantes who have one water right get the water for 24 hours, two water rights 48 hours, one-half a water right 12 hours, etc.

When it's your turn to irrigate—usually at either six o'clock in the morning or six in the evening—you open your compuerta, or headgate, that lets the water out of the acequia madre into your regaderas (lateral ditches), which feed your fields, orchards, or gardens. Irrigating gardens is tricky because over the last generation the system has been geared to service hay and alfalfa fields, which can effectively be watered on a two-week rotation. Gardens can't; even if flood irrigated, they need water more frequently. I'll talk more specifically about the controversy that arose in El Valle over how those of us who have gardens are able to get the water when needed, but each community has to work this out, especially as more and more folks bring back the gardening tradition that receded once the cash economy reached norteño villages after World War II.

So that's how the water gets to the fields and gardens. Who manages this system is a story of strong tradition complicated by personality, demographics, and politics. The irrigation system is governed by an acequia comisión, comprised of three comisionados: a president, a secretary, and a treasurer. These commissioners are elected by the acequia parciantes, usually for two-year terms, and they are essentially an executive committee that oversees any work or repairs to the acequia, keeps records and account books, and makes all decisions pertaining to acequia administration. Day to day management of the acequia is the domain of the mayordomo, also elected by the parciantes or appointed by the commission, to oversee the scheduling of water delivery to each irrigator.

When we arrived in El Valle in 1992 my neighbor Tomás Montoya was the president of the Acequia Abajo, the acequia that waters our lower field; his brother Arsenio was another commissioner, and a third brother Orlando was the mayordomo. Tomás was also a commissioner on the Acequia Arriba, which waters our upper field and orchard.

Because he was our neighbor and we were living in a house built on his former property (he sold the land to a young Anglo farmer who began a house, ran out of money, and sold it to us), he took us under his enormous wings (he was about six foot four) that encompassed just about every facet of our new lives in El Valle.

We certainly needed his help. The house we bought was a two-story solar adobe that lacked everything but plumbing and electricity. We had to lay the tile floor, plaster the walls, divide the upstairs into two bedrooms and lofts, install a wood stove (we tied Tomás's son Fred to a tether on the 30 foot high roof to lower the stove pipe through the hole in the tin), and make insulated curtains for the eight-foot high windows. Outside, the young farmer had planted the upper field in quinoa, of all things, but had let it go to weed and we were faced with batches of burdock, the plant whose seed burrs were the inspiration for Velcro, and every other prickly, horrible weed ever blown into New Mexico. Tomás plowed over what he could with a light tractor sweep and told us what to plant: brome, timothy, rye. He showed us how to guide the acequia water through the laterals to the far corners of the field.

He came over with his fence fixing equipment and helped repair the ancient barbed wire structures that divided our fields from his so his cows couldn't get in. And that was a bigger blessing than it appeared, because, as he explained to us, the law of the land stipulated that the property owner was required to fix fences to keep his neighbor's animals out, not the other way around. He provided the manure for our garden every spring. He cut

Orlando and Tomás Montoya

our hay crop in the summer. He loaned us his generator when the electricity went out for four days (the electricity in El Valle went out a lot). He gave us steaks when he butchered a cow.

So this man with a generous nature incorporated us into the community because we were buen vecinos, the highest compliment he could pay anyone, based on our receptiveness as well as our reciprocity: we provided him with produce from our garden, eggs from our chickens, fruit from our trees, and half the hay crop. There were few boundaries in our exchange system. When his wonderful cow dog Cuete got sick, probably poisoned, I took him to the vet (Tomás paid) and kept him warm in our mudroom (few people other than gringos let their dogs in the house). He took us out to lunch on our birthdays and occasionally took me shopping for a dress. We went dancing on Sundays in Las Vegas. Mark eventually became a commissioner on the Acequia Abajo in the early 2000s as did I in 2006.

By then the commission on the Acequia Arriba had been taken over by several men of the younger generation (Tomás was in his sixties when we moved to El Valle, and the younger men were in their forties, the same age as Mark and me) who had moved back to El Valle after completing their educations and working outside the community for a number of years. One of the younger men's family had been feuding with the Montoyas over another issue that carried over to the governance of the acequias, the only venue where these kinds of power games could play out. The ensuing years saw increased contestation over the way the acequias should be run, as the younger men challenged Tomas's generation for influence and power in the village. I'll explore the nature of this challenge in a later chapter, which reflected the changes that were occurring outside the El Valle community in the larger world of water governance.

Three

Acequias—Organize!

As with any group of people who organize to protect their interests from the power elite, there is danger both within and without. The history of the labor movement in this country is fraught with the brutality inflicted by corporate bosses from without as well as endemic corruption from within. The revolutionary political movements that rose up over the course of many centuries, including the one many of us participated in in the 1960s and 70s, were subsumed by the status quo and fragmented by disagreements on strategy and goals within the ranks.

Acequia communities striving to remain intact against neoliberal policies are often romanticized as models of democratic institutions and traditional cohesiveness but see their own share of internecine bickering. The New Mexico Acequia Association, as well as the regional associations that work under its umbrella, haven't been immune from this dynamic. The NMAA was formed in 1988 but became inactive during the early 1990s. Then in the late 1990s a group of folks including Nicasio Romero, an artist and activist from Ribera, Lynn Montgomery and Ida Talalla from Placitas, John Carangelo from La Joya, and John Brown (now with the *New Mexico Water Dialogue*) reorganized and issued its first newsletter called *Acequia!* that laid out the issues the community faced: water transfers, historic preservation, interpretation of the public welfare doctrine, and adjudication. Other articles in the newsletter addressed industrial and urban development threats to acequias, water rights forfeiture and abandonment, the high cost of challenging a water rights application through the Office of the State Engineer, and bills pending in the state legislature that could affect acequia users.

Soon after, however, a group of acequia activists from Mora and San Miguel counties joined the association and were elected to the governing board. These included Antonio Medina, who became chair of the board, Harold Trujillo, Michael Coca, William Gonzalez, and Facundo Valdez, who was named director. Many of the members who had been involved in the resurrection of the organization felt they were being marginalized and left but continued to organize within their own communities. Then, shortly after the election, Valdez had to resign because of health problems, and Paula Garcia, a young Mora native who came out of the planning department at the University of New Mexico, was appointed director. She remains in that position today.

As the NMAA was organizing so, too, were other regional associations across the state. One of the oldest and most influential was the Taos Valley Acequia Association (TVAA), formed in 1986 by Eduardo Lavadie and Alfred Trujillo, representing the 55 acequias in the Taos Valley that were part of the Abeyta Adjudication with Taos Pueblo, which I will discuss in detail later. It grew out of the efforts by these activists who were involved in the Committee to Save the Rio Hondo when threatened by the development of condominiums in the Valdez area and Taos Ski Area development. The TVAA also took the lead in developing various strategies such as water banking and water conservation programs, which eventually led to the adoption of a new state statute in 2003 that allows acequias to set up water banks to protect rights that aren't being put to beneficial use (along with another provision that requires the approval of acequia commissions to transfer water from the acequia, which I will also talk about later in the book).

The TVAA also saw its share of internecine conflict when Palemon Martinez became involved in the organization and brought in Geoff Bryce as Executive Director and Fred Waltz as attorney. Unfortunately, Lavadie died, and Trujillo left over disagreements with Martinez concerning management of the organization, but has remained active in the acequia community, particualy as an advocate for the Rio Hondo. (Martinez's role as president of the TVAA board will be explored more fully in later chapters dealing with the Abeyta Settlement.)

Bryce was killed in a car accident on June 16, 2004 in Taos. I remember a workshop designed to impart better organizational and communication skills that I participated in with Geoff, many years ago in Santa Fe. We had broken down into affinity groups; Geoff and I were in a group focused on water issues. Also in the group was an environmentalist from the southern part of the state, who immediately started complaining about what he considered the wasteful agricultural practices of the acequia community and the need to implement instream flow legislation (water rights that belong to the river). In a quiet, non-confrontational way, Geoff quickly set him straight about the environmental, social, and cultural importance of acequias and reminded him that if he wanted to participate in meaningful dialogue about water issues he better educate himself *tout de suite* about acequias. The environmentalist decided to join another affinity group.

Many of the other associations that formed, such as the Rio de Chama Acequia Association, did so because of ongoing adjudications, while others anticipated being adjudicated despite the agonizingly slow process that kept extant adjudications in negotiations or legal proceedings for years.

The NMAA quickly grew into a much larger and more influential group in the 2000s and reorganized its governing structure to reflect that. It redrafted its bylaws and organized an Acequia Congreso made up of at-large acequia representatives and acequia association representatives. The Congreso also elected a Concilio, or working board, that would meet at least bi-monthly to conduct the day-to-day business of the association in coordination with the Director. The NMAA continued to focus on three efforts: capacity building through workshops and leadership teams to meet the educational and organizational needs of acequias; policy advocacy through monitoring, analyzing, and developing legislation concerning water management at the state level; and organizational recruiting to better represent acequias and acequia associations statewide.

On a more theoretical level, the NMAA recognized that it must play a role in identifying the intrinsic values of rural communities that the acequia system supports as a bulwark against commodification. On the state level this required working to protect existing water law and clarifying concepts like public welfare and beneficial use, which are enshrined in state law but have been open to interpretation. On the local level it meant working on regional water plans that recognize the autonomy of traditional water courses or watersheds and the prohibition of transferring water from one watershed to another.

I was one of the at-large representatives of the Concilio because of the work I did with Antonio Medina on the Rio Pueblo/Rio Embudo Water-

35

shed Protection Coalition. A few years after we moved to El Valle Mark and I were asked to join this coalition of groups that came together when the local downhill ski area, Sipapu, applied for a permit from the Forest Service to expand, increasing its vertical drop by one hundred percent. While the proposed expansion didn't elicit the kind of organized, public opposition that the proposed Santa Fe Ski Area expansion did (see Chapter Twenty-Six on ski area expansions), many local people were worried about cumulative impacts of the expansion on both water resources and traditional communities. Carl "Cat" Tsosie of Picuris Pueblo, put out the word to see who might be interested in joining the coalition. A diverse group of people showed up: acequia associations from Vadito, Embudo, and Dixon; the Eight Northern Pueblo Council; land grant activists; Carson Forest Watch; Amigos Bravos; the Sierra Club; former Sipapu employees; and representatives of the Mora Water and Land Protective Association, who were concerned expansion would affect their northeast side of the Sangre de Cristo Mountains as well. The head of that group was Antonio Medina, president of the board of the New Mexico Acequia Association.

One of the primary goals of the NMAA is to help acequias form regional associations, to prepare for adjudication and to address issues of concern within their own watersheds. We tried to do just that in our Rio Pueblo/Rio Embudo watershed, but the results were not pretty.

In 1996 several major business ventures that would need large amounts of water loomed on the horizon: development of the Summo copper mine near Picuris Pueblo; the proposed Sipapu Ski Area expansion; and cities such as Santa Fe and Rio Rancho looking to buy up agricultural water rights to implement development plans. Mark and I started working with two Peñasco school teachers, Ben and Verna Gurule, to see if there was sufficient interest in area acequias to organize a Peñasco Area Acequia Federation.

Peñasco is the largest village in the cluster of communities in southern Taos County located along the Rio Pueblo, Rio Santa Barbara, Rio Chiquito, Rio Embudo, and Rio de las Trampas. The children from the smaller villages—Tres Ritos, Placita, Vadito, Llano, Chamisal, Ojito, El Valle, Las Trampas, and Ojo Sarco—are bused to the independent school district in Peñasco, where several grocery stores, gas stations, and restaurants serve a community of about 600 people. Picuris Pueblo sits on the west end of the village where the Rio Santa Barbara and the Rio Pueblo meet to form the Rio Embudo, which flows down to the Rio Grande. Peñasco is unincorporated, and like many of the other unincorporated villages of el norte, acequia commissioners constitute the only governing body in the area.

Things got off to a slow start, but in November of that year, 27 parciantes, representing acequias on the Rio Pueblo, Rio Santa Barbara, Rio Chiquito, and Rio de Las Trampas, met at the old bank building in Peñasco to discuss the adoption of bylaws and other steps necessary to organize this group. Using the bylaws of the Taos Valley Acequia Association as a model, the group was able to agree upon a 10-page list of bylaws to formalize the organization and establish procedures to elect officers. The group also created a committee to do an inventory of all the acequias using water from these four rivers and determine a contact person from each acequia. Once an inventory was compiled, the group would need the participation of 51 percent of the acequias in order to have legal standing and elect officers. At a subsequent meeting in December, representatives of the downstream Dixon and Embudo acequias were in attendance and expressed their desire to work with the group.

A standing-room only crowd filled the old bank building in Peñasco on January 11, 1997 to hear David Benavides, water law expert with Northern New Mexico Legal Services, provide a brief overview of the adjudication process and then address other pressing water issues such as acequia registration, instream flow, Native American water rights, and water banking. "It's probably safe to say that the Peñasco area will not be adjudicated before the year 2000," Benavides said, "but the important thing is to keep exercising your water rights by irrigating as much of your irrigable property as possible."[10] (The year 2000 has long come and gone with no adjudication, of course.)

David addressed the question of unregistered water rights by reassuring parciantes that unless their warranty deeds stipulated that water rights had been retained by the previous owner, those rights automatically remain with the purchased land. He pointed out, however, that those people who had purchased land after 1991 needed to fill out a Change of Ownership form with the Office of the State Engineer (OSE) to secure their water rights. He also said that while it's not absolutely necessary to file a declaration with the OSE, it may prove to be advantageous during the adjudication process. He cautioned parciantes not to declare a priority date, however, until all of the historical research of their acequias has been completed.

David also addressed the issue of Native American water rights, as the adjudication of Picuris Pueblo's water rights will be part of an adjudication in the Peñasco Valley. He stressed the importance of establishing a good relationship between the Pueblo and Hispano and Anglo communities. "There is a long history of cooperation between Pueblos and Hispanics in New Mexico," Benavides said, "and it's critical that these communities not allow the adjudication process to pit them against one another." The biggest difference between Native American water rights and all others is that the federal government recognizes the Pueblos' right to expand their water use as their population increases; all other water rights are limited by state regulations drafted in 1907 when all waters had already been apportioned (more on this later). Benavides mentioned the long-standing water rights battle in the Pojoaque Valley (Aamodt Adjudication), and cautioned that in the Peñasco area parciantes needed to work together with Picuris Pueblo before the adjudication process began.

Finally, the Peñasco Area Acequia Federation sent out notices to all mayordomos and commissioners of area acequias that a meeting would be scheduled in June for a vote to see if 51 percent or more of the area acequias wanted to formalize the Federation as the umbrella group for all of them. I attended that meeting with Tomás, who was enthusiastic about the idea of the Federation, but who had heard that there were some in the community who planned to object to the formation of the Federation, claiming it was "too soon" and that too many people were still unaware of exactly what a federation or acequia association meant. One of the main politicos in the Peñasco area, Mary Mascareñas, who ran the Democratic machine and served on various committees and boards in Peñasco, came into the meeting with a cohort of supporters and delivered the message that because she and others hadn't been involved in organizing the Federation it was indeed "too soon" and so no vote was taken. As I write this chapter in 2016 there is still no acequia association or federation in the Peñasco Valley. Fortunately, as I mentioned previously, neither is there an adjudication process in motion in the Valley.

Probably every community or region in el norte has its local patron (in this case a patrona) who functions as its representative in the political process, be it in the Democratic or Republican party, on the school board, on a community center board, and usually as a commissioner on the acequia. Mary did all of that, and in my opinion, not very benevolently: she controlled the Taos Democratic Party; ran the Peñasco School Board; was on the Taos County Planning and Zoning Board; sat on the Peñasco Area Community Association board; and served as commissioner on her local acequia. Soon after we arrived in El Valle, however, there was an uprising. It started first in the Democratic Party, where the progressives organized and threw out some of the patrones, including Mary. Then some progressives ran for the school board and Mary disappeared from that venue. Finally, others came together and voted her off the community center board. But slowly, over the years, Mary worked her way back into some of these positions, with the same tenacity she'd employed previously. It's too bad she didn't use some of that energy to form a Peñasco area acequia association.

Four

Filing a Water Transfer Protest

Before I begin the discussion of all the fights over water transfers that took place throughout the 2000s I should explain the mechanics of transfer protests. All applications to transfer water rights must be submitted to the Water Rights Division of the Office of the State Engineer, the agency that administers the state's water resources with authority over the supervision, measurement, appropriation, and distribution of all surface and groundwater in New Mexico. For those of you who might not be familiar with the agency, the Office of the State Engineer (OSE) began as the Office of the Territorial Engineer that oversaw the adjudication of water under New Mexico's Territorial Water Code in 1907. Once the territory became a state in 1912 it adopted the water code and the Territorial Engineer became the State Engineer. The most famous—and perhaps most powerful—of these engineers was Steve Reynolds, who served from 1956 to 1990. He's the one who popularized the expression "water runs uphill to money," and while some might say he facilitated that movement others credit him with being a realist when it came to recognizing the state's limited water supply and the infeasibility of many water augmentation schemes. Instead, he advocated moving existing water rights from agriculture to industry to underwrite economic development. He was also the driving force behind the state's attempt to create a conservancy district in Taos County, which I reference in the Prologue. Today, the OSE, and its partner agency the Interstate Stream Commission, rarely encounter a water project they don't endorse—projects like the Indian Camp Dam and conservancy that disenfranchise local farmers by creating bureaucratic and commercially controlled water systems, or the damning of the Gila River, the last free flowing stream in the state (see Chapter Thirty-three).

An application to transfer water rights states the point of diversion, the place of use, and the quantity of the rights. Once the Water Rights Division of the OSE reviews the application for approval or amendment the applicant must publish it in a newspaper of general circulation in the area where the right is located for three consecutive weeks. Anyone wishing to protest the transfer must file a protest with the OSE within 10 days after the last date of publication. Protestants must prove they have standing in the case by demonstrating that the transfer will either impair their existing water right, is contrary to the conservation of water, or is detrimental to the public welfare. The public welfare criterion was added to the state statutes in 1985 and has never been defined in case law. I will discuss this in greater detail later in the book.

Pursuing a water transfer protest is like participating in a trial: the OSE appoints a hearing examiner; there is a pre-hearing conference to set a schedule; both protestants and applicants must provide a witness list, proceed with discovery, call witnesses, etc.; then, the examiner makes a recommendation to the State Engineer who approves or disapproves the transfer. To wend your way through this process you obviously need a lawyer. Or not. You can represent yourself, just as you can in a court of law, but it ain't easy.

Fortunately, there are New Mexico water lawyers who have ably represented many protestants over the years, often *pro bono*, in transfer cases. One of the ablest is Peter White, who represented protestants in the Top of the World (TOW) water transfer protest. He also worked on the Rio Hondo water sharing agreement, tried to bring peace to the warring factions in Ojo Sarco, and intervened in an internecine dispute in El Valle that I will detail later in the book. Ironically, he worked for the OSE before he retired and started representing all of us who usually ended up doing battle with that agency.

Peter has long been critical of the way the OSE functions in water transfer protests. He believes that the OSE purposely tries to dismiss protests through technicalities—for instance, trying to deny protestants standing— placing undue burdens on those seeking to deny transfers. He's outlined several areas of concern in OSE policy: 1) the legitimacy and quantity of water rights being transferred need to be determined; 2) the Rio Grande Compact always needs to be raised as an issue of public welfare; 3) the OSE uses a loophole in the state regulations that allows municipalities to hold water rights for 40 years without having to put them to beneficial use;

4) water judges in each district can't be disqualified even though they often have conflicts of interest; and 5) the OSE is always reluctant to enforce priority administration because so many municipalities have junior water rights. White emphasizes that water sharing is a more equitable solution to the state's water adjudications, but that sometimes priority must be invoked to protect acequias and rural communities.

Doug Wolf, Peter's co-counsel on the TOW protest, worked for the New Mexico Environmental Law Center. He also represented those who protested Sipapu Ski Area and Summer Resort's proposal to change agricultural water rights to commercial rights for snowmaking and to transfer downstream water rights to the ski area (more on this later). Through this very contentious fight Doug always kept his cool and was able to meet and communicate with the Sipapu defenders who often demonized the protestors. Doug was also the lead attorney in the fight against the 1997 attempt by Intel Corporation, the giant computer chip factory based in Rio Rancho, outside of Albuquerque, to transfer 2,027 acre feet of water, worth $4 million, near San Marcial in Socorro County, to its three wells that provide 2.9 million gallons of water daily to the plant.

The New Mexico Environmental Law Center was founded by attorney Doug Meiklejohn, whom I first met when he was an assistant New Mexico Attorney General and involved in the negotiations over the Cibola National Forest Plan in the 1980s, which I discuss in my book *Culture Clash: Environmental Politics in New Mexico Forest Communities*. I'm pretty sure Doug always thought of me as a hot head, from his bureaucratic perch (it was very unusual for an agency like the Attorney General's Office to get involved in an environmental battle with the Forest Service, so he gets a lot of credit there). But he approved Doug Wolf's representation in the TOW and Sipapu protests, and I thank him for that. Over the years he has also guided the law firm in its representation of pueblo communities fighting uranium mining and rural communities challenged by other water transfer applications.

David Benavides is the longtime land and water attorney at New Mexico Legal Aid. He's the go-to-guy on just about everything related to acequias and land grants, and as I will describe later in the book, has helped acequias that have been challenged by the United States Forest Service over their rights to conduct maintenance and repairs on their diversion dams and ditches that lie within the national forest. He was my behind the scenes guide when I protested *pro se* (advocating for oneself) a water transfer by El Prado Water and Sanitation District that was part of the Abeyta, or Taos Pueblo Settlement (see Chapter Thirty-two). Enrique Romero, a promising young attorney who was born and raised in Nambe and whose father, Orlando Romero, is a prominent New Mexico historian, worked with David for several years before transferring to the New Mexico Acequia Association.

Malcolm Ebright doesn't like to admit he's a lawyer. But I have to include his work as an historian who has conducted enormous archival research to help acequias determine their priority dates in the adjudication process. Other attorneys who have worked with the acequia community include Fred Waltz, Mary Humphrey, Connie Odéz, Jennifer McCabe and Peter Shoenfeld, who represented Taos County in its protest of the Top of the World water transfer (Chapter Thirty-eight), former UNM professor Em Hall, and Simeon Herskovits, who I will discuss later in the chapter on the Taos Regional Water Plan. Simeon was instrumental in drafting a Public Welfare Statement, first for the Taos Regional Water Plan and then as an ordinance for Taos County, in an attempt to define the criteria of public welfare in protests to water transfers.

On what I call the dark side we have the Stein and Brockman Law Firm. One of the state's most powerful water lawyers, Jim Brockman has represented many water brokers in the state, including Richard Cook, the Española businessman who challenged on constitutional grounds the 2003 state statute that gives acequia commissions the authority to deny water transfers if they would prove detrimental to the integrity of the acequia, (the statute was upheld). A listing of the Stein and Brockman Law Firm clients reveals an almost entirely urban roster, from Las Cruces to Española.[11] The firm has also been one of the driving forces behind attempts to limit due process in water transfer protests. Brockman appeared before the state legislative Water and Natural Resources Committee in July of 2015 to promote Senate Bill 665 that was introduced in that year's session to change the requirements for filing a protest of a water transfer or appropriation with the Office of the State Engineer. The bill proposed to change the regulations in three ways: 1) require that a protestant provide evidence of standing "up front" in the protest letter submitted to the OSE; 2) limit the participation of a protestant to those issues identified in the letter of protest; and 3) allow applicants to request the recovery of attorney fees and costs for "frivolous" protests.

Attorney Connie Odé and New Mexico Acequia Association director Paula Garcia testified at the same hearing that OSE regulations, as currently written, provide important protections of the public interest. Section 72-2-17 of the Water Code provides specifically that in the conduct of State Engineer hearings, "opportunity shall be afforded all parties to appear and present evidence and argument on all issues involved," and "a party may have and be represented by counsel and may conduct cross-examination for a full and true disclosure of the facts." They pointed out that because political subdivisions of the state (acequias or mutual domestic water associations) have automatic standing to protest and participate and cannot be restricted in the evidence or arguments they can present, other parties and individuals should be accorded these same rights. As for allowing applicants to recover attorney fees and costs for "frivolous" protests, this would have a "chilling effect" on public participation. The definition of "frivolous" is wholly subjective, and there already exist adequate remedies to determine early in the process both the basis of a protestant's standing and the nature of the claims.

Brockman currently represents El Prado Water and Sanitation District, one of the parties to the Abeyta, or Taos Pueblo Adjudication, and challenged my standing as a protestant to the district's proposed application to appropriate water from two deep, Rio Grande wells near the Gorge Bridge (more on this later).

Then there are the ones who end up working for whomever pays the bills and in that process participate in multiple representations where conflict of interest is rampant. Many of the attorneys who've represented various parties in state water adjudications participate in a revolving door exercise moving from representing private clients, counties, and the state, all of which have conflicting claims in the adjudications. John Utton, who works for a private law firm, has been a contract attorney for the County of Santa Fe since the 1997 application to transfer Top of the World water rights to San Ildefonso Pueblo. As a protestant to that transfer I've had many dealings with John over the years as he tried to negotiate a settlement with us to drop our protest. His most ambitious offer came in 2004 when he told us if we dropped our protest he would recommend to the county that it not pipe TOW water south of Otowi Gauge. The 588 afy would be used only for the water delivery system to non-pueblo residents in the Aamodt Adjudication, north of the gauge. In 2006 a formal settlement offer made another commitment that the county would not acquire, transfer, or use water rights from community acequias in order to satisfy its obligation to acquire an additional 750-acre feet per year of water rights under the Aamodt Settlement Agreement. We turned down John's offer (the offer would eventually be enacted), stating that water should stay in its area of origin and purpose of use, and that the OSE should deny transfers that underwrite inherently inequitable adjudications like the Aamodt that threaten the integrity of another region or subregion's water resources. Once the Aamodt Final Decree was signed by the Secretary of the Department of the Interior John went to work for the state in the Abeyta Settlement.

Five

We Find Out About Top of the World

It came as a shock when we first learned in 1997 that Santa Fe County had bought up approximately 600 acre feet of water rights (consumptive use) from Top of the World Farm (TOW) in northern Taos County (El Valle is the southern most village in this county). The county planned to transfer those rights to a takeout on San Ildefonso Pueblo, just north of the Otowi Gauge, and pipe them south of the gauge to the Buckman Well Field, Santa Fe's main source of water. As I referenced in the Introduction, the Rio Grande Compact divides New Mexico into three basins—upper, middle, and lower—which act as de facto barriers to the transfer of water from northern New Mexico to the middle or lower basins. This water transfer was seen as a brazen attempt to circumvent these barriers by diverting water above the Otowi Gauge and piping it to an area south of the gauge that could set a precedent for other municipalities and developers to acquire water rights in northern New Mexico and transfer them to the lower basins. The city of Santa Fe was also a partner in this project, although city officials claimed that they would only be diverting San Juan/Chama Project water rights that they already owned. (San Juan/Chama Project water comes from tributaries to the San Juan River, which flows through the Azotea Tunnel under the Continental Divide into Heron Lake in northern New Mexico, and then flows into the Rio Chama. It was completed in 1978 to access New Mexico's share of Colorado River water.)

The Top of the World water rights are groundwater rights, diverted through wells on the Farm, that would be retired and transferred to San Ildefonso Pueblo, where they would be taken out of the Rio Grande. The rationale for this transfer was that if you stop pumping groundwater at TOW the water will migrate to the Rio Grande and flow downhill to the Pueblo (much more on this later in the book). The TOW wells, beginning in the 1950s, had watered a breadbasket of produce (potatoes, sugar beets, pinto beans, alfalfa, barley, and many kinds of vegetables) in this area referred to as Sunshine Valley, between SH 522 and Ute Mountain near the Colorado border. When the area was adjudicated in the Red River Adjudication most of the farmers were allotted the amount of water they had been pumping. Production continued into the 80s, until sell-offs and arguments over ownership shut down much of the production.[12]

Members of the New Mexico Acequia Association found out about Santa Fe County's purchase of the water rights and the transfer application was protested by nineteen groups and individuals, including the Acequia Madre de Las Vegas, Acequia Junta y Cienega in Embudo, the Taos-based environmental group Amigos Bravos, and other individual parciantes (Mark and I were protestants). Our protest raised issues of impairment, conservation, and public welfare, the three criteria upon which a protest can be based, citing the effects of historic pumping on the surface flows of the Rio Grande; the lack of a county conservation plan; and issues of public welfare such as moving water rights out of areas of origin, the impact on traditional agricultural uses, and moving junior water rights from the upper basin to the middle basin.

Santa Fe County Utilities Director Estevan Lopez and Santa Fe City staff were surprised by the fierce opposition to the project, presumably because the water rights weren't acequia water rights. David Wolf, also with the county utility, had this to say: "I don't think we could have predicted which communities would perceive this as a threat."[13] They quickly asked to meet with the protestants hoping to head them off, but as the NMAA members pointed out, the removal of land from the agricultural base and the transfer of water rights out of the northern basin sets a dangerous precedent for all of northern New Mexico, including the acequia community.

It was also a shock to find out that Estevan Lopez was my neighbor. He lived in one of the small neighborhoods that surround the town of Peñasco. He served on the school board for several years and was a member of the Santa Barbara Grazing Association, a group of 20 or so cattlemen who had permits to graze their animals in the beautiful Santa Barbara Allotment, which includes the Pecos Wilderness. He was also a Santa Barbara Land Grant heir. So what was he doing as director of the Santa Fe County Utilities that wanted to move Top of the World water from Taos County, where he lived, to Santa Fe County, where he worked? I don't really know the answer to that question, but I watched him move from director of the Utilities department to the head of the Interstate Stream Commission, a branch of the Office of the State Engineer, and finally to the Bureau of Reclamation where he was appointed director in 2014.

In March of 1999 the Office of the State Engineer (OSE) convened a pre-hearing on the TOW transfer only to find out that the water rights were under disputed ownership by Wrangler Properties and the four individuals applying to transfer them. OSE hearing examiners decided that this question was a "threshold" issue that must be resolved by the county, the farm owners, and the parties that claimed ownership of the water rights before the hearing could proceed. Attorneys for the Water Rights Division of the OSE, with the support of attorneys for the protestants, then claimed the issue of violation of the Rio Grande Compact also constituted a "threshold" issue. The protestants' lawyers, Peter White and Doug Wolf, would subsequently raise other "threshold" issues that dragged the transfer hearing process into the early 2000s. These included questions as to whether the rights that would be used were ground or surface water; questions as to the place of use; lack of a county water conservation plan; questions regarding the technical and financial feasibility of an infiltration gallery, or takeout diversion; and issues of access on Pueblo land.

In the summer of 1999 we learned that Taoseño Tom Worrell had purchased Top of the World Farm. Worrell was a notorious developer whose land and historic property acquisitions in the town of Taos had created considerable controversy. His private residence burned down as a result of arson. Our lawyers received copies of deeds verifying that in June a Worrell-owned company called Macho Grande de Rio Grande Ltd., a British Virgin Islands company, had indeed purchased 3,166 acres of land from Wrangler Properties. Unfortunately, Macho Grande subsequently signed a quitclaim deed to the disputed water rights being transferred to Santa Fe County, opening the door for the water transfer to proceed. According to a spokesperson at Dharma Properties, Worrell's Taos-based company, the intent of the purchase of Top of the World Farms was to "keep the water rights in Taos County." Why the company then signed off on the disputed water rights was the $64,000 question.

I have a folder about four inches thick that contains all the documents pertaining to the Top of the World Farm protest that never ended—literally. Before we could even get to the substantive issues, the Aamodt Adjudication of the Pojoaque Valley subsumed the TOW protest. This adjudication, and its relationship with TOW, will be more fully explored in subsequent chapters. Suffice it to say for now, when the sitting judge in the adjudication, Edwin Mechem, ruled in 2001 that the four pueblos being adjudicated—Pojoaque, San Ildefonso, Tesuque, and Nambe—were limited to their domestic water use that was established between 1846 (the year the United States seized control of New Mexico) and 1924 (the year of the Pueblo Lands Act that sought to resolve disputes over pueblo land and water rights), political hell broke loose. The pueblos' development plans would never be met by such a limited water supply, and in the wake of the decision, Senator Pete Domenici met with both the pueblos and the Pojoaque Valley Irrigation District (PVID) to push for a negotiated settlement of the adjudication to preclude Mechem's decision. Domenici insisted there was consensus for a regional water delivery system, which could potentially supply all domestic water needs within the valley.

Under continuing pressure from Senator Domenici, and despite fierce opposition from the non-pueblo residents of the Pojoaque Valley who did not want to give up their wells for a delivery system, Santa Fe County abandoned the project to use the TOW water rights at the Buckman Well Field and instead slated them to supply the water delivery system as part of the Aamodt settlement. In 2006 the county bought an additional 1,100 afy of water rights at Top of the World to complete the needed water rights for the water delivery system. While the Aamodt settlement negotiations continued, our TOW protest sat in limbo until Santa Fe County, in 2015, applied to transfer the entire 1,700 afy of rights it had acquired. Subsequent chapters will fill in the details between these years from the first protest in 1999 to the 2015-second protest of all the TOW water rights.

Six

Instream Flow

In 2016 the environmental group WildEarth Guardians, formerly Forest Guardians, filed a lawsuit demanding that State Engineer Tom Blaine force the Middle Rio Grande Conservancy District (MRGCD) to prove that it is putting its allotted water to "beneficial use," i.e., that the farmers in the district are actually irrigating the District's 65,000 acres with the permitted water. WildEarth Guardians wants whatever water the district isn't using for what is called instream flow, for bosque vegetation and wildlife. While there may indeed be accounting issues within the District, any water that's not being used for irrigation either remains in the reservoirs, the river, or is counted as return flow, so it's very unlikely this lawsuit will move the issue of instream flow towards a legal definition (the Office of the State Engineer has filed a motion to dismiss the lawsuit and the court has yet to act, as of this writing).

Environmentalists have been trying for a number of years to require the state to keep water in the Rio Grande between San Acacia and Elephant Butte as instream flow to save the silvery minnow. Their previous legal actions have also been directed at what they perceive as the bad boy MRGCD, which governs the river from Cochiti Pueblo in the north to Isleta Pueblo in the south and all the farmland in between. Created in 1923, it eventually incorporated the 71 existing pueblo and Mexicano acequias and newer community ditches into its system of canals and drains, and has for years been accused of failure to account for its enormous water use and lack of conservation management. But what the environmentalists continually fail to acknowledge is the connection between the conservancy district and the acequias. While the acequia community doesn't necessarily see eye to eye with the MRGCD in terms of sustainable water use, it does recognize that they both share many of the same interests in water policy. Acequia advocates have said over and over again in public meetings, in roundtable discussions with these environmentalists, in newspaper articles, and at the state legislature, that defining instream flow as a federal water right or as a beneficial use is directly tied to the commodification of water rights that have been traditionally defined as community rights tied to their lands of origin. Once state water law is subordinated and water becomes a free market commodity sought after by developers, urban areas, or the federal government, acequia water rights are vulnerable.

Parciantes are already being marginalized by not being able to actually use their "appropriative rights." Historically, of course, water was shared as a community resource with less regard to appropriative or priority rights, concepts that were formalized when New Mexico became a state. But even with the imposition of priority and private property concepts, acequia parciantes have continued to share their village water, particularly in times of drought. Now, as more and more northern New Mexico parciantes become involved in organic and specialty farming, they face the threat of losing these rights.

In 1998, then New Mexico Attorney General Tom Udall was asked by state senators Dede Feldman and Carlos Cisneros to render an opinion regarding the controversial issue of instream flow, which they defined as leaving water in a stream bed where it is "used" by way of providing aquatic and riparian environment for fish and wildlife. (Several legislative proposals, called water conservation acts instead of instream flow, had been already put forward.) Before issuing an opinion, the Attorney General asked the Office of the State Engineer (OSE) to prepare an opinion regarding both the legal and administrative issues related to instream flow. Parciantes and acequia associations from all over northern New Mexico attended a meeting with then State Engineer Tom Turney on March 19 to hear a presentation from the legal division of his office regarding its analysis.

Attorneys DL Sanders and Stephen Farris addressed the question of whether New Mexico law "permits the state engineer to afford legal protection to instream flows for recreational, fish or wildlife, or ecological purposes." Their answer essentially was that although neither common law nor state statute recognize the concept of instream flow, applications can be made to the state engineer requesting such use, and permission can be granted based upon current standards and guidelines. Because of this, their recommendation to the attorney general was that it was not necessary to pass legislation for the state to recognize instream use as an appropriate water right.

Sanders and Farris provided some historical information to explain how they arrived at this conclusion. Former state engineer Steve Reynolds was of the opinion that instream flow is not a valid water right because it has no point of diversion, or means of quantifying or differentiating that right from the other water rights in the river. His successor, Eluid Martinez, felt that because there is no unappropriated surface water in New Mexico, any instream flow right would have to be a transferred right, which could account for its measurability. If someone applied to transfer a water right to instream flow, he was prepared to proceed through the official protest procedure where all parties would be at the table to hear issues of beneficial use, public welfare, conservation, etc., and proceed to a court opinion. Tom Turney, the state engineer at the time of the hearing, was of the opinion that in order to distinguish a water right for instream flow all water rights would have to be gauged. But because the best available gauges have large margins of error, the difficulties of accurately gauging water rights was enormous.

Farris and Sanders also pointed out that other western states that legally recognize instream flow use on paper actually have no realistic way of guaranteeing that the water remains in their rivers. Most states, like New Mexico, have established priority rights through adjudications and historical documentation and must abide by these priority dates. Any attempt to claim priority for instream flow would open up a huge can of worms and could very well result in priority fights with Native Americans.

While most of those parciantes present—including representatives from the Taos Valley Acequia Association, the state Acequia Commission, the New Mexico Acequia Association—agreed the OSE would be the better agency to make decisions regarding instream flow, as opposed to the state legislature, there was general consensus that the OSE needed to have some regulations in place that would guide any future decisions regarding instream flow applications. Palemon Martinez, president of the Taos Valley Acequia Association, pointed out that former state engineer Steve Reynolds called instream flow a "beneficial non-use" and that administratively, enforcing instream flow would be a nightmare not only for the state engineer but at the local level as well. While Turney agreed with Martinez, he said that there are perhaps places where it might be appropriate to recognize an instream flow, or "minimum flow" right, such as between El Vado Dam and Abiquiu Lake, where the flow is artificially adjusted by dam releases, or on a section of the Red River where there are no other diversions.

Parciantes also expressed their concern that they would have to bear the financial burden of protesting individual instream flow applications before the OSE, and that any decisions favoring instream flow rights could set a bad precedent. Turney announced that the OSE had just approved lowering water application protest hearing fees from $300 per day to a flat fee of $25. It also amended regulations to allow acequias, corporations, or organizations to be represented by an authorized official, employee, or member of the particular entity.

Subsequently, on Friday, March 27, Attorney General Tom Udall and Assistant Attorney General Alletta Belin announced that in their opinion New Mexico constitutional, state, and case law permits the state engineer to afford legal protection of instream flow. They concurred with the state engineer that applications submitted for approval must be transfers from traditional diversionary use, not new appropriations, and that gauging devices would have to be used to measure any instream flow right.

Udall and Belin arrived at this decision by analyzing the opinion that "it is beneficial use, and not diversion, that is the constitutional hallmark of a water right." They found that neither constitutional law nor state statute indicate that there is a requirement for a diversion in order to establish a water right, and that instream flow could constitute a beneficial use (although beneficial use is not defined by statute). While there is some New Mexico case law that does support the opinion that there must be a point of diversion to establish a water right, those decisions have been criticized and should not be applied in any general way. Because of these findings, Udall and Belin agreed with the OSE that it is not necessary to legislate instream flow: the OSE is legally mandated to hear water right transfers for the purpose of instream flow if approval of the transfer is "conditioned on installation of accurate and continuous gauging throughout the permitted stream reach."

In a June 1998 op-ed for *La Jicarita News*, John Brown, longtime editor of *The Water Dialogue*, had this to say about some of his environmental friends who continued to push for instream flow (less than a year after the AG decision the environmental group Rio Grande Restoration tried to get an instream bill passed in the state legislature):

"Most acequias and parciantes are not currently allowed to take all the water they're entitled to under law (the state's 'duty of water' to each farm). What they actually get in drier years is based on 'average historical supply,' and amounts to only 60 to 70 percent of their appropriative 'rights.' Acequias already share the pain in drought years. As a result, farms are not as productive as they might be, and farmers and acequia-based communities are being economically marginalized. I don't think environment-friendly folks who think seriously about this issue really want this to happen, but the policies they advocate will hasten the demise of New Mexico's traditional villages and landscapes, particularly in the north.

"A fundamental mistake in the thinking of both economists and 'free market environmentalists' is the notion that water is just another tradable commodity, a private good whose highest and best uses will be discovered in the marketplace. They're wrong about that. Water has a community value as well as a commodity price. For many New Mexicans in pueblo and Hispano traditional communities, the value of water is stated in spiritual terms. If a cynic is one 'who knows the price of everything, and the value of nothing,' the economic argument is nothing but cynical. Rights to water are use rights, not absolute private property rights. Water is owned by the state in trust for the common good, and water rights depend on beneficial use. Impairment of a third party's right is one bar to transferring a right . . . . But it is not the only one. A transfer can be forbidden if it is contrary to conservation or to the public welfare."[14]

Our neighboring state, Colorado, passed an instream flow rights bill in 1973 but the concept is limited in scope by the Colorado Water Conservation Board, the only entity that can appropriate the rights. They of course have very junior priority dates, which means, as David Owen explains in his 2017 book, *Where the Water Goes: Life and Death Along the Colorado River*, "that during dry periods, when exercising them [instream flow rights] would be the most useful to whatever river systems they're connected with, they inevitably get called out by something senior. The CWCB has the power to acquire water rights with older priority dates by buying or leasing them from willing sellers or lenders, but it doesn't have the power to acquire them by eminent domain."[15]

Seven

Protecting Acequia Pre-existing Rights on Federal Land

In the mid and late 1990s the acequia community in El Valle continued to function as it always had under the guidance of Tomás and the other older men on the commissions. Many of these men, all born and raised in El Valle, had been away for years working the mines of Colorado, herding sheep in Wyoming, or working in the canning factories of California. During their absence their wives and children irrigated the fields and gardens that sustained them. By the time I arrived in1992 the men were back in the village, either retired or scamming together a livelihood in an area where jobs were few and far between. Tomás at one time drove the school bus and fire crew buses for the Forest Service, ran a gas station and pool hall in the village, worked briefly as a sheriff, and had a grazing permit as part of an association that ran cattle in the forest above the village.

They managed the acequias conscientiously, if not seriously, meaning there was a lot of joking around, teasing, and fun in the acequia community. Every parciante had a personal relationship with the mayordomo, who came to your house to let you know when it was your turn to get the water. Jacobo Romero, whom Bill deBuys wrote about in his book *River of Traps, Life in a Mountain Village,* rode his caballo. Orlando, who was the mayordomo when we arrived, road his ATV, which he *referred* to as his caballo. We all got together and cleaned the acequia or hired a cousin or nephew or peon to clean it for us at the annual spring limpieza, and often there was a free lunch cooked by someone's wife or girlfriend and occasionally there was a party with a band and potluck dinner. (More women started cleaning the ditch in the 2000s as the men got older and more reliant on peones to work, men and women.)

But there were structural problems ahead. The three presas, or dams, in El Valle were constructed long ago of logs that had badly deteriorated in the harsh winters, sun baked summers, and periodic floods on the Rio de las Trampas. The flood of 1997 just about took out the Acequia de Abajo presa, so in 1998 the commission contacted the Acequia Rehabilitation Program of the Interstate Stream Commission (ISC), which helps fund acequia rehabilitation and maintenance projects. Mark soon came on board as a commissioner, along with Arsenio Montoya (Tomás's brother) and Clarence Macareñas, with Tomás as mayordomo, and with their combined talents we were off on a five-year long project. Mark worked through the bureaucratic process of getting the necessary permits—including an environmental assessment—to access funding through the ISC while Tomás, Clarence, and Arsenio worked their contacts as lifelong community members to hire our contractor, get additional funding from Taos Soil and Water Conservation District, and donations from the Presbyterian Church's Self-Development of People Committee and the McCune Foundation. In October of 2002, the community met to celebrate the completion of a gabion basket, concrete-capped dam that will hopefully serve the community through a hundred year flood. We raised enough money to pay for the entire $100,000 presa without charging the parciantes a cent.

I want to give Mark some extra credit here. While we all worked on this project (I wrote several of the grant proposals), Mark dedicated a phenomenal amount of time to this project without any recompense other than the respect of the parciantes. It was a bureaucratic nightmare, wading through all the rules and regulations of the Acequia Rehabilitation Program, getting clearances for the environmental assessment, working with the contractor and acequia engineer (we had a great friend in the engineer, Mike Meyer) on an almost daily basis, writing grant proposals, and coordinating the entire project so that everything came together when it was supposed to.

But at least he didn't have to contend with an even greater bureaucratic nightmare, the claim by the United States Forest Service (USFS) that any acequias that are located on national forest land have to get special use permits from that agency to conduct maintenance and repairs on their ditches. Legal arguments to confirm acequia pre-existing rights were played out over a number of years; during the process the parciantes and acequia associations suffered financial and emotional hardship.

For over a year, beginning in 2000, the parciantes of the Nacimiento Community Ditch Association (NCDA), near Cuba, argued with Santa Fe National Forest over access rights to its acequia and diversion dam near

San Gregorio Reservoir in the San Pedro Parks Wilderness Area. When the association approached the Forest Service about wanting to do maintenance work on its acequia, which entailed improving the existing log and sandbag structure on Clear Creek with a rock and mortar and/or log headgate diversion, the Forest Service told NCDA that it needed a special use permit for its entire acequia system, not just the proposed work on the diversion. The association, represented by Community and Indian Legal Services lawyers David Benavides and Margaret Carde (a division of New Mexico Legal Aid), claimed that rights-of-way for water conveyance, established prior to 1891, come under an 1866 Congressional Act that grants easement without the necessity of a permit or other authorization, and that wilderness restrictions are subject to existing rights.

The Forest Service, on the other hand, claimed that the 1976 Federal Lands Policy Management Act (FLPMA) "includes the right to reasonably regulate the exercise of vested water rights and accompanying rights of way obtained under the 1866 Act where such rights and rights of way lie within national forest." What this legalese meant is that even though parciantes have established easements and acequias, the Forest Service claims it has the authority to regulate them.

Over the course of the next few months the association and its lawyers met with forest representatives to discuss an equitable balance between NCDA's valid and historic rights and the need for management of public lands. However, the Forest Service, in a May 30th letter to Community and Indian Legal Services, remained intransigent in its insistence that it had the authority to regulate these uses. This time its argument was that "entirely apart from FLPMA" the Secretary of Agriculture retains the right to "reasonably regulate the exercise of vested water rights and accompanying rights-of-way obtained under the 1866 Act where such rights and rights-of-way lie within a National Forest." But what constitutes "reasonable" was under question, be it under FLPMA or the Secretary of Agriculture. A Colorado water lawyer, Peter Fleming, had written an article in *Natural Resources Notes* that the Forest Service Manual, an internal agency guidebook, states that pre-FLPMA rights of way can be regulated only to the extent such regulation does not reduce the rights conferred by the original right of way grant. Therefore, "no federal authorization is necessary to maintain or make minor changes to the water facility in order to maintain the capacity of the facility as it existed prior to the adoption of FLPMA."

Finally, at the end of 2001, the Forest Service recognized the association's right to operate and make minor improvements on its acequia without a special use permit. In a letter dated September 26, then Regional Forester Eleanor Towns (Region 6 includes New Mexico and Arizona) wrote Benavides that "no special-use authorization is required for the presence or use of the [NCDA] ditch," and that "no special-use authorization is required to conduct normal maintenance or minor improvements to maintain the capacity of the ditch." She also stated that because a "portion of the ditch system is within the San Pedro Parks Wilderness, the use of mechanized equipment, motorized equipment, and non-native materials must be evaluated carefully." She directed the staff of the Santa Fe National Forest to work with the NCDA to implement these decisions.

In a subsequent December letter, Cuba District Ranger Roberto Rodriguez informed Benavides and Carde that under the directive from Towns he had decided that no special use permit for maintenance and minor improvements of the ditch was necessary, but that a special use permit would be required for the construction of a new diversion dam. This was an especially significant statement, as over the next ten years the issue of whether a USFS permit was required for the construction of new diversion dams would raise its head many times as acequias sought, like we did in El Valle, to replace their worn out log structures. And Regional Forester Towns's decision came too late for Virgil Trujillo, who was cited by the Española Ranger District for taking equipment into the forest without a special use permit and ended up paying a fine for the work he had done to maintain his acequia.

Trujillo is a well-known land grant activist from Abiquiu, on the west side of the Rio Grande on the Rio Chama. He served as ranch manager at Ghost Ranch, a longtime Presbyterian retreat and community facility, was a member of the board of directors of the Quivira Coalition, and a highly respected rangeland conservationist. He is also a parciante who owns a water right on the Lopez Ditch in the old community of Vallecitos, above Abiquiu, in the Santa Fe National Forest. In the early 1970s the Forest Service bulldozed the main ditch, which lies on national forest land, when they were chaining to create pastureland. Trujillo's uncle, who owned land fed by the ditch, asked that the Forest Service restore the ditch but had to eventually go to the Forest Supervisor in order to get restitution. The Forest Service paid for his uncle to restore the ditch but also installed a water line from Vallecitos Creek three miles to an allotment pasture, without establishing a water right, and in the process destroyed the diversion dam and rendered a nearby spring useless.

Virgil Trujillo at Ghost Ranch workshop

In 1994 Virgil Trujillo bought this land from his uncle's family. In the spring of 2000 he took a bulldozer across USFS land to his property, Rancho Alegre, to build earthen catchment basins. He asked permission of the Forest Service to clean the catchment basins on the Oso and Vallecito Allotments where he is also a parciante, but the agency denied him permission.

Trujillo went ahead with the maintenance work on his basins and the diversion dam, which lies on USFS property. Several days after Trujillo began the work, John Miera, Española District Ranger, and law enforcement personnel issued Trujillo a citation and ordered him to stop work immediately. Miera claimed that Trujillo had illegally taken heavy equipment across Forest Service roads and pipeline easement to work on his dam, which could impact archeological sites and a wetland. Trujillo countered that the Forest Service had already bulldozed the original diversion dam and the new easement along the pipeline, but he agreed to stop work.

Trujillo believed that as a land grant heir and parciante, he, like the members of the NCDA, holds pre-existing access rights, which are not subject to regulation by the Forest Service, to maintain and use his ditch. Relying on this principle, he pled not guilty in federal court. After the judge listened to his explanation, he ordered Trujillo and the Forest Service to work out a settlement within 30 days. When Trujillo, Miera, and range staff biologist Donald Serano met out in the field at the ditch, Miera insisted that Trujillo needed a special use permit to use the ditch. Trujillo said he knew nothing about a special use permit and told Miera that because the ditch pre-dated Forest Service tenure no permit was necessary. According to Trujillo Miera then told him, "I'll tell you if you can put water in the ditch." Trujillo responded, "You better cite me right now because I'm putting water in this ditch this afternoon and you better be prepared to cite everyone in northern New Mexico if you think you have the authority to stop people from exercising their water rights."

After a second meeting Trujillo felt it was obvious that the Forest Service wasn't interested in an equitable settlement and was intent upon prevailing. However, Trujillo, whose career has been based on finding innovative solutions to land management problems, felt that an adversarial relationship with the Forest Service was counter productive and at the next court hearing offered to do the restoration work, under the direction of the Forest Service, if the fines were dropped. The judge approved this civil settlement, but much to Trujillo's surprise, the Forest Service then raised the issue of criminal charges and insisted that he pay $1,400 in damages and a $300 fine. Trujillo asked to meet with the Forest Service to see if they could again negotiate a settlement, but according to Trujillo, the Forest Service and its attorney threatened to seek $7,000 in damages if the case went to trial. Back in front of the judge, Trujillo said, "I don't want to plead guilty but I can't afford not to." Although the judge told him he wouldn't let him plead guilty if he didn't believe that he was guilty, Trujillo said he "couldn't afford the battle or the trips to Albuquerque." The judge accepted his plea and imposed a $300 fine, but it was agreed that Trujillo could do $1,400 worth of restitution in labor or advice. As a final insult, the Forest Service wanted him to be paid $50 a day for his work and to be placed on probation, but Trujillo protested and the judge dismissed these requests.

When *La Jicarita News* interviewed Trujillo about this incident he said it was "a black cloud that will always hang over me. But I hope the other parciantes who are fighting this same battle will be able to get the Forest Service to recognize that it doesn't have the authority to require a special use permit or regulate our pre-exiting water rights."[16] *La Jicarita* spoke with both Wayne Thornton, Director of Lands and Minerals at the Regional Office, and Mike Fraser, Recreation Lands Staff Officer at the Santa Fe National Forest, about cases like Trujillo's that were dealt with before Towns's letter essentially changed the Forest Service position regarding the 1866 Act. They both agreed that the Forest Service needed to make sure that this information had been sent out to all the ranger districts; a copy of Towns's letter had already been sent to John Miera, Española District Ranger. According to Thornton, the letter from Eleanor Towns provided the framework for district officers to have a wide latitude in verifying the validity of a ditch—records, oral histories, state records, etc.—and according the parciantes the right of way for routine maintenance and minor improvements without a special use permit unless there was specific case law to the contrary.

Española District Ranger John Miera would come back to haunt many more parciantes and acequias as he moved through the Forest Service ranks to other districts, including the Camino Real in Peñasco, and eventually to the Forest Supervisor's Office in Taos, where he became head of Special Permits. I will discuss these ensuing cases in a later chapter.

Eight

San Luis Valley Water Wars

The story of the vast reservoir of water that sits below the San Luis Valley's Baca Ranch in southern Colorado provided fascinating fare to the papers that covered environmental and social issues in the west in the late 1990s, including *La Jicarita News*. The Baca Ranch's history is inextricably tied to that of New Mexico's land grants. In 1863 the U.S. Congress agreed to settle the Luis Maria de Baca land grant dispute in the Las Vegas area by agreeing to a land swap that gave Baca's heirs five sites, each 100,000 acres in size, located anywhere in what had formerly been Mexico. The Valles Caldera National Preserve in the Jemez Mountains of New Mexico is one of those former grants; the northernmost is the Baca Ranch of the San Luis Valley.

The "Baca" has seen many owners over the years, including William Gilpin, the first governor of the Colorado Territory, until in the 1980s it fell into the hands of Canadian oil millionaire Maurice Strong and his American Water Development company. They hatched a scheme to pump 200,000 acre feet of water per year from beneath the ranch to the Front Range (the water short county between Denver and Colorado Springs). That plan died an ignoble death at the hands of Valley farmers, ranchers, and environmentalists, aided by the county government, asserting that pumping water in the San Luis closed basin would adversely affect existing wells and riparian areas.

The San Luis Valley is geologically divided into two sections by a wall of impermeable rock running east and west, roughly through the middle of the valley near the towns of Center and Hooper. Water on the south side of the subterranean barrier flows into the Rio Grande; water on the north side is trapped in what geologists term a "closed basin." In articles written for his *Colorado Central Magazine*, Ed Quillen said that conservative estimates suggested there are several billion acre feet of water (one acre foot equals approximately 330,000 gallons) trapped deep beneath the surface. Furthermore, scientists claim it receives an additional million acre

63

feet per year from run-off.

The state of Colorado appropriates approximately 40,000 acre feet of this water per year through its federally and state funded Closed Basin Project to meet Colorado's obligation to New Mexico via the Rio Grande. This still leaves hundreds of thousands of acre feet of recharge water which, according to Colorado law, may be unappropriated.

The closed basin water again became an issue after Strong sold the 100,000 acre Baca Ranch (located near the town of Crestone) to Falloran Investment of San Francisco, whose managing partner was Gary Boyce, a pistol-toting, Humvee-driving, hand-tooled knee-high cowboy boot-wearing former San Luis Valley resident who went to California as a young man and came back a millionaire. Boyce, through his Stockman's Water Company, attempted to reopen the door to the sale of the water rights to urban areas on the Front Range by drilling wells to export 100,000 to 150,000 acre feet per year. To facilitate this plan he got two constitutional amendments on a Colorado state ballot that would have subverted the power of the local conservation districts that opposed the water transfer. One proposal would have required the costly installation of water meters on many irrigation wells in the San Luis Valley, while the other required local irrigators to pay four times the market rate for water pumped from beneath state trust lands in the Valley. Through the determined efforts of the Rio Grande Water Conservation District both of these amendments were soundly defeated, so Boyce decided to pursue the possibility of sale in the other direction, south, to New Mexico. To "level the playing field" Boyce filed a lawsuit against the Closed Basin Project, which delivers water to New Mexico to meet Rio Grande Compact requirements, so that he could sell ranch water to meet Compact needs. Boyce also began talking to the New Mexico-based environmental group Forest Guardians that was lobbying for a change in the Compact. He saw the possibility to use the Closed Basin Project's cheap and available plumbing to sell some of the water beneath his ranch to New Mexico to meet its federal environmental law requirements (at $5,000 to $10,000 per acre foot, 60,000 acre feet equals between $300 and $600 million). Boyce, therefore, realizing he and Forest Guardians had a common goal, made contributions to the environmental group through his Stockman's Water Company. When *La Jicarita* questioned Boyce about the reason for these contributions, he claimed Forest Guardians " . . . were raising the right issues" and he wanted to help "underwrite their research."[17] He refused to disclose the amount of his contributions. Forest Guardians meanwhile filed a notice of intent to sue state and federal agencies in an attempt to dismantle the Rio Grande Compact, which it claimed unfairly favors agricultural water users and prevents the state from enforcing the Clean Water Act and the Endangered Species Act.

In April of 2000 a new twist was added to this water saga. A bipartisan coalition in Congress proposed to change the status of Sand Dunes National Monument, at the south end of the Baca Ranch, to a national park. While such a change in status might result in any number of cumulative impacts (just ask the residents of Moab, Utah, near Arches National Park, or those in Montrose, Colorado, near the Black Canyon of the Gunnison, how national park status has changed their communities), the issue at the Sand Dunes was water. According to Republican Congressman Scott McInnis, sponsor of the legislation, the primary goal in changing the monument's status was to protect the closed basin water rights in the Baca from development.

That, of course, could only be implemented with the purchase of the ranch from Falloran and Boyce. But as Ed Quillen pointed out in *Colorado Central*, there was no incentive for Boyce to sell water rights that he paid $15 million for to the federal government for the appraised value of $35 million when he could conceivably get $750 million for development rights.

When we were covering the issue no one seemed to know for sure if The Nature Conservancy—the organization that was leading the negotiations to buy the ranch in anticipation of the Sand Dunes status change —was making any headway in purchase negotiations with Boyce or the other investors of Falloran Investments, which owned 50 percent of the Baca Ranch. It was also unclear what the Conservancy would eventually do with the 100,000 ranch, if acquired. Ralph Curtis of the Rio Grande Water Conservation District told *La Jicarita* that there were three distinct parts of the ranch for which the legislation proposed management. The first was called the sand sheet, or the dunes that actually provide sand to the monument, which would become part of the national park. The second area included the pastures and riparian areas that would be managed by U. S. Fish and Wildlife as a wildlife refuge to recharge the groundwater aquifer. The northeast part of the ranch, called the Mountain Tract, abuts the Sangre de Cristo peaks (it includes the 14,154 foot Kit Carson Peak) and could be managed by the Forest Service as wilderness.

Somehow The Nature Conservancy persuaded Boyce to refrain from filing a water rights application and instead sell the Baca Ranch to the Conservancy, which would hold it in escrow until the federal government's purchase. In November of 2004, the final federal appropriation to repay the ranch's $34.5 million purchase price was approved and it was then divided among three federal agencies: 53,135 acres were included in the Great Sand Dunes National Park and Preserve; almost 13,000 acres were added to the Rio Grande National Forest; and the 31,000 remaining acres were included in the Baca National Wildlife Refuge. There would be subsequent controversies over the federal government's right to all of the unappropriated water lying underneath the Park, and over split estate subsurface mineral rights when an oil and gas company came calling. But the Rio Grande Compact remains intact and closed basin water is not flowing down the Rio Grande to save the silvery minnow.

Nine

Lomos Altos Water Transfer Protest

Notification of intent to transfer water rights has been a contentious issue for many years. As it stands now, notice of a water transfer must be published for three consecutive weeks in a publication of general circulation in the areas that could potentially be affected by the transfer. Acequia advocates have several times pushed the state legislature to consider amending the statute to further ensure that citizens who could potentially be affected by such transfers are alerted and given ample opportunity to protest. However, all such proposals have either died in the legislature or been vetoed by a governor, a clear indication that developmental interests that benefit from such transfers continue to control the political process to the detriment of the public at large. It's particularly distressing that the Office of the State Engineer (OSE) also seems to cater to these interests. In the following water transfer case the agency had to be ordered to revisit its initial decision and require that notice be republished in a paper of general circulation.

This case was also unique in that it went all the way to the New Mexico Supreme Court, guided by the untiring efforts of Placitas resident Lynn Montgomery. *La Jicarita News* co-editor Mark Schiller and I lived for twenty years in Placitas, on the north end of the Sandia Mountains in Sandoval County, where we built a house and had two children. The gentrification of the area, driven by its proximity to Albuquerque and aggressive developers, eventually drove us out, in 1991, and continued growth has overwhelmed this traditional land grant community. Mark and I, along with Lynn Montgomery, one of the Lomos Altos protestants, worked to try to control growth through county regulation and developer oversight, but more and more local folks joined in the development boom as contractors and commuting Albuquerque suburbanites soon became the predominant population.

The water situation in Placitas was precarious even when we lived there.

The village itself is supplied with domestic and irrigation water from spring-fed ponds that periodically dry up as drought affects run-off from the Sandia Mountains. The wells that serve the vast outlaying areas (houses currently extend miles up SH 165 from I-25, through the village, up to the national forest boundary of the Sandias, and out for miles north of the village towards San Felipe Pueblo) depend on rivers of underground water that fill rock fissures and are affected by the same run-off from the Sandias. When we built our house in the 1980s our first well went dry, as did those of most of our neighbors. As the subdividers came in the late 80s and 90s, they drilled very deep wells that accessed the Rio Grande basin.

In 1998 Lomos Altos Inc., the agent for two subdivisions in Placitas (the developer, Bob Poling, was a longtime Placitas resident), gave notice that it was seeking to transfer 4.85 acre feet per year of water from the Peralta Main Ditch, 4.2 acre feet per year from the Old Belen Ditch, and 6.0 acre feet per year from the Isleta Diversion Dam (located far south of Placitas in Valencia County) to an approximately 500 foot deep well that serviced the subdivisions (because the acequia water and the development's well are within the same Middle Rio Grande Basin, the applicant can claim the retired acequia water as offsets for the well, which will be discussed a little later in this chapter). As stated above, New Mexico state law requires that notification be made for three consecutive weeks in a publication of general circulation in the areas that could potentially be affected by the transfer. Lomos Alto chose to publish its notification in *El Hispano*, an Albuquerque based Spanish language newspaper that is distributed by subscription. The Placitas based Sandoval Environmental Action Community (SEAC) became aware of the proposed transfer after the prescribed period to lodge protests had expired. The group protested to the OSE, claiming that Lomos Altos purposely sought to evade the public notice provision by publishing its notice in a paper that was not widely circulated in the area. The OSE denied this appeal and SEAC subsequently appealed the OSE decision in state district court. In late July of 1998 Judge Kenneth Brown upheld the SEAC appeal, stating that the publication in *El Hispano* clearly intended to evade the public notice provision and deny citizens the right of due process.

In the wake of Judge Brown's decision, Lomos Altos was required to re-advertise its notice (this time it appeared in the *Albuquerque Journal*) and the transfer was appealed by local homeowners Bob Wessely, Catherine Harris, and Lynn Montgomery, who was the mayordomo of a nearby spring-fed acequia. At the time 45 homes existed within the 257-acre sub-divisions and 106 additional homes had been platted.

The protestants, represented by Taos attorney Mary Humphrey, claimed the transfer would impair their existing water rights and be contrary to sound conservation practice and the public welfare. Using information provided by hydrologist Reid Bandeen, Humphrey argued that the aquifer from which the subdivisions draw their water intercepts water that feeds springs and perennial streams in the area. Therefore, if development such as Lomos Altos were allowed to proceed, each new water user would have a negative incremental effect upon the springs and streams in the area and the riparian areas that depend upon them. Harris, who had lived in the vicinity of the subdivisions since 1975, testified that her hand-dug 32-foot well, which she relied on for domestic water, went dry that summer after being a reliable source for more than 20 years. She claimed the proposed transfer would further impair the groundwater and springs on her property. Lynn Montgomery testified that the proposed transfer would impair the hydrology of the spring-fed acequia he manages, La Rosa de Castilla, which has been in use since the 1840s. The protestants claimed the transfer constituted a new appropriation of groundwater because depletions would not be offset at the protestants' source of water.

Expert witnesses Consuelo Bokum of 1000 Friends of New Mexico and Bill Dunmire, a botanist and instructor at UNM, testified that increased depletion of the springs and perennial streams would destroy fragile wetlands and riparian habitat, eventually making the entire area a piñon-juniper desert and destroying the ecological diversity most people in the community treasure. Humphrey also argued that water use records for the subdivisions demonstrated that some homeowners within the subdivisions were using enormous amounts of water and that the developers had no guidelines for water conservation, provided no incentive to conserve, and had no means to enforce conservation.

Lawyers for the subdivisions claimed that a surplus of water exists in the vicinity of the well and that the proposed transfer would have little if any effect upon the surface water, springs, and groundwater in the area, despite Humphrey pointing out that all New Mexico rivers are fully appropriated. They also vigorously questioned whether the protestants, despite living in close proximity to the subdivisions, would be directly affected in any way, and that they therefore did not have legal standing to protest the application.

The OSE found for the developer and granted the transfer in 2000. The agency ruled that any depletions that would occur to La Rosa de Castilla Spring would be "de minimis" (immeasurable). It also argued that the applicant only has to offset depletions at the transfer location and that the depletions from the applicant's pumping are "de minimis."

Montgomery contended that this was an arbitrary and meaningless term that could ensure developers win all protests brought by upland, spring-fed acequia parciantes and would eventually cause their acequia sources to dry up. He further claimed that the burden of proof had been placed on him rather than on the applicant, as the law requires. "Attorneys and officials for the State Engineer have demonstrated an unfair and unprofessional bias favoring new users and are openly hostile to acequia rights," Montgomery told *La Jicarita*. "We have a 1912 district court judgment granting the parciantes of La Rosa de Castilla all of the waters from this source, and we have presented evidence that local groundwater pumping is going to deplete our spring flows. The Applicant and the OSE also found that these effects would occur but to a lesser degree. Nevertheless, the State Engineer chose to ignore all this and dismiss the protest as 'de minimis.' We feel it is imperative that we continue this case to the bitter end, as all acequias are under attack."[18]

Concurrent with the Lomos Altos protest Lynn was a protestant *pro se* (representing himself) in another case where a company had applied to transfer 31.7 acre feet of water from agricultural land south of Albuquerque to a gravel pit 3.4 miles downhill from La Rosa de Castilla Spring. When *La Jicarita* interviewed him about this case he had this to say about the criteria of public welfare and how it relates to priority administration, which could be applied to the Lomos Altos situation as well:

"While there has not been much public welfare precedent concerning water rights transfers, private interests must bow to the common interest

70

Lynn Montgomery

and the State, which holds the water in trust for the public, has a duty to see to the public interest and defend it. This requires defending the resource. Anything that reduces the efficiency and health of the water resource reduces its usefulness and value. . . . Priority administration is the only means the State has to manage the water day to day, in emergencies, and during water shortages. It is critical that the State enforce priority, so that New Mexicans can continue to control and manage their water resource. When priority administration is unenforced, which seems to be the current policy, the seniority of water rights becomes meaningless. The State Engineer has stated that about 85 percent of surface rights are unadjudicated. If the State does not protect old, unadjudicated rights in some fashion, then the

State cannot claim to be carrying out priority administration. If one cannot protect and defend a water right, one cannot keep it. Thus a massive selling off of senior water could occur. The State Engineer has made public statements that he believes water rights need to be moved from agriculture to other uses and has supported legislation to create water banks to facilitate this. This demonstrates an aversion to carrying out priority administration and little regard for traditional rights, communities and their economies."

The protestants appealed the OSE decision to District Court. In July 2003, the judge, in a summary judgment, granted the application. But this ruling then allowed the protestants to file an appeal (still represented by Taos attorney Mary Humphrey) before the Court of Appeals, where Lynn believed they would get better consideration of the legal issues.

The Court of Appeals rendered a split decision against the protestants. One of the judges disagreed with the OSE argument that there was "extra" water in the stream system that supplies the protestants' spring: "I am not convinced that whether a system that is 'hydrologically connected' in the entire MRGAA [Middle Rio Grande basin] answers this case's problem of small location-specific springs being impaired by groundwater pumping for a 106-unit residential development. Relinquishing surface rights in Valencia County might not have much to do with making sure there is enough water in Las Huertas Canyon to feed a spring. Under our case law, impairment of water rights is a factual question to be resolved on a case-by-case basis."

This was an encouraging statement that recognized the need to have a much clearer definition of impairment based on fact, not OSE policy. The judge raised the issue that these transferred water rights are essentially "paper" water rights and that surface water rights in Valencia County that are being retired so that groundwater well rights in Bernalillo County can be pumped don't necessarily insure against impairment. The protestants again appealed their case, this time to the New Mexico Supreme Court. *Amici Curiae* (an organization or person not actually party to the litigation who will be impacted by the decision and therefore entitled to contribute to the court record) briefs on behalf of the protestants were entered by 1000 Friends of New Mexico, Amigos Bravos, and the New Mexico Acequia Association. Briefs on behalf of the applicants were entered by the cities of Alamogordo and Las Cruces, the County of Santa Fe, and El Prado Water and Sanitation District (part of Taos), concerned that any ruling that this was indeed a new appropriation would hurt their ability to transfer water.

At the Supreme Court hearing the lawyer for the applicants tried to put a good spin on the case by claiming that the developer was trying to be a good community member by installing a water system for his development rather than allowing individual wells. What she failed to say was that this community water system would still have to pump enough water to serve over a hundred houses whose combined square footage would probably exceed 500,000 square feet of fancy kitchens, multiple bathrooms, Jacuzzis, and outdoor watering for landscaped patios. And that it was only one of dozens of similar developments that use just as much water.

On December 5, 2006 the Supreme Court issued its opinion. The Court denied that the transfer request should be considered a new groundwater appropriation and that surface depletions at the move-to location should be considered *per se* impairment. It also determined that district court erred in granting summary judgment because there was an unresolved dispute regarding the extent of depletion at the move-to site and that the summary judgment notice failed to provide the protestants notice that the issues of water conservation and public welfare were subject to summary judgment.

The Court sent the case back to district court to determine: 1) the measure of existing water rights and the extent of depletion at the move-to location; 2) whether this depletion constitutes impairment of existing water rights, and 3) whether the applications are contrary to water conservation or detrimental to the public welfare of the state. In other words, the protest, after lingering for six years, would be heard all over again in district court. Peter White, who represented the *Amici Curiae* 1000 Friends of New Mexico, the New Mexico Acequia Association, and Amigos Bravos in the original protest, assisted Mary Humphrey for the protestants.

But the Supreme Court also ordered the District Court to conduct an adjudication of all water rights in the area that could potentially be impacted by the decision in the Lomos Altos case. In its remand order the Supreme Court stated: "[W]e remand to the district court for a *de novo* proceeding to consider all existing water rights at the move-to location, or extinguish those rights, the extent of depletion at the move-to location, and determine whether this depletion constitutes impairment of existing rights." The Supreme Court also directed "[f]or the impairment analysis, the State Engineer must either include the total amount of water rights contained in . . . non-party declarations [or other evidence] or formally extinguish them. The State Engineer can extinguish these rights through various means, including a forfeiture proceeding or an abandonment action." (These are the two ways that water rights can be lost under New Mexico law. Forfeiture is non-use of a water right for four consecutive years, followed by a written notice from the Office of the State Engineer, and then followed by one additional year of non-use after the notice. New Mexico courts haven't actually provided a precise definition of abandonment but it is usually denoted when they find that someone has intentionally given up their water right, e.g., constructed a house on irrigated land.)

This opened a Pandora's Box of proceedings that brought in over 100 new parties with new lawyer representation that complicated the case beyond the scope of my exploration here. The main argument that essentially ended the case, however, was that the OSE would have had to instigate an adjudication of the stream system to satisfy the court order and that was never going to happen. Finally, the applicant Bob Poling withdrew the water transfer application and that was the end of this long, complicated, potentially precedent setting case. Montgomery was glad for that but disappointed that once again arguments for conservation and public welfare would not be heard in a court case where legal precedent could be set. This case demonstrates so painfully the many obstacles that protestants to water transfers face.

Ten

With Dedication *and* Dysfunction, the Acequias Persevere

We got the water yesterday for the orchard and upper field. The first irrigation of the season is brutal; the lateral ditches have filled in with dead grass and debris, the water inevitably flows over the side of the ditch, and you have to run around hoeing and shoveling it free while filling "sackos," or burlap bags with dirt to line the sides of the eroded laterals to keep the water moving toward what it is you're trying to irrigate. It took me all afternoon to guide the run-off orchard water onto my garlic patch, so far the only greenery besides grass that's in cultivation.

One of our neighbors calls the corner of the field to which he can never get the water "Arizona" (Bill deBuys in *River of Traps*). We have a Sahara, a Gobi, and a Death Valley. No matter how many feeder ditches we dig off the main acequia, no matter how fast we get the water, or how much water we get, there are bare, brown spots that will never receive the sparkling waters of the Rio de Las Trampas.

Watering the vegetable garden is a lot easier as everything is on a drip irrigation system—we turn a few valves on and off and the plants are wet in a matter of hours. Over the years, however, as our garden grew, especially with a thick patch of water hungry raspberry bushes, we wanted to also irrigate the garden from the acequia. This was problematic for several reasons: in the irrigation rotation we get the water only once every couple of weeks, often enough to water fields but not a garden; and pumping water from the acequia closest to the garden initiated a battle of wills between the commissions that governed our two acequias, a power struggle within the community that was emblematic of struggles within the acequia community at large.

In the early 2000s Mark was elected to the commission of the Acequia Abajo, along with Arsenio Montoya and Clarence Mascareñas (Tomás continued as mayordomo). Trouble had already been brewing between the Acequia Abajo and the commissioners who ran the Acequia Arriba, younger men who had challenged Tomás's position as a commissioner and had succeeded in voting him off the Arriba ditch. With the addition of Mark on the Acequia Abajo, the two ditches delineated different management philosophies, which played out in a variety of ways.

The Abajo sought to embody the more traditional methods that had kept the acequia community based and community driven. Despite the changing demographics of the community—older and absent parciantes—the commission asked every parciante to participate in la limpieza, cleaning the ditch in the spring, or hiring a relative or friend to work for him or her. The Arriba, in its valuation of efficiency, began pushing for the ditch to contract out the cleaning to a crew instead of the parciantes. The Abajo also recognized the traditional hierarchy given to crops, based on the years when parciantes grew much more of their own food than we do today: gardens are first in priority, then orchards, and then hay fields. Because the rotation among our 17 water rights holders took almost two weeks, the commissioners embraced methods to insure gardeners got the water more often. We added a provision to our bylaws that allowed parciantes to pump water from the acequia to our gardens with the permission of the parciante whose turn it was to irrigate. Thus, Mark and I were able to keep our raspberries well watered and to also start a potato patch within striking distance of the ditch. The Arriba denied any such right on that acequia, to maintain the priority of their hay fields.

Another important issue over which we argued was whether we voted one-parciante-one vote or by the number of water rights we held. The Acequia Abajo endorsed the more democratic system of one person one vote and incorporated that into our bylaws. The Acequia Arriba, whose commissioners were the largest landowners in the village, continued to vote by derecho, or water right.

When a governing body decides that all decisions must be made "by the book" in the name of efficiency and so-called fairness, the result is usually anything but fair. As relations between the two acequias became more acrimonious, many parciantes quit going to the meetings to avoid the arguments and bad feelings that inevitably flared up. Even Tomás quit going to the Acequia Arriba meetings. Mark and I continued to attend the meetings of both acequias to make sure we stayed abreast of the action.

76

It's always a bad idea to involve the Office of the State Engineer in acequia affairs, but unfortunately, because of the litigious nature of the acequia community, that agency, or district attorney offices, are often called upon to intervene in internecine disputes. The question of voting methods was heard in district court when the community of La Lama, north of Taos, had to grapple with the issue after a wealthy Anglo landowner challenged the voting process on his acequia to gain control. The rest of the community joined against him, hired a lawyer, and successfully challenged his position in court. The ultimate decision was that each acequia association has the right to determine its own voting practice, either by derecho or by parciante. La Lama community, like Acequia Abajo, immediately adopted the more democratic system into its bylaws.

I became a commissioner on the Acequia Abajo in 2006, "taking on" the role of secretary of the acequia with its innumerable headaches. This is from a piece I wrote about El Valle after I'd been on the commission for a number of years:

"Two parciantes are fighting over who is responsible for the capacity of their lateral ditch, which is outside the purview of the acequia commission but has drawn us in anyway because we're trying to promote cooperation. There's a debate over a water right that is generations old and now divided into percentages that no one knows the genesis of. The mayordomo quit halfway through the season. We now have to contract work for cleaning the ditch, which is something alien to the tradition of each parciante cleaning, or hiring someone to clean, the ditch communally, which we abandoned a year ago because none of the parciantes showed up and neglected to make sure someone would be there to do the work for them. There are so many divided water rights among absentee landowners and family transfers that I can barely keep track of who I bill for what amount of money."

Drought hit el norte in 2011 and I discovered that my agricultural exemption had been revoked; I filed a protest. Ater I filed I discovered that horses do not qualify as stock in the agricultural regulations (based on a 1999 state court decision). After raising a hay crop on both of my irrigated parcels for more than 20 years I continued to irrigate but let the pastures rest for two years; my horse and a neighbor's mules ate the standing grass.

The county appraiser told me I needed to either cut the hay as a crop or put cows in the pastures to re-qualify for the agricultural exemption as my three years under the new drought regulation had expired. Tomás, who cut my hay and put his cows in my fields for those twenty years, died in 2009; his son sold the cows the following year. I asked another neighbor who still raises cattle to put them in the field the following fall and would try to find someone to cut the hay the next summer. The drought made it more difficult to get the irrigation water to the areas of the field usually kept in good shape by the monsoon rains. As this book goes to press in 2018, we're facing the worst drought ever (aridification; much more on this later in the book) and the entire county will have to qualify for agricultural exemption.

So we struggle on during the good and the bad, the fun and the frustration, as those before us did, and those who will hopefully be here when we're gone.

Eleven

Will Top of the World Water Get a New Destination?

Most adjudications of water rights are regulated by the state, but when an Indian reservation with federal treaty rights is adjudicated the federal government also holds a reserved water right for the Indians. This was established by the landmark case of *Winters v. U.S. of 1908* when the United States Supreme Court determined that when Congress set aside lands for a reservation there was also a reserved right for sufficient water for the reservation. The reservation's priority date is its date of establishment.

Indian water rights may not be conveyed without Congressional consent as the United States holds legal title to Winters rights as the trustee for the Indians. Pueblos in New Mexico may have their water rights adjudicated under the Winters Doctrine or under the Mechem Doctrine, which was established in the Aamodt Adjudication (Edwin L. Mechem is the judge who heard the case). This doctrine holds that the pueblos retained their aboriginal rights to water because they had been Mexican citizens who were afforded the protections of the Treaty of Guadalupe Hidalgo.[19]

In 1952 Congress passed the McCarran Act that allowed tribes and pueblos to conduct adjudications in state court. Thus, when Native American water rights are involved in an adjudication the process usually involves federal, local (county) and state government agencies, the tribes or pueblos, and non-Indian water users. Because of the complexity of the process, as an alternative to lengthy and expensive lawsuits, the Indians often agree to negotiate settlements with the other parties to the adjudication. As demonstrated in an adjudication such as the Aamodt, this certainly didn't guarantee an expeditious process: the now more than 50-year old Aamodt case is one of the longest in federal court history.

In 2001 a ruling by U.S. District Court Judge Edwin L. Mechem on the Aamodt Adjudication once again brought the longstanding controversy over water use in the Pojoaque Valley to the front page. The decision stated that the involved pueblos — Pojoaque, Nambe, Tesuque, and San Ildefonso — were limited to their domestic water use that was established

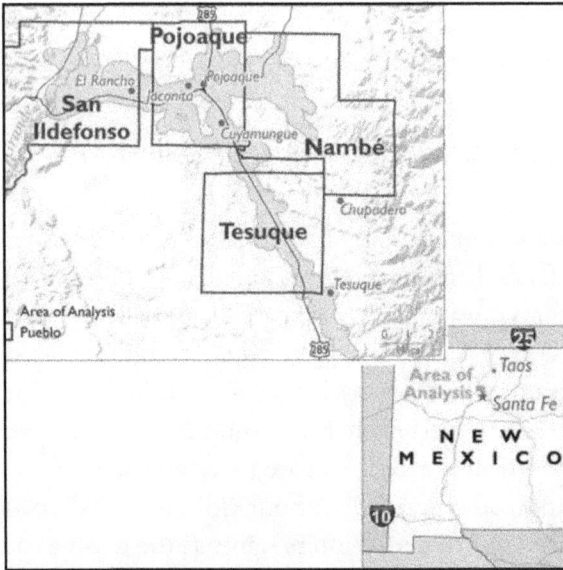

between 1846 (the year the United States seized control of the New Mexico territory) and 1924 (the year of the Publo Lands Act that sought to resolve disputes over pueblo land and water rights).

In a previous district court decision in 1985, Mechem had limited the pueblos' stream water rights to the acreage irrigated between these same two dates. In August of 2000 the parties to the suit began mediation with an Arizona state court judge to try to reach a settlement. Despite Mechem's ruling, settlement hearings continued.

Mechem's decisions, if upheld, might have seriously impacted pueblo development plans, such as the golf courses at Pojoaque Pueblo or the casinos at Pojoaque and Tesuque. The decisions would have also impacted domestic water use at all the pueblos because, as San Ildefonso Pueblo attorney Peter Chestnut pointed out, "1924 was a time not only when the population was smaller but things like indoor plumbing hadn't come to the pueblos." He told La Jicarita that the pueblos felt a negotiated settlement was going to be better for all parties rather than going back to court for a quantification of rights.

In the wake of Mechem's decision, New Mexico Senator Pete Domenici met with both the pueblos and the Pojoaque Valley Irrigation District (PVID) and claimed there was consensus for a regional water delivery system that could potentially supply all domestic water needs within the valley. However, at a February 22 Pojoaque Regional Water Planning meeting valley residents and representatives of the PVID made it abundantly clear that what they wanted was a wastewater treatment system, not a water delivery system. They pointed out that while some existing wells had a contamination problem, a water delivery system would benefit new uses at the expense of existing water rights. David Ortiz, president of the PVID, told *La Jicarita* he suspected that Domenici was being pressured by the city and county of Santa Fe to push the water delivery system so that the plumbing was in place to eventually send water to Santa Fe. Orlando Romero, board member of the PVID and well-known historian, said that it would be "political suicide" for Domenici to promote a water delivery system rather than a waste treatment system. Others at the meeting raised the same concerns and pointed out that the San Juan/Chama water that Santa Fe was looking to divert to solve its future water needs was limited and was "not really going to save them. We're not going to negotiate one drop of water."[20]

Remember, the city and county of Santa Fe were then exploring the feasibility of an infiltration gallery on San Ildefonso land that would divert Top of the World water rights from the Rio Grande alluvium to the Buckman Well Fields via a pipeline. Romero pointed out that this project was fraught with problems, including the difficulty of "dealing with the quasi-sovereign status of the pueblos" and the fact that it had not been determined if water from such a diversion was ground or surface water (this issue was being debated in the Top of the World water transfer protest hearing before the Office of the State Engineer).

People at the meeting also discussed the issue of whether a water delivery system would facilitate and encourage unwanted growth in the valley. Ortiz pointed out that a water system could serve more people at a higher density. In a conversation with *La Jicarita* Romero added that Nambe was already suffering from developers exploiting the family subdivision provisions that allow three-quarter acre lot splits. He talked about a twelve-acre lot of formerly irrigated land that was being subdivided into three-quarter acre plots. "I'd like to know where the acequia rights from this land are going, and if they're being sold or leased why aren't the local people being given the opportunity to acquire them?" Acequia water that is lost to the community depletes groundwater recharge, so that the water table drops and wells go dry. As someone at the meeting pointed out, "It's all the same water."

"People in the valley are not going to give up their wells," Romero insisted. At the time a well owner was entitled to pump three-acre feet per year, whereas the State Engineer had been inconsistent in determining what amount of water a community was entitled to use per household when it committed its well water to a mutual domestic association. More-over, this water could only be used for indoor, household domestic pur-poses while a well could be used to water livestock and irrigate.

Both Ortiz and Romero believed that the State Engineer should file suit on behalf of the state if the pueblos were using water rights that they might not own to facilitate development. The State Engineer took the position that its direction must come from the courts because it lacked jurisdiction to adjudicate Indian water rights. San Ildefonso attorney Peter Chestnut stated that the pueblos would like to see a regional water delivery system within the Pojoaque Valley and supported Domenici's efforts to ac-quire funding for a feasibility study. In response to the concerns expressed by PVID members that a water delivery system would jeopardize their ex-isting groundwater rights, Chestnut minimized their concerns: "State law says that the determination of groundwater rights is based on beneficial use, and most people don't use anywhere near three-acre feet. It's closer to a quarter to half-acre foot, so they wouldn't in fact be losing any water." Chestnut acknowledged, however, that because these rights had not been adjudicated, there was no accurate measurement of use.

While the people at the regional water planning meeting (see Chapter Thirteen about the development of regional water plans) were obviously concerned about the burgeoning growth at Pojoaque Pueblo and the at-tendant water demands, they emphasized that the relationship between valley residents and the pueblo was critical and were fearful that it was being eroded beyond repair because of these water issues. In the 1987 book *Water and Poverty in the Southwest*, authors F. Lee Brown and Helen Ingram quote several people who express typical reactions to this divide: from a Hispano activist, "It's easy to understand why neighbors that had for generations lived together side by side were now caught in a legalistic vortex that seemed to care little about intermarriage, social customs or anything else;" and this from a tribal member, "I would just like to say that it's unfortunate, very unfortunate, that a lawsuit of this nature pits neigh-bor against neighbor."[21]

Folks at the meeting also acknowledged that it was developers like those in Las Campanas, the wealthy sub-development north of Santa Fe, who were responsible for the even greater threats of poorly planned and thirsty growth that affected the entire county. They feared that rural communities and their water would be sacrificed to urban interests that were unable or unwilling to control this kind of growth and demand for water. As one person at the meeting bluntly put it, "Use of precious water for golf courses is a sin."

While possible solutions were also discussed — tax incentives for preservation of agricultural lands, land trusts, transfer of development rights, water conservation, regional water planning, and water banking to protect water locally — the frustration and fear for the future were palpable.

And rightly so. As Aamodt settlement negotiations continued over the next few years, lawyers for Santa Fe County, the Office of the State Engineer, and several protestants met to discuss the status of the Top of the World water transfer case. Representing the county, attorney John Utton told the group that the county would like to consider applying the water from Top of the World to the Aamodt Settlement. Utton outlined the potential agreement, which included both the construction of a water delivery and wastewater treatment system that would service 2,200 existing residences in northern Santa Fe County. In return for the system, residence owners would retire their existing underground water rights. The agreement also called for acquisition of 750 acre feet of water rights for future expansion of the community water delivery system.

Most important to the water transfer protestants, however, was the water delivery system's feasibility study: the preferred alternative would divert water from the Rio Grande via the San Idefonso infiltration gallery for delivery both above and below Otowi Gauge. Paula Garcia, director of the New Mexico Acequia Association, and Peter White, one of the lawyers for the protestants, continued to maintain their concern that this transfer could set precedent for developers and municipalities below the gauge to shop for water rights above the gauge even if the county agreed not to purchase acequia water rights. Over the next few years the negotiations between Santa Fe County and the protestants would take several turns, as would the settlement agreement among the defendants in the Aamodt adjudication. Stay tuned.

Twelve

2003 State Statute Gives Acequias More Power to Protect Water Rights

Throughout the late 1990s and early 2000s acequia associations worked to establish water conservation and banking programs. In 1998 the Taos Valley Acequia Association (TVAA), which represents 55 acequias in the Taos Valley, and the Rio Chama Acequia Association, which represents 27 acequias in the Chama valley, in conjunction with the Office of the State Engineer (OSE), formulated a set of guidelines to initiate a pilot acequia conservation program. First, a community acequia would submit an application to the State Engineer for approval of a water conservation program. The application must include water conservation measures recommended by the Natural Resources Conservation Service. Second, the State Engineer staff would devise a conservation plan and implementation schedule for approval by the State Engineer. Guidelines could also establish a legal basis for an acequia to "bank" water apportioned to the acequia that wasn't being used, thus protecting it from forfeiture (non-use of a water right for a period of four or more years). This "banked" water could be used within the acequia or leased to other acequias or water users for a prescribed period of time.

Concurrently, the state legislature looked at several bills that dealt with water conservation and banking. The "The Water Conservation Act" would have required the state engineer to incorporate water conservation into the evaluation of water rights applications, water planning, permits, etc. The New Mexico Acequia Association passed a resolution opposed to that bill because it could have separated a parciante's water right from the collective right of the acequia to divert sufficient water to the parciante's land. The bill could have actually worked as a "disincentive" for parciantes to conserve water.

Two water banking bills were also brought up before the Water and Natural Resources Committee the same year. The "long" version, which would have established a new central agency to govern a statewide water banking program, raised many questions and failed to get committee recommendation. Acequia advocates testified that water banking should be administered at the local level, within acequia associations and watersheds. The "short" version of the bill didn't provide for a banking agency but specified that a banking program would protect against forfeiture of rights. The committee endorsed the concept of a banking program based on the guidelines set up by the Taos Valley Acequia Association, but the NMAA felt that before any banking bill passed, parciantes needed to work with the State Engineer on defining water banking, setting regulations, and determining if temporary transfers then allowed were adequate to conserve water and protect parciantes from forfeiture. In general, the association agreed that there needed to be more research and critical analysis of how water conservation, banking, and instream flow fit together and how they could impact the integrity of acequias.

In a January 1999 "Puntos de Vista" column for *La Jicarita* water lawyer Peter White encouraged acequias to adopt water banking as a better means of protecting their water rights and maintaining control of their water rights at the local level:

"It is important to distinguish between water banking systems and water conservation programs. In water banking a water right would be assigned or transferred to a water bank that could allow the right to be used by the other water users under the acequia, or, if the other users had a 100 percent water supply, the water right could be leased for a new water use. An assignment of a water right would not transfer the legal title to the bank. Title would remain with the water right owner. A transfer would convey title to the bank. In either case the bank could receive payments from the lease of water for any new uses and it could set conditions controlling new uses of water. If overall water use is not increased, water from lands that are not being irrigated could be used to establish a water bank without State Engineer approval. Such a system is merely a private contractual arrangement between the water right owner, the water banking entity, and the new water user."[22]

In the spring of 1998 the Acequias de Chamisal y Ojito Association drew up a Declaration of Water Conservation Program "to make available a supply of water and water rights for management by the Acequias de Chamisal y Ojito for the benefit of its members and itself, which would include but not be limited to storage of water." What the Acequias de Chamisal y Ojito essentially did was set up a water bank to protect individual parciantes, unable to irrigate their land for whatever reason, from forfeiture and abandonment (the taking of irrigable lands for other purposes). The bank would then "allow the Acequias de Chamisal y Ojito complete control and power over the use of such water right for the benefit of the Acequias de Chamisal y Ojito and its members." Water would be kept within the community acequia system and ownership would be maintained by the water right owner who contracts the water to the association. This same contract would determine who would be responsible for fees and labor of the water right.

In response to all of this the New Mexico Acequia Association sponsored a workshop on the issue of water banking on April 17, 1999 in Las Vegas (cosponsored by the Rio de las Gallinas Acequia Association). David Benavides, staff attorney with Northern New Mexico Legal Services, opened the discussion by posing the problems and concerns water banking could address: 1) to prevent loss of water rights due to nonuse; 2) to protect acequias from outside threats such as municipalities and developers; and 3) to reestablish community control of its water resources.

Essentially, water banking was a mechanism to assign, lease, or convey individual water rights to an entity, preferably an acequia, that would put the rights to beneficial use or otherwise protect them from being lost to the community. State statute dictated that if an acequia owned a water right, rather than an individual parciante, that right could not be lost because of nonuse or condemnation.

Once the acequia was in effect "banking" these rights, it could use the water within the acequia as needed (unless the acequia was using 100 percent of its water entitlement, which is very unusual). The acequia could further protect and beneficially use these rights by drafting covenants to prevent the transfer of the right out of the acequia. In fact, at the time, a Manzano area land grant was considering making a declaration that its water rights were community rights, not individual rights, and the rights would always be kept within the acequia system, in their area of origin.

Geoff Bryce, Taos Valley Acequia Association Program Director, told the workshop that its pilot water conservation program guidelines had been rejected by the OSE and that the association was working to revise the guidelines. Several additional issues TVAA would address in this revised program included protection of water rights from abandonment based on hydrographic survey information, and assurances that acequias would be able to lease banked water only within the service area of the acequia. Even though the process had been long and arduous, TVAA wanted to continue to push for this program because of the legislative bill that would have set up a statewide banking program. Both the TVAA and the NMAA continued to promote acequia-based water banking programs.

Arnold Lopez, representing the Acequias de Chamisal y Ojito, reported that the OSE had not responded to his acequia's Declaration of Water Conservation Program, so the association has proceeded independently with the program. Twelve parciantes had contracted with the association (which includes nine acequias in the two communities) to place their water rights into the community water system, which would have all rights of management. The parciantes retained ownership of the rights.

Finally, David Benavides discussed what advise he would give acequias that wanted to set up their own banking programs, given the two examples of the TVAA water conservation program with the OSE and the Acequias de Chamisal y Ojito independent banking program. While we waited to see if the OSE granted approval to the TVAA conservation program, or if the Chamisal association was challenged, acequias could do two things. In the public arena, acequias could submit applications to the OSE to allow alternate places of use of water rights (for example, moving the water rights not being used on one field of the acequia to a different field). Privately, acequias could turn over the authority of water use to the acequia commission. As a community effort, parciantes would assign management of their water to the acequia, a gesture that could reinforce the idea that water rights are a community resource and are not for sale to the highest bidder.

Ultimately, in 2003, all of this discussion was rendered moot when the state legislature passed legislation that allows acequia systems to bank unused water (water that would be reallocated within the acequia system) and to adopt a provision in their bylaws that gives commissioners the authority to deny proposed water transfers if they would impair the acequia's operation. Here are the two statutes:

73-2-55-1. Water banking; acequias and community ditches (2005)

An acequia or community ditch may establish a water bank for the purpose of temporarily reallocating water without change of purpose of use or point of diversion to augment the water supplies available for the places of use served by the acequia or community ditch. The acequia or community ditch water bank may make temporary transfers of place of use without formal proceedings before the state engineer, and water rights placed in the acequia or community ditch water bank shall not be subject to loss for non-use during the period the rights are placed in the water bank. An acequia or community ditch water bank established pursuant to this section is not subject to recognition or approval by the interstate stream commission or state engineer.

73-3-4.1. Commissioners; additional duties; approval of changes in place or purpose of use of water; appeals. (2005)

Pursuant to rules or bylaws duly adopted by its members, an acequia or community ditch may require that a change in the point of diversion or place or purpose of use of a water right served by the acequia or community ditch, or a change in a water right so that it is moved into and then served by the acequia or community ditch shall be subject to the approval by the commissioners. The change may be denied only if the commissioners determine that it would be detrimental to the acequia or community ditch or its members. The commissioners shall render a written decision explaining the reasons for the decision. If the person proposing the change or a member of the acequia or community ditch is aggrieved by the decision of the commissioners, he may appeal the decision in the district court of the county in which the acequia or community ditch is located within thirty days of the date of the decision. The court may set aside, reverse or remand the decision if it determines that the commissioners acted fraudulently, arbitrarily or capriciously or that they did not act in accordance with the law.

These statutes went into effect in March of 2004, and in 2006 the Acequia Abajo de El Valle incorporated them into our bylaws, which every acequia must do in order for them to be legally binding. In 2007 it came as no surprise that Española businessman Richard Cook was the first water rights owner to challenge the law, or that he was represented by the law firm of Stein and Brockman of Santa Fe. Cook has a long history of adversarial dealings with rural communities, particularly with regard to his sand and gravel business that opened mines in Velarde and El Guique, north of Española. The Stein and Brockman law firm has long represented clients who want to transfer agricultural water rights to municipalities and has also tried to derail two of the states regional water plans.

Cook challenged the decisions by the commissioners of two norteño acequias, San Jose de Hernandez Community Ditch, and La Acequia del Gavilan, in Ojo Caliente. In the Acequia del Gavilan case Cook wanted to use his water rights to offset evaporation from a pond on another property he owned near Ojo Caliente. In the Hernandez case, Cook's company, Peña Blanca Partnership, wanted to transfer water rights off the ditch and use them in a subdivision the company owned in Española. Every parciante—except Cook, of course—on the Gavilan acequia opposed the transfer, and the Hernandez acequia association also overwhelmingly opposed the transfer of 75 acre feet per year of water from its ditch.

Cook's lawsuit (the two cases were combined as one case) was heard in Judge Daniel Sanchez's district courtroom in September, in front of a large crowd of acequia supporters including members of the New Mexico Acequia Association, the Rio Arriba County Manager, and the commissioners from the Gavilan and Hernandez ditches. Attorneys from New Mexico Legal Aid—David Benavides and Ryan Golten—along with Kristina Martinez, represented Acequia de Hernandez, and Connie Odé and Mary Humphrey represented Acequia del Gavilan. Cook was represented by Katherine Hall of the Stein and Brockman Law Firm. After opening statements Sanchez limited arguments to a single issue: the constitutionality of the new state statute. Hall argued that the statute denied Cook his private property rights under the provisions of the New Mexico Constitution, which, she claimed, would allow him a *de novo*, or new trial without deference to previous judgments, if his water transfer requests were denied by the Office of the State Engineer, the agency responsible for reviewing all transfers before the promulgation of the new statute in 2003. She asserted that the statute, which allows transfer applicants a more limited appeal, was therefore "an unconstitutional taking of property without just compensation." The new law stipulated that if an applicant appeals the acequia's denial of a transfer request the court will consider only whether the commissioners "acted fraudulently, arbitrarily or capriciously, or not in accordance with law." Under an OSE review the applicant can appeal the State Engineer's decision in district court, which allows for "substantial review" of the evidence.

Attorneys for the acequias argued that the legislature had the authority to override the OSE's authority and that the new statute did not require a *de novo* appeal of an acequia commission's decision. They pointed out that in the case of the commissioners' reviews of Cook's request there already existed "substantial evidence" in the form of recordings, letters, and minutes that were available for the judge to review. They also argued that unless Cook could prove that he had been denied any economic benefit of the use of the water by the transfer denial there was no taking of private property rights. On the Acequia de Hernandez he owned the land from which he wanted to sever the water rights, and on the Acequia del Gavilan the water rights were already severed from the land.

Sanchez deferred his ruling and announced he would make a decision on the constitutional issue on October 11. But on September 26 he issued a ruling that took everyone by surprise (particularly when it was delivered to the press before it was delivered to the defendants' attorneys). Sanchez decided that the case would be a *de novo* appeal because not doing so would constitute "giving some water rights owners more procedural protections than others" and "rais[ing] the specter of denying the Appellants of a constitutional right." This decision essentially negated these acequias' authority to deny the transfer but didn't rule the statute unconstitutional.

A year later, on October 20, the New Mexico Court of Appeals reversed District Court Judge Daniel Sanchez's decision that Cook was entitled to a *de novo* appeal. The appellants judges concluded that the statute violates neither constitutional provision and that district court erred in its decision that the cases should be heard as *de novo* appeals. It remanded them back to district court to be heard "for further proceedings under the appropriate statutory standard of review." The attorneys for the acequias and Richard Cook agreed to try to negotiate a settlement, but in the end Cook withdrew his transfer applications and the acequias—and the state statute—were vindicated.

Thirteen

State Water Plan

At the Santa Fe hearing on the State Water Plan in the summer of 2003 environmentalists, acequia parciantes, farmers, ranchers, and city residents all told the Interstate Stream Commission (ISC—authors of the plan) that unless growth in Santa Fe and Albuquerque was limited we would run out of water—period. At the Las Vegas and Taos hearings the same message was conveyed, this time from the heart of acequia communities that could be the big losers in a water market game. And at the three-day Town Hall meeting in Albuquerque, it was pounded home even harder: no amount of water conservation, water banking, water delivery systems, desalination plants, or combinations thereof were going to solve our water woes if we didn't do something to stop the developers from turning Albuquerque into Los Angeles and Santa Fe into a desert wasteland.

Planning staff at the ISC drafted the water plan, at the behest of Governor Bill Richardson (also mandated by the state legislature in 2003), that divided the state into 16 regions and stipulated that each region would develop its own water plan under the direction of the ISC. It took a year's worth of public hearings and consultation with State Engineer John D'Antonio and members of the Water Trust Board (WTB), comprised of representatives of diverse constituencies including acequia and irrigation communities, Native Americans, environmentalists, and various state agencies. The final draft version of the plan was presented to the governor and the ISC for their approval in mid-December. Implementation of the plan was both statutory (authorized by state statute) and legislative; the latter would be necessary to fund state agencies responsible for carrying out the plan's various components.

La Jicarita interviewed ISC director Estevan Lopez, in charge of the plan's promulgation, who said, "The criticism of cities is, where does growth end? Or should we be looking at stopping growth? These discussions need to be opened up even if they're difficult and emotional. I don't know if this will provide solutions but at least you start getting at some of the root issues instead of one side saying, 'We can't have any more growth because we don't have enough water,' and the other side saying, 'You're just saying that so you can control growth. Let's have a discussion about the growth, then."[23]

While that dialogue did take place in many of the public hearings on the plan, the final version largely ignored this debate and devoted many pages to "making more water": "creating" more drinking water with desalination plants; conserving water through more efficient delivery systems; banking water (temporarily reallocating water); and of course, buying and selling water on the open market. A policy statement in Section C.2 of the plan reads, "The State shall promote water markets that enable the efficient movement of water rights within the State in accordance with the applicable legislative and legal safeguards." The plan goes on to say, "As water demands from expanded existing and new uses increase, the demand for marketing of water through these voluntary transfers of existing water rights will grow." (The word voluntary was added to the language in the Draft Final.)

This is the direction water policy has been headed the past 20 years: commodification and movement of water to the "highest and best use," meaning, of course, whoever can come up with the most money gets the most water. Sitting as "Representative of the Environmental Community" on the Water Trust Board was Denise Fort, chair of the Western Water Policy Review Advisory Commission that issued the "Water Management Study: Upper Rio Grande River Basin" that I discussed in the Introduction. The study states, "We recommend federal agencies in the [Rio Grande] Basin do more to mitigate the constraints to competition that keep water and other resources in low-value uses while high value demands go unmet." The report goes on to say that acequia associations and irrigation and conservancy districts have exercised undue influence on legislation pertaining to water distribution in the state and the Rio Grande Compact that "reflects the agrarian economy . . . that existed at the end of the 1920s, not today's highly urbanized economy." Even new innovations such as water banking programs, which the 2003 legislature approved, should, according to the report, only be supported by federal agencies if they determine "that the bank will facilitate voluntary transfer of water to highest-value uses."

The commodification of water has long been a concern of the New Mexico Acequia Association. At the October 2003 hearing in Santa Fe on the Draft Water Plan, Paula Garcia, director of the NMAA and representative of acequia parciantes on the Water Trust Board, asked that the water plan protect acequia water rights under the Treaty of Guadalupe Hidalgo and that acequia communities be treated as a distinct entity along with Native American pueblos. She objected to the language in the plan that essentially defines the Office of the State Engineer as a "facilitator" of water markets rather than a "regulator" in this process that threatens the water rights of rural northern New Mexico. Trudy Valerio Healy, the Water Trust Board representative of irrigation districts, shared Garcia's concerns. "Some rural areas may sell their water to urban areas, then become ghost towns," she warned.

ISC director Lopez and State Engineer D'Antonio pointed out that the plan was a "working document" that would evolve over time to incorporate public concerns and technical information that continues to be gathered. In response to Garcia's concerns, which were raised by many others at all the public meetings, the final version references that "acequias assert certain protections under the Treaty of Guadalupe Hidalgo" and that "Nothing in the State Water Plan will impair or limit the claims that these Native American and acequia water-rights holders assert."

In the meantime, the OSE continues to adjudicate stream systems, which essentially privatizes water rights that have been used as common rights in acequia and pueblo communities for hundreds of years. The adjudication process is also an adversarial one, pitting the state against individual water users who must defend their water rights in a lengthy, litigious process that takes years to complete.

This process of privatization has larger implications in the global water market. As Maude Barlow and Tony Clarke point out in their definitive book on water privatization, *Blue Gold: The Fight to Stop the Corporate Theft of the World's Water*, "Citizens of the most privileged countries simply take water for granted or are able to buy it . . . [and] their lifestyles — SUVs, lawns, and golf courses" are a leading factor in "consumption disparity between rural and urban areas, the rich and the poor."[24] Global water cartels will certainly not provide water to all, and those they do will pay dearly for it, like the citizens of Cochabamba, Bolivia, who successfully fought off a consortium led by Bechtel Corporation (a previous corporate manager of Los Alamos National Laboratory), with whom the Bolivian government contracted to take over the municipal water system.

Could this be the scenario in New Mexico? Certainly the tension between urban and rural and rich and poor will be exacerbated as water is increasingly commodified and sold on the open market. That's why so many of the policies implemented by our city councils and county commissions and now codified in the State Water Plan make little sense to the people who came to the Water Plan hearings and told the planners that New Mexico is a desert state with a carrying capacity they think has already been exceeded.

Albuquerque and Santa Fe built diversion dams to access San Juan/Chama water rights that may eventually be nonexistent. As aridification intensifies, the flow from these tributaries into Heron Reservoir may be reduced to a trickle, especially in light of the fact that upstream Navajo rights are senior rights that will keep the water from ever entering the diversion tunnel. Buying acequia water rights, which Healy fears will turn our rural villages into ghost towns, will also turn our tourist economy into a fond memory —or not so fond for some folks—once the fields, wildlife habitat, and open space the acequias support dry up. If "management" of our water resources—that is, conservation, new diversion projects, the purchase of water rights, new technology, and conjunctive use (combined surface and groundwater)—merely facilitates unlimited residential and commercial growth, we may be headed towards social and environmental collapse.

To buy into the "grow or die" argument is to fail to recognize the difference between economic growth and economic development. Many years ago, Maria Varela, longtime New Mexico community activist, wrote a paper on this issue: "Growth increases the amount of money running through a community's economy but may not increase that economy's capacity to steer its own direction. Growth is characterized by dependence on outside capital, technologies and management talent. Economic development, conversely, increases the capacities of the people in the community to attract and pool capital and acquire technologies and management skills. Most of the wealth stays in the community." Our finite water resources must be used to support economic development, not growth, and until the powers that be also acknowledge this concept, the State Water Plan is, as one citizen commented at the hearing on the draft plan, "full of sound and fury, signifying nothing." Those were prescient words.

Fourteen

State Engineer's Proposed Active Water Resource Management Regulations (AWRM)

In 2004 State Engineer John D'Antonio wrote an op-ed piece in *The New Mexican* defending his office's "Proposed Active Water Resource Management Regulations" (AWRM) promulgated to "effectively manage and conserve our water resources, particularly in this time of drought." I wrote an editorial in *La Jicarita News* that said, "His defense might hold water (pardon the pun) if this was a world that was equitable and fair, where developers don't pursue unlimited growth, politicians aren't complicit, and water doesn't flow uphill to money. While we all need to conserve our water resources, unless there is equitable distribution of that water it's hard to focus on its conservation. And with D'Antonio's proposed regulations, there may be further erosion of that equity."[25]

The proposed regulations called for the appointment of regional water masters who would have the authority to administer water rights in their districts, including priority administration and alternative administration, or water sharing. Through these water masters the Office of the State Engineer (OSE) would have the authority to require measuring devices on points of diversion and return flow. The OSE would allow junior users to "rent" a priority date from senior water rights holders when water use was curtailed because of a priority call, without going through the normal water rights transfer process that allows the public to protest a proposed transfer. Protests would be allowed only after the transfer decision was made and it would be incumbent upon the protestant to show that the approval was "arbitrarily and capriciously granted."

OSE representatives got an earful at hearings in Santa Fe on the proposed regulations, almost all of it negative. Former state engineer Eluid Martinez, testifying for the city of Española, claimed the OSE would be unable to enforce the regulations. Sterling Grogan of the Middle Rio Grande Conservancy District cautioned that OSE personnel could not enter private property to regulate head gates and that the proposed regulations didn't take into account the collaborative efforts to manage unadjudicated water. Lynn Montgomery, Placitas acequia mayordomo, gave a passionate indictment of the regulations as an assault on traditional agricultural users and an attempt to manage the resource from the top-down instead of at the local level.

John Brown, director of the *New Mexico Water Dialogue*, speaking on his own behalf, pointed out that the proposed regulations were inconsistent with the State Water Plan and contrary to state statute. Paula Garcia, director of the New Mexico Acequia Association (NMAA), concurred with Brown that the State Water Plan recognizes that acequias must be protected by prior appropriation law and are furthermore protected by the Treaty of Guadalupe Hidalgo. She also claimed that the so-called Replacement Plan that would allow junior water users to take on senior water users priority dates was unconstitutional and in violation of due process. And finally, she pointed out that holding one hearing in Santa Fe on such an important issue was a burden to members of the public who have to take time to travel from all over the state to attend at their personal expense.

The proposed regulations used the phrase "Expedited Marketing" as a rationale for minimizing "costly and time-consuming administrative procedures" (as does the State Water Plan). Only 15 to 20 percent of the state's stream systems have been adjudicated and these proceedings often last 20 or more years. What "Expedited Marketing" really means is allowing junior water users—urban, suburban, industrial—to shop around for water rights to underwrite growth and development. In a paper delivered at the *New Mexico Water Dialogue* 2001 annual meeting, New Mexico Legal Services attorney David Benavides had this to say about the prior appropriation system:

"Our problem here in New Mexico is that some of the most junior users, like the City of Albuquerque, Intel, and the City of Rio Rancho, expect to get their full water right every year, and moreover, they think no one should question their junior water right in a dry year. So not only did we over-appropriate our water supply, but we have junior water users who are taking water like senior users, resulting in the continued use of water each year at unsustainable levels. The important point is that we have the statutory tools to reduce water use to more sustainable levels, and there is nothing illegal or anti-private-property rights about using them. It's just that no one wants to start that war.

"The question of how to ration water to get to a sustainable level is a question of environmental justice. The principles of environmental justice encourage us to choose, among all the environmentally sustainable options for resource management, those options that address the most important issues facing society, particularly issues of inequity, poverty, and lack of opportunity. . . . [D]o we believe in righting historical wrongs, even if that means that the larger public does not get something it might desperately want?"

In response to these comments and concerns the OSE subsequently released its revised Active Water Resource Management Regulations in November of 2004. At a hearing at the Roundhouse, State Engineer John D'Antonio and OSE attorneys told the audience that while they had made what they felt were significant changes to the regulations—the "overarching statewide framework"—they would also devise specific rules for each region where priority administration would likely occur: the San Juan River Basin, Rio Chama Basin, Nambe, Pojoaque, and Tesuque rivers, the lower Rio Grande Basin, Upper Mimbres Basin, Rio Gallinas Basin, and the Lower Pecos River Basin.

Many of those who commented on the proposed regulations expressed concern whether due process was sufficiently provided with respect to Replacement Plans (the ability of junior water users to lease senior water rights without going through the formal water transfer process) and the strategy for expedited marketing and leasing. The OSE response to these concerns was to clarify that replacement plans would only be available in regions where a Water Master District had been declared, a Water Master appointed, and priority administration had been initiated. According to the OSE, Replacement Plans "do not adjudicate your water rights but are only an interim determination for administration and can be superseded by the courts." Replacement Plans would be limited to two years, which the OSE claimed would prevent developers from transferring water rights without a full public hearing.

The OSE also claimed that with expedited marketing and leasing, the proposed regulations did not attempt to move water to a "highest and best use" but "treat all beneficial users equally." However, in its written response to the public comments the OSE stated, "[it] is essential to protect, for example, a steady drinking water supply for municipalities, many of which have junior priorities." At the hearing, one of the attorneys stated, "We will not deny drinking water and showers to urban dwellers." The response went on to say, ". . . the State Engineer believes that cultural and other values will nevertheless be protected. For instance, acequias and community ditches are expressly exempted from Expedited Marketing and Leasing provisions." This refers to the 2003 legislation (NMSA 1978 72-2-9.1) that authorized the OSE to promulgate new regulations for priority administration and hydrologic models to promote expedited marketing and leasing but expressly exempted acequias and community ditches from these rules.

Although the acequia community generally favors efforts by the OSE to administer water rights to protect senior water users, many believed that these proposed regulations were contrary to state statute and denied due process. In comments submitted to the OSE, the NMAA said, "A Replacement Plan is, in effect, a transfer of the senior water right. In order for a transfer to be done legally, it must include the various public protections regarding public notice and an opportunity to protest." Many believe that Replacement Plans are the same as water leases and should be subject to administrative protest before the transfer takes place, not after, as the new regulations stipulated.

While the proposed regulations provided for policies and procedures for alternative administration that was based on water sharing agreements, the NMAA believed the proposed regulations were unclear how a water sharing agreement would be determined and who would make that determination. Alternative administration should explicitly recognize long-standing agreements among acequias for shortage sharing. Customary practices and laws predate the United States and have been codified into New Mexico state statute.

Parciantes questioned the assurances from the OSE that the proposed regulations did not support the movement of water to the "highest and best use" as the state continued to look for new water sources to supply unlimited growth and development, particularly in the county and city of Santa Fe. Several parties to the Aamodt adjudication were at the hearing and expressed concern that the water delivery system in the proposed settlement to the adjudication could well supply not only the domestic water they would have to give up by capping their wells but further growth in Santa Fe County. While the pueblos would be afforded all their water rights and additional water rights for future development, the acequia communities remained vulnerable to urban and suburban pressures for more water. As one woman in the audience put it, "It's all about money."

The OSE finalized the revised regulations in December of 2004. Today, looking at the OSE website, the stream systems that have been identified as "high priority" for AWRM management are: Lower Pecos River Basin; Lower Rio Grande Basin; San Juan River Basin; Upper Mimbres Basin; Rio Gallinas Basin; Nambe-Pojoaque-Tesuque Basin [Aamodt Adjudication]; and the Rio Chama Basin. According to the website, "Each basin team includes a project manager, hydrologist, attorney, communication manager, personnel manager, and technical support staff."

Fifteen

Pueblo Water Rights Doctrine

The promulgation of Active Water Resource Management (AWRM) coincided with the Rio Gallinas water rights adjudication and its entanglement with what is known as the Pueblo Water Rights Doctrine. This doctrine involved the Office of the State Engineer (OSE), the city of Las Vegas, the Rio Gallinas acequias, and the Storrie Project Water Users in a lawsuit that would determine water allocation not only in the Gallinas Basin on the east side of the Sangre de Cristo Mountains but in the entire state. The Pueblo Water Rights Doctrine not only claimed that municipal water rights were superior to water rights of adjacent irrigators, i.e., the acequias, but also allowed the municipality to take as much water as it needed as the town grew, expanding its water use indefinitely.

The Pueblo Water Rights Doctrine originated in Los Angles, California, when lawyers for the city argued there was an historic basis for assuming municipal rights took precedence over other water users in the laws of antecedent sovereigns, Spain and Mexico, whose validity was protected by the Treaty of Guadalupe Hidalgo. Citing the 1783 Plan of Pitic, which the Spanish government used as a template for the settlement of communities in California, Texas, Arizona, Colorado, and New Mexico, California lawyers claimed "the doctrine recognizes the right of the inhabitants of Mexican or Spanish colonization pueblos [towns] to use as much of an adjoining river or stream as necessary for municipal purposes. The doctrine [also] contemplates the expansion of the pueblo's right to use water in response to increases in size and population, and if necessary, the right can encompass the entire flow of the adjoining water course." In other words, a municipality could take as much water as it needed and go on indefinitely expanding its use to encompass the entire aquifer without regard to the needs of other water users dependent on the same source.

The litigation of the Pueblo Water Right claim on the Rio Gallinas started when a group of acequia farmers made a priority call in the late 1950s due to extreme drought conditions. The Agua Pura Company, a private water delivery franchise, was taking what little water there was. The State Engineer brought in a Water Master who issued an order to Agua Pura to stop diversions; the company refused and the litigation began. Public Service Company of New Mexico (PNM) bought out Agua Pura; the Town of Las Vegas, which was not yet incorporated, joined in the lawsuit, and it was then that the Pueblo Water Right claim was made by the municipality (the town eventually took over the PNM water system).

A 1958 New Mexico District Court decision, referred to as the Cartwright Decision, recognized that the Pueblo Rights Doctrine, as affirmed by the California courts, applied to New Mexico. (UNM Law Professor Em Hall wrote a lengthy analysis of the Cartwright Decision in his paper "Bringing Water Law to the Gallinas River.") Local politician Donaldo "Tiny" Martinez, who served as San Miguel County District Attorney, district judge, the local Democratic Party Chairman, and a state representative, was largely responsible for pushing the idea of the Pueblo Water Rights Doctrine.

Before I go into the details of the Pueblo Water Rights Doctrine case and the ultimate decision, I want to reference an article that Rio Gallinas parciante and former Northern New Mexico Legal Services paralegal William Gonzales wrote for *La Jicarita* in 1999. Gonzales's article gives the history of the establishment of the Rio Gallinas acequias and city of Las Vegas priority dates, which would play out in the determination of the Pueblo Water Rights Doctrine lawsuit. In the mid-1830s Hispano settlers in the Las Vegas area built their acequias before they established their permanent homes, as happened in many other New Mexico land grant communities. In the 1933 adjudication of water rights in the city of Las Vegas, the town was given an appropriative right of 2,600 acre feet per year of Rio Gallinas water, with a priority date of January 1, 1881. Water rights were also adjudicated for the Gallinas Canal Water Storage and Irrigation Company (1888) and the Storrie Lake Water Users Association (1909), and the acequias (1835-1880), giving them first priority in the "Hope Decree."

Then in 1991 the OSE reopened the Rio Gallinas adjudication in an attempt to resolve the Pueblo Water Rights Doctrine claim by the city that had been in the courts since 1958. This time the OSE engineered a negotiated settlement in 1997 that would have given the city 2,200 afy with a priority date of 1835 and 1,900 afy with a priority date of 1881. In exchange for this agreement the city would withdraw its claim to a "Pueblo Water Right."

Eleven community acequias and the Storrie Lake Water Users Association contested the settlement in an expedited inter se district court hearing in February of 1997. The judge ruled that the city was entitled to only its original appropriation of 2,600 afy and a priority date of 1881, as stipulated in the Hope Decree. The city appealed that decision to the New Mexico Court of Appeals, which upheld the district court ruling.

In his *La Jicarita* article Gonzales described the water situation in 1997 this way:

"Where do we go from here? Is the City of Las Vegas now going to ask the New Mexico Supreme Court to rule on the Pueblo Water Right Doctrine once and for all? Will the city decide to continue further litigation in an attempt to obtain more water rights and ask the Supreme Court to hear yet another case? City leaders don't seem able to decide. One day it's the Pueblo Water Right theory with unlimited water rights and the next day it's the appropriation theory with 4,100 acre feet and a split priority date. One thing for sure, the city currently owns rights to 2,600 acre feet of water on the Gallinas River with an 1881 priority date. Another certainty is that the city is currently using more water than it has a right to. Acequia leaders are concerned the city will continue to over-divert water and will continue litigation. This over diversion continues to affect the availability of water for acequia members and has a tremendous impact on the entire agricultural community that depends on the water. Additionally, litigation costs continue to mount."

In 2004 the New Mexico Supreme Court ruled in favor of the OSE that the Pueblo Water Rights Doctrine "is incompatible with water law in New Mexico, and violates public policy," primarily because of the principle of beneficial use. This was a complicated—and somewhat inconclusive—decision. The court asserted "that an appropriator can only acquire a perfected right to so much water as he [or she] applies to beneficial use." Applying this principle, the court "recognized that water users have a reasonable time after an initial appropriation to put water to beneficial use" even though "a municipality may be given a more substantial 'reasonable time' for its population growth than a typical water user." The Pueblo Rights Doctrine, the decision went on to say, is "not limited by the reasonable time requirement . . . instead, [it] contemplates an indefinite expansion to meet growing demands of an increased population, regardless of how small the population of the initial pueblo and how long it takes the pueblo to expand. This aspect of the pueblo water right intolerably interferes with the goals of definiteness and certainty contemplated by prior appropriation" that is the most fundamental principle of New Mexico water law.

In addition, the decision asserted "that the pueblo rights doctrine unduly interferes with the state's regulation of water rights" with regard to its duty to meet interstate water delivery requirements to Texas and its duty to conserve a vital resource. But the court then remanded the case to District Court "to determine the most appropriate equitable remedy that will balance the City's reliance on Cartwright [the original 1958 pueblo water right claim] with other water users' reliance on New Mexico's system of prior appropriation." While David Benavides, the Legal Aid attorney representing the acequias, said that in general he thought the inconclusive decision wouldn't resolve all the conflict between the city of Las Vegas and the acequias, he did say, "I don't think the acequia community ever has to worry about another municipality trying to appropriate water through the pueblo rights doctrine again." While Benavides was technically right that acequias ultimately didn't have to face appropriation of their rights via the doctrine, several cities—Albuquerque and Santa Fe—tried to raise the claim but were rejected by the courts.

According to Gonzales, Benavides was also right in his pessimism that the decision would resolve the water battles between the city and the acequias, which continue today. The OSE failed to complete the adjudication of acequia water rights until a new judge, Special Water Master Stephen Snyder, working under the AWRM regulations, forced the adjudication to proceed. After years of settlement talks, in March of 2018 Snyder recommended to the presiding judge that the City of Las Vegas's appropriative water rights of 2,600 afy with a priority date of 1881once again be divided with 1,200 afy of that assigned an 1835 priority date. The City acknowledged that under these terms there would likely be a 300 afy shortage of water per year and proposed a payment of a million dollars, which the water master raised to a $1.7 million payment to the acequias to be paid out on a per acre basis. Gonzales pointed out that this is a one-time payment while the 300 afy shortage is on a yearly basis. The City also acquired increased storage capacity at Storrie Lake.

The acequias tried to convince the court that instead of assigning these priority dates they agree with the City to draw up a water sharing agreement where both entities, the acequias and the City, would be willing to share in times of shortage. According to Gonzales, while the OSE ostensibly observes a sharing agreement, the City has been unfairly favored. The OSE has installed meters on all the acequias and updated the City's diversion gates, which are automated. The OSE oversees delivery requirements and rotations schedules that are in opposition to traditional practices that took into account drought and other contingencies that were handled by the folks on the ground actually using the water. Many acequia acres have already been lost due to the state taking the position that they were abandoned during over diversions by the City, Agua Pura, and PNM.

Water Master Synder retired and a new water master, who actually lives in Las Vegas (Snyder lives in Santa Fe), presides over the administration of the basin's water rights, which Gonzales said improves the logistical situation but ultimately aids in the bureaucratization of a system that was once based on need and fairness, and yes, a priority date that the courts seem unwilling to acknowledge. As Em Hall put it in his comprehensive analysis of the Cartwright decision, "In the end, the river remained the same as it always had been: water short and problem rich."

Sixteen

Women of El Norte

I remember the first time I met my vecino Tomás, the mayor-domo on the Acequia Abajo, which waters our lower field. He came down the driveway to tell me (I don't know where Mark was) we could have the water the next day, tentatively shaking the hand of not only a gringo but a *gringa*. I didn't know which category gave him more pause, and still don't, because as soon as we proved our worth—that we could be buen vecinos—neither mattered. I wasn't treated any differently than Mark as a neighbor, fellow parciante, or friend.

It's important to remember that during the many years men like Tomás had to leave the villages of northern New Mexico to make a living in the mines of Colorado or the factories of California, their wives took care of all the household and outdoor needs, which were extensive. In those days kitchen gardens provided much of the food consumed by the family, hay fields provided forage for the cows, sheep, and goats that had to be herded and cared for on a daily basis, village molinos ground the wheat into flour, and firewood had to be brought in from the common lands to be cut and split. When we moved to El Valle in 1992 these men were largely retired and were the ones who served as acequia commissioners and mayordomos. But even in those early years there were women who filled those roles in el norte villages: Jane Stanley was a commissioner in Vadito for many years; Tanya Leherissey was (and is) the mayordoma in Llano San Juan; Esther Garcia of Questa served as a commissioner on the Cabresto Irrigation District as well as mayor of the village; and Carol Miller helped her Ojo Sarco acequia fight the Forest Service over access rights. I became a commissioner in 2006 and women started showing up to help clean the ditch at the annual spring limpiezas around that time as well.

In the larger acequia community women have played predominant roles for many years. As I discussed previously, Paula Garcia became the director of the New Mexico Acequia Association when it was reorganized in the late 1990s and continues in that role today. I served on the NMAA board for several years with Josie Lujan, a member of the Santa Cruz Irrigation District in Chimayó, and Janice Varela of Pecos (now a San Miguel County Commissioner) was the longtime community organizer at the NMAA. In the literary and academic world, native Taoseña and former UNM professor, Sylvia Rodriguez is the author of one of the definitive books on acequia culture, *Acequia: Water Sharing, Sanctity, and Place;* Phaedra Greenwood wrote *Beside the Rio Hondo* and is a longtime member of the Committee to Save the Rio Hondo.

Trudy Valerio Healy, also a native Taoseña, is a partner with her husband Ed in the Healy Foundation, which has funded numerous water and acequia projects and advocates, including *La Jicarita News*, for many years. Daughter of Juan Valerio, longtime acequia commissioner in Ranchos de Taos, Trudy also served on the Water Trust Board, the state-appointed committee that approves funding for state sponsored water projects, until the Republican Governor Susana Martinez nudged Trudy, a loyal Democrat, off the board.

Trudy was best friends with Butchie Denver. Butchie seemed to be involved in everything: Democratic party politics, government account-ability, county land use planning, water and acequia issues, anything and everything that mattered to the citizens of Taos County. Butchie was always there, at all those interminable county commission meetings, all those county planning meetings where volunteer citizens struggled to help the staff come up with a viable land use plan or subdivision regulations.

God knows, Butchie never gave anybody any peace. She'd show up in their office—county commissioner, planner, attorney, town mayor—track them down at home, or confront them in public to express her displea-sure when they failed to contribute to the common good. Seeing her in action was like watching a bulldozer in the guise of a southern California surfer girl, with her blue eyes, shoulder length blonde hair, and mostly sandaled or bare feet. Which is where she came from, actually: Los An-geles. How she ended up in New Mexico is a long and complicated story that involved being married to the actor Bob Denver back east, but she made it here about 40 years ago and things haven't been the same since.

Tony Trujillo, Butchie's partner of 38 years, was the one who charac-terized Butchie and two of her comadres, Trudy Valerio Healy and Fabi

Butchie and members of the Taos County Commission (and Bill Whaley, second from right)

Romero, as Las Brujas. It was Bill Whaley, longtime editor of *Horse Fly*, the alternative Taos newspaper that addressed all things political, who ran with it over the years as he reported on their doings. Las Brujas first worked their magic on the Taos County Democratic party machine back in the 1990s when the usual suspects ran everything under a patronage system reminiscent of the baddest patrón of them all, Rio Arriba County Emilio Naranjo (progressives in that county were taking the Naranjo machine on at the same time). Las Brujas, along with other progressives in the party, managed to kick them out and install a new chair. They then went after an inept county commission, county manager, and other assorted misfits and actually helped elect a commission that actually *did* do something for the common good.

Obviously not a woman, but a friend of a lot of us women, Bill Whaley published his memoir, *Gringo Lessons: 20 Years of Terror in Taos* in 2015, which documents the many crazy years he spent trying to make a living in Taos by bringing entertainment to the community: music in bars, movies at the Taos Plaza Theater, plays at the community theater. He left for a while in the 90s to go back to his home state of Nevada and finish his degree, but he came back and this time brought us muckraking journalism in the form of *Horse Fly*, which like Butchie, never gave any politico, particularly the corrupt ones, any peace. *Horse Fly* eventually segued into *Taos Friction*, an online journal that continues the investigations in grand style. The bad gringo will return in a sequel called *Taos Redux: The Horse Fly Years*.

I didn't meet the infamous Butchie until the 2000s when we both began working on the Taos County Regional Water Plan. As I discussed earlier, the New Mexico State Water Plan, promulgated in 2003, divided the state into 16 regions and stipulated that each region would develop its own water plan under the direction of the Interstate Stream Commission.

We served on the subcommittee whose task was to help define what constitutes the "public welfare" when water rights are transferred. Remember, the criteria the Office of the State Engineer uses to approve or disapprove proposed water rights transfers are: 1) whether the transfer will impair other water rights; 2) whether the transfer is contrary to the conservation of water; and 3) whether the transfer is consistent with the public welfare. This last criterion has never been defined; that's what Butchie and I and several others on the steering committee tried to do. I'll tell this story in later chapters. Suffice it to say, the special interests that want to move water rights around with impunity came together to sabotage our efforts. But Butchie and our cohort persevered, and in 2010 Taos County passed its own ordinance setting up a Public Welfare Advisory Committee to review all proposed water transfers within or from Taos County to assess their consistency with the public welfare. I served on that committee along with Tanya Leherissey and Glorianna Atencio, a parciante from Arroyo Hondo.

Butchie would periodically get disgusted and say she was going to quit getting involved in Taos politics. She'd stay home for a while, in her La Lama home filled with her beautiful retablos, tin work, and rehabilitated trasteros. She'd spend time with Tony and her beloved cat until something would really piss her off and she'd storm back down the mountain to confront whoever needed to be taken to task. One day my son heard a message from Butchie on my answering machine, telling me I *had* to go to a meeting because she couldn't, and he said to me, "Boy, she really sounds like she's mad at you." She wasn't, but if she had been it would have been a compliment. As Trudy Healy told the *Taos News*, if you got Butchie's attention that meant "you were worthy of her scorn. If she thought you were just an idiot, she would ignore you, and that was probably worse."

(Butchie died on June 25, 2012, not long after being diagnosed with cancer. It came as a shock to all of us, friends and coworkers alike. She always had our backs, and we were unsure how to proceed without her. I knew that at 74, having experienced the many disappointments that any activist acutely feels, she was tired. May she rest in peace.)

Seventeen

Taos County Regional Water Plan and Public Welfare

It was wishful thinking that the Taos County Regional Water Plan Steering Committee, which began meeting in 2004, would have a plan all done and delivered by 2005. As a steering committee member and reporter for *La Jicarita* I would be involved in this confounding enterprise for the next six years.

The purpose of the plan, part of the Interstate Stream Commission's (ISC) regional water planning program (16 planning regions in the state), was to characterize water supply, current and future water demands, and alternatives for meeting future water needs in Taos County. The task of the steering committee, comprised of representatives from major water user groups and water management agencies such as acequias, county and municipal governments, federal and states agencies, and individual farmers and ranchers, was to help identify issues and concerns of local communities, review and discuss alternatives as they were developed, and be a conduit for information to their constituencies.

The Taos Regional Water Plan encompasses all of Taos County as well as a slice of Rio Arriba County in the Embudo watershed. North to the state line the region includes the Pueblo of Taos, at the base of Taos Mountain, and the small communities of El Salto, Arroyo Seco, Des Montes, Valdez, Arroyo Hondo, San Cristobal, Lama, Questa, Costilla, and Amalia. The northernmost communities—Amalia, Costilla, and Questa— have experienced some of the boom/bust fallout of the Chevron Questa molybdenum mine that opened and closed over the years of 1920 to 2014 as the price of the metal rose and fell. It was permanently closed in 2014 and is now an Environmental Protection Agency Superfund site. The communities of San Cristobal, Arroyo Hondo, Valdez, Des Montes, El Salto, and Arroyo Seco still retain their acequia culture and are members of the Taos Valley Acequia Association, but because of their proximity to Taos have gradually gentrified as wealthy Anglos bought land and renovated houses. With the loss of much of the younger generation there are

112

fewer parciantes to water smaller fields as housing fills in. For example, the Atalaya Acequia in Arroyo Hondo, at five miles the longest in the community, has the fewest parciantes. These communities had been engaged in previous struggles to protect the Rio Hondo against development: the Committee to Save the Rio Hondo fought both the United States Forest Service and the Taos Ski Valley over expansions in the 1990s and is again involved in negotiations as I write this book as the new billionaire owner Louis Bacon seeks expansions.

The most southern communities in the region in the Peñasco area, on the Santa Barbara and Las Trampas land grants—Tres Ritos, Vadito, Placita, Llano, Chamisal, Vallecito, Ojito, El Valle, and Las Trampas—often feel like the orphans of Taos County, complaining of less attention and fewer services. As we'll see in the next chapter about the Abeyta Adjudication Settlement, which governs water in the Taos Valley, the southern most communities have kept a watchful eye on how any portions of the settlement might affect the viability of their water supply.

The Taos Regional Water Plan steering committee would work with the information provided by the professionals: the New Mexico Bureau of Technology to analyze subsurface geology; private water specialists who would collect data on private wells, springs, and surface water; and the Soil and Water Conservation District that was mapping groundwater levels. Committee members submitted issues that needed to be addressed in the Plan: identifying current supply (surface and groundwater) versus use; water quality; conservation development; drought and affects on supply; agricultural return flows; off-road vehicle use; sediment loading; urban and non-urban sprawl; removal of non-native vegetation; loss of irrigated lands; preserving and protecting water rights; protection of watersheds; transfer of water rights; protection of Otowi Gauge and subsequent accounting related to the Rio Grande Compact; definition of highest and best use; and prohibition of "out of county" transfers.

By 2005 the Plan had been derailed when the consulting contractor failed to supply adequate information on water supply and Taos County terminated its contract. A new firm, DB Stephens and Associates of Albuquerque, was brought on board to complete the water planning effort.

In May, the steering committee set up several technical teams to advise and watchdog the consultant. A technical group of agency people such as Peter Vigil of Taos Soil and Water Conservation District, and Palemon Martinez, of the Taos Valley Acequia Association, would help provide critical information regarding groundwater and surface water supply and quality. A demographic team would look at population projections and growth issues. A legal team would coordinate the attorneys who were involved in various aspects of the plan and monitor how it developed with regard to state water law. Most importantly, in my mind, Brian Shields of Amigos Bravos, the Taos-based environmental group, brought up the issue of public welfare, which is one of the criteria in judging water transfer applications, and the steering committee agreed that a separate team should work with the consultant on examining public welfare case law. It was pointed out that the Top of the World water transfer application was still pending, eliciting a conversation about the necessity of preventing water transfers out of Taos County. While acequia commissions by then had the authority to prohibit water transfers from their acequias, many of them had failed to incorporate this authority into their bylaws. Over the course of several subsequent meetings everyone on the committee agreed that the number one goal was to preserve regional water sources for Taos citizens, both physically and legally.

By 2006 a subcommittee of the Taos Regional Water Plan Steering Committee had been set up to draft a Public Welfare Statement that would be incorporated into the regional water plan (disclosure: I was a member of that subcommittee). The State Water Plan specifically called for regions within the state to establish criteria for evaluating the public welfare within their regional water plans, and the Taos steering committee hoped its Public Welfare Statement could be a precedent setting document, as public welfare, while a criterion in the management of New Mexico's water resources, has never been legally defined.

One of the few cases that actually addressed what "public welfare" might mean was the Ensenada Ditch case in northern Rio Arriba County near Tierra Amarilla. Back in the mid 1980s a developer tried to transfer water rights from that ditch to a proposed ski area. The acequia protested the transfer, the State Engineer ruled against the acequia, but it then appealed to district court Judge Art Encinias, who overruled the State Engineer. This is part of what he said in his decision: "Here, it is simply assumed by the Applicants that greater economic benefits are more desirable than the preservation of cultural identity. This is clearly not so. Northern New Mexicans possess a fierce pride over their history, traditions, and culture. This region of northern New Mexico and its living culture are recognized at the state and federal levels as possessing significant cultural value, not measureable in dollars and cents."[26]

Coincidentally, one of the few times the words "public welfare" were used by the Office of the State Engineer to deny a water transfer was in Taos County. During the hearing on the controversial Las Sierras resort development water transfer application in the early 1990s, then state engineer Eluid Martinez denied the transfer request, basing his decision on the fact that a transfer might draw down area wells and hamper the historical flow of the Rio Pueblo, the Arroyo Seco, and the Rio Lucero. In his decision Martinez wrote, "The public welfare is not well served by approval of only a portion of the water supply required for a proposed planned development project in which the ultimate water requirements are known. Ultimate cumulative effects to existing water rights resulting from the use of water within the proposed Las Sierras development project are not known and therefore a determination cannot be made as to whether those effects would not constitute impairment." He also acknowledged that because New Mexico state statute does not recognize preferential uses of water, local agencies should determine whether water uses for agricultural and traditional purposes should be protected: "Whether a given area is to be preserved for traditional uses, such as agriculture, or converted to new uses such as subdivisions and commercial enterprises is more appropriately decided by local governmental entities charged with land zoning and development activities."[27] (Taos Pueblo supported the water transfer protest filed by members of the Las Colonias-West Mesa Preservation Association because of the possibility that the transfer would lower the water table under the Buffalo Pasture Wetlands.)

The decision was appealed to district court, but Judge Peggy Nelson dismissed the appeal. Several months later the owner of the land and water rights terminated his agreement with the developers and the transfer became moot. Without a hearing in the New Mexico Appellate or Supreme

Court, State Engineer Martinez's decision was not binding and did not become case law.

The Public Welfare Statement and Implementation Program of the Taos Regional Water Plan was a comprehensive attempt to manage the area water in a sustainable manner. In particular, it laid out the criteria for determining whether proposed water appropriations or transfers from the Taos Region to other regions and within the Taos Region from one sub-watershed to another were inconsistent with the public welfare. The individual criteria included: cultural protection; agrarian character; ecological health; long-term economic development potential; recreation/tourism; public information; water budgets; conservation/restoration; and conjunctive management. The Implementation component of the program called for the formation of a local review board that it suggested "will be better qualified than the State Engineer to evaluate the Public Welfare criteria of the Taos Region," just as former State Engineer Martinez acknowledged. It would evaluate the potential impacts of proposed water appropriations and transfers on the public welfare and advise the OSE and local governmental entities as to whether these appropriations or transfers were consistent with public welfare. The board would be comprised of members who represented the various water interests within the Taos Region, including the Taos County Commission, the town of Taos, unincorporated communities, Taos Pueblo, Picuris Pueblo, the acequias, the mutual domestic water associations, domestic well owners, and regional watershed groups. In evaluating each individual public welfare criterion, the review board would also consider the cumulative effects of all other existing and reasonably foreseeable appropriations and transfers that might affect the same sub-watershed, together with the potential effects of the proposed transfer.

While the State Water Plan called for each region to establish its own public welfare criteria, there was no legal requirement that the OSE agree to the findings of the local review board. While an OSE lawyer wrote a brief years ago that supported the position that agency decisions should be defined by regional water plans, the OSE has a long history of rubber-stamping water transfers that underwrite growth and development in our urban and suburban areas. We hoped that Public Welfare Statements like the one in Taos would be a step in the right direction, but a court decision upholding a case based on this public welfare criteria, as in the Las Sierras district court decision, is necessary to establish precedent and get us farther down the road towards more equitable management of our water resources.

Unfortunately, the Public Welfare Statement and Implementation Program got high jacked by the powers that be before any results could be evaluated. While some of the already completed Regional Water Plans had drafted public welfare statements that were approved by the Interstate Stream Commission, there were delays and internecine fights within the planning areas instigated by special interests that didn't want to see what they interpreted as "restrictions" on their ability to move water to the "highest and best uses," i.e., urban and industrial growth and development. In our case it was the parties to the Taos Pueblo Water Rights Adjudication, or the Abeyta Settlement, who began to undermine the Public Welfare Statement and Implementation Program. The following chapter looks at the Abeyta Adjudication, whose parties, just like those in the Aamodt, spent years negotiating a settlement, and their role in scuttling the efforts to provide oversight of water transfers both within and from Taos County.

Eighteen

Abeyta, or Taos Pueblo Adjudication

The Taos Pueblo Water Rights Settlement, or Abeyta Adjudication, governs only one pueblo, Taos; the other parties include the Taos Valley Acequia Association (representing 54 acequias), the town of Taos, El Prado Water and Sanitation District, and the mutual domestic water associations. It is a complex mix of agreements among its parties to equally distribute and protect water resources within the Taos Valley. While the parties to this settlement emphasized their desire to minimize effects on water users outside the Taos Valley, the settlement was contingent on acquiring uncontracted San Juan/Chama water, imported from the San Juan Basin. These 2,990 acre feet (afy) of water (this amount was later reduced by 300 afy, which went to help fulfill the terms of the Aamodt Adjudication) would go primarily to Taos Pueblo (2,440), but 500 afy was slated for the Town of Taos and 50 afy for El Prado Water and Sanitation District. Taos Pueblo is entitled to its Historically Irrigated Acreage Right of 5,712.78 acres (22,508.35 afy), but shall "forbear" disruption of non-Indian irrigators in the Taos Valley by limiting its irrigation to 2,322.45 acres of recently irrigated land.

The Abeyta would also use a "mitigation well system to offset the surface water depletion effects resulting from future groundwater diversions and consumption." Mitigation wells, which reach 1,000 feet or more into the deep aquifer, would be used to offset at least 50 percent of any Taos Valley tributary surface water depletions resulting from future groundwater pumping. Because pumping water from these deep wells does affect stream flows in the Rio Grande, users would have to obtain offsets of water to compensate for these depletions. These offsets could be acquired by changing the point of diversion of water taken from Rio Grande tributaries (water purchases from wells) or using San Juan/Chama project water. All of these groundwater and surface water depletion effects would be calculated using a groundwater flow model that was incorporated into the proposal, called the Settlement Model.

118

At a 2006 meeting of the Taos Regional Water Plan steering committee, the Stein and Brockman Law Firm, which represented El Prado Water and Sanitation District, one of the parties to the Abeyta Adjudication, submitted a letter objecting to the Public Welfare Statement and Implementation Program included in the draft plan, which I discussed in the previous chapter. Several other parties to the Abeyta, and the Taos County Association of Realtors (whose name also appeared on the Stein & Brockman letter as a client) submitted letters predicated on the Stein and Brockman letter, raising the same issues. Over the course of several years parties to the Abeyta, who were also members of the Taos Regional Water Plan steering committee, had been in negotiations on their proposed settlement at the same time Water Plan members had been meeting and therefore did not regularly attend the Plan meetings (with the exception of Palemon Martinez of the Taos Valley Acequia Association (TVAA), who managed to attend many Plan meetings as well as the Abeyta settlement meetings), so their concerns were being expressed at the eleventh hour (the draft was supposed to be completed by December 31 of 2006).

The bottom line for all of them—the TVAA, El Prado Water and Sanitation District, the town of Taos, Taos Pueblo—was that there be no oversight or restrictions on buying and selling water rights required to implement the settlement. The other objectors—real estate interests, Taos Ski Valley, the town of Red River—wanted no restrictions on their ability to move water to facilitate growth and development. They tried to disguise these concerns with the claim that the Implementation Committee was contrary to state law and duplicating the process already overseen by the Office of the State Engineer (OSE). It seemed like a tempest in a teapot: the Implementation Committee could only function in an advisory role, and ultimately, any protested water transfer applications would be decided, as always, by the State Engineer.

The lawyers for these Abeyta parties and other interest groups seemed to be raising three fundamental arguments: 1) water is a private property right, not a public resource that can be regulated for the public good; 2) economic development has precedence over other water management concerns; and 3) approval of the Taos Regional Water Plan Public Welfare Statement would prevent successful settlement of the Abetya Adjudication.

Their concerns reflected a bias towards protecting their negotiated settlement, which includes only the Taos Valley, while the Taos Regional Water Plan is the management plan for the entire Taos area, including all of Taos County and part of Rio Arriba County. In the settlement there are provisions for transferring water rights to offset any "Future Groundwater Diversions" by the Town of Taos and El Prado Water and Sanitation District, rights that could conceivably come from sub-watersheds within the Taos planning area. The parties to the Abeyta failed to acknowledge that the burden of these settlements sometimes falls on people who weren't sitting at the table, and any proposed transfer of those water rights should also have to meet the criteria laid out in the Public Welfare Statement.

The law firm's letter stated that "The Public Welfare Statement, combined with the Conservation Statement [also drafted by a subcommittee of the Taos Regional Water Plan], would result in the denial of all future transfers of water rights in the Taos Valley" and in the proliferation of domestic wells. They obviously were fearful that any future water applications made by the municipalities would indeed be contrary to the Public Welfare and they would be faced with the reality of actually tying growth to the availability of water. And finally, all the papers ended with some form of statement that the restrictiveness of these proposals would result in a taking of private property without just compensation. The Taos Pueblo letter concurred with this assessment with the additional overlay of its claim of sovereignty.

Members of the regional water planning subcommittee that drafted the Public Welfare Statement met with the Abeyta parties on more than one occasion and made revisions to the Public Welfare Statement to address their concerns.[28] They added this language to the statement: "Provided that the Abeyta Settlement is finalized and receives all required court approvals, this Regional Water Plan proposes that appropriations or transfers of water within the area of the Taos Valley Stream System, as defined in the draft Abeyta Settlement Agreement . . . are presumed to be consistent with the Public Welfare and Conservation of Water." The statement went on to say, however, "To the extent that implementation of the Abeyta Settlement requires appropriation or transfer of water from other sub-watersheds in the Taos Region, this Regional Water Plan proposes that such appropriations or transfers to be subject to Public Welfare review." However, some of the Abeyta parties still submitted comments to the Interstate Stream Commission (ISC), which oversees the regional water plans, challenging the idea of a local review board.

The steering committee and planning team took a draft of the Taos Regional Water Plan to the public during the last two weeks of October and got an enthusiastic response. At large turn-out meetings in Questa and Taos folks expressed their support for the priority strategies that had been identified to meet current and future water needs: watershed management; water quality protection; public education; protection of traditional agriculture (acequia protection); infrastructure improvements; keeping water rights in the region; and managing growth. The Public Welfare Statement and Implementation Program was also enthusiastically received at the public meetings and much of the discussion centered on the review board. One participant in Questa pointed out that it would help protect communities by creating greater accountability at the OSE. There was also discussion that it was important to have a repository of information regarding the plan and its implementation, and a board could play that role. Many Taos area residents agreed with the Public Welfare Statement subcommittee that a local review board would provide additional oversight to the transfer process that all too often occurs under the radar screen, without public input, and to the benefit of water users outside the Taos region. The regional water planning process is only a framework for water management, but if the Taos plan was approved by the Interstate Stream Commission many of the concepts laid out in the plan would be implemented through ordinance and with funding from the New Mexico Water Trust Board.

Show Down at the ISC

But ultimately, all of this was for naught. The Taos Regional Water Plan was presented to the ISC on Wednesday, November 28, 2006 at the Roundhouse, in Santa Fe, and as expected, the commission voted to delay approval of the Plan, including the Public Welfare and Conservation Statement, until "the parties can reach consensus." There would never be consensus between the opponents and proponents of the Plan, of course, because the former wanted unconstrained water markets while the latter believed that oversight and public awareness were critical to the public welfare.

Apparently then State Engineer John D'Antonio also believed in unconstrained water markets. During the hearing he admonished all of us on the steering committee for not reaching consensus and insisted that the current process, whereby water rights holders can protest transfer applications on the basis of three criteria—impairment, conservation, and public welfare—was perfectly adequate. Apparently D'Antonio thought that his office could continue to make those decisions without local involvement and in a process that is extremely burdensome to those who must hire lawyers to represent them at protest hearings that often drag on for years.

When ISC director Estevan Lopez asked Alan Vigil, former Taos County Planner and chair of the Regional Water Plan Steering committee, if Taos County was likely to establish a public welfare advisory committee regardless of whether the ISC approved the plan and public welfare statement, Vigil answered: "We don't have 40 years to come up with consensus. We're going to go ahead with public welfare implementation." Taos County Attorney Sammy Pacheco, while more politic in his answer, said, "We'll wait to see what the ISC committee decides," but expressed that the plan and public welfare statement had the full support of the county commission.

The ISC refused to approve the Taos Regional Water Plan, which included the Public Welfare Statement and Implementation Program, until all the stakeholders agreed to sign on. They sent us back to Taos to try to come to this consensus at two scheduled mediation sessions, but essentially the plan was hijacked by the powers that be. The expression "not at the table" is often used to indicate that someone's input was not represented in a process, whether by intention or omission. At the March 7 meeting of the Taos Regional Water Plan, members of the Public Welfare Committee who drafted the Public Welfare Statement and Implementation Program, were designated the "Stakeholders" and literally were "not at the table": we were consigned to the audience while all the "Decision Makers" were physically there. The Decision Makers, or Taos Region elected officials, included all the municipalities, water districts, and Abeyta Adjudication parties who had objected to the Public Welfare Implementation Program because they wanted to buy and sell water rights on the open market with no oversight.

I had already dropped out of the negotiation process prior to this meeting when I saw where we were headed. But I went to the second mediation meeting to cover it for *La Jicarita News*, and even I was surprised by the blatant maneuvering of the ISC. Rosemary Romero, who was mediating the meeting, made it clear that only the Decision Makers were going to address implementation, and Stakeholders were not to participate. When several Public Welfare Committee members objected to the undemocratic way the meeting was being run, they were told that the steering committee and Public Welfare Committee had done their job and were no longer part of the process. It was time for the Decision Makers to draft an implementation component for the plan.

I wrote an editorial about the meeting for *La Jicarita News* that raised a ruckus in the Middle Rio Grande Water Assembly (the support group for the Middle Rio Grande Regional Water Plan) after Lynn Montgomery distributed the article to all its members.[29] John Brown, who was the editor of the *Water Dialogue*, wrote a letter objecting to my claim that the ISC didn't want public welfare to apply to a water management strategy that encourages water transfers from agricultural lands to urban areas. Steve Harris, founder of Rio Grande Restoration and owner of a commercial rafting company (and a longtime proponent of instream flow), called my editorial "sour grapes." While John conceded that the ISC may have capitulated to developmental interests in the Taos Regional Water Plan, he believed that "generally" the ISC is not "in bed" with development interests. He suggested that "state water policy administrators are seeking to avoid conflict, and especially the litigation of competing claims on a scarce resource, which they're anxious not to get in the middle of . . ." because they lack data and don't have the resources.

Michael Jensen of Amigos Bravos also wrote a letter to the Assembly stating "the ISC/OSE never wanted to have public welfare applied to intra-state water transfers and is perfectly happy passing the buck to the Regional Water Plans, as long as they don't do something crazy like actually developing an implementation plan that is in step with the 'values' contained in the Public Welfare Statement."

Taos County Steps up to the Plate

As the lead organization in drafting the Taos Regional Water Plan, Taos County rose to the occasion in 2010 and passed a Public Welfare and Implementation Ordinance setting up an "Educational and Informational Committee" to review all proposed water transfers and applications in the Taos area under the public welfare criteria. The county was witness to the efforts of the parties to the Abeyta Adjudication Settlement to eviscerate the Public Welfare Statement and were prepared to move forward in crafting an ordinance to provide oversight, regardless of whether the Regional Water Plan, with the Public Welfare Statement intact, ever got approved by the Interstate Stream Commission. So members of the Public Welfare Committee, particularly the chair, Taos attorney Simeon Herskovits, pitched in and helped draft the ordinance.

The Taos County Commission failed to approve the ordinance the first time it appeared on the agenda, arguing that there was still some opposition to the ordinance that needed to be heard. Most of that opposition was from Palemon Martinez of the TVAA, who continued to oppose any oversight of water that might be targeted for the Abeyta Settlement. Butchie Denver, in a magnificent gesture of protest, sent the commission her letter of resignation from the Planning Commission, the Land Use Update Task Force, the State Water Plan Ad Hoc Committee, the Growth Management Steering Committee, and the Taos County Complex Committee, stating: "You ignored the ten meetings that the Public Welfare Committee had with these people [representatives of the Abeyta parties], trying to accommodate any reasonable suggestions and requests they came up with in an effort to come to some kind of consensus; but each time they wanted more until, ultimately, we simply felt it was a waste of time. There are 18 different drafts of the Public Welfare Statement to show for these meetings, but it still wasn't enough. Only the complete gutting of the Public Welfare Statement would suit them, which we were unwilling to do."

But finally, on Tuesday, October 26, 2010 the Taos County Commission approved a Public Welfare Ordinance[30] that established "an advisory and informational committee," comprised of volunteers from throughout the county, that would analyze and recommend to the commissioners whether proposed water transfers within or from the county are consistent with, or contrary to, public welfare requirements and whether the county should protest the transfer. The ordinance passed unanimously despite a last minute derailment effort by Martinez, repeating objections that he had raised over the long history of the ordinance's development: that it was overreaching, that it might infringe upon acequia commissioners' rights to deny or approve transfers, and that it might conflict with the terms of the Abeyta Settlement. He also claimed, once again, that there hadn't been enough public input. The commissioners were quick to address his objections by pointing out that the ordinance would work to protect all county stakeholders and water resources, not just acequias and mutual domestics within the TVAA, and allow the county to make informed protests of proposed water transfers that are not in the best interest of the citizens of Taos County.

Nineteen

"Taking On" Los Alamos National Laboratory

The year 2006 was also a big year for *La Jicarita News*—it's 10th anniversary. To celebrate that event we decided to "take on" the behemoth on the hill, Los Alamos National Laboratory. After covering the Cerro Grande Fire in 2000 that scorched 48,000 acres of the Jemez Mountains surrounding the Lab and threatened to destroy the Lab itself, we'd been paying more attention to this destructive institution so bound up in the economic and cultural web of northern New Mexico. I was asked to serve on the board of Concerned Citizens for Nuclear Safety, the non-profit watchdog group that was born when the Waste Isolation Pilot Plant was first proposed to house low-level defense nuclear waste near Carlsbad, New Mexico, and then segued into a LANL watchdog organization headed by Joni Arends, a long time activist and environmental attorney.

Over the years we investigated and documented all aspects of the Lab's dysfunction and invidious effect on the lives of New Mexicans: the continued promulgation of nuclear weapons development; management corruption and fraud; the failure to protect workers' health; discrimination and retaliation towards workers; and air and water contamination. The first article we published dealt directly with the pollution of groundwater from toxic sites on Lab property. Here's the article Mark wrote in the June 2006 issue of *La Jicarita News*.

LANL Toxic Legacy Threatens New Mexico Water Supply
By Mark Schiller

There's a specter haunting northern New Mexico, the specter of Los Alamos National Laboratory (LANL). LANL is widely regarded as the word's biggest death factory, devising, constructing, and testing the weapons, nuclear and otherwise, that form the arsenal of the "big stick" behind American foreign policy. Less well publicized, however, is the legacy of toxic pollutants with which LANL has poisoned New Mexico water, air, and land in its sixty plus years of creating weapons of mass destruction.

Although concerned activists, the New Mexico Environment Department (NMED), the Environmental Protection Agency (EPA), and current and former Lab employees have all voiced grave concerns about how the Lab uses and disposes of contaminants, the Lab's policy of hiding behind "security designations" and the protection it enjoys from our congressional delegation as the centerpiece of our economy, have historically worked to suppress information critical to exposing environmental infractions.

In March of 2005, however, the federal government finally acknowledged more than 1,400 sites on LANL property that required clean up because of groundwater contaminants, toxins, explosives, nitrate, and perchlorate. As a consequence, LANL signed a consent agreement with the NMED for "fence to fence" cleanup of LANL by 2015. Not surprisingly, given its past record, the Department of Energy (DOE) has already reneged on that agreement by requesting 90 million dollars less than the proposed cleanup agreement outlines for fiscal year 2007. With a total operating budget in excess of two billion dollars, LANL clearly can't blame budgetary restrictions for this shortfall. Both Senators Domenici and Bingaman believe this will result in missed cleanup deadlines and violations that could result in fines totaling millions of dollars.

Now an ad-hoc coalition of groups, calling itself LANL Water Watch, has filed a "Notice of Intent to Sue" the DOE and the Regents of the University of California, which oversees LANL, for violations of the Clean Water Act. The coalition consists of community and environmental groups including: Amigos Bravos, Concerned Citizens for Nuclear Safety (CCNS), Embudo Valley Environmental Monitoring Group, Partnership for Earth Spirituality, Rio Grande Restoration, and Tewa Women United. Citing reports and studies done by the NMED, EPA, and LANL itself, the notice of intent asserts that the Rio Grande and tributaries that flow through LANL property as well as groundwater from area wells are being threatened by contaminants from the Lab.

The coalition's press release states that "many tributary streams to the Rio Grande, either wholly or partially on LANL property . . . are designated as polluted by the NMED. Most of the streams are polluted with PCBs, gross alpha, and selenium." Some of the canyons running through LANL have also tested positive for mercury, perchlorate, and chromium.

By contrast, the coalition notes that "the Rito Frijoles and Capulin Creek, both tributaries to the Rio Grande from the Pajarito Plateau not on LANL property, are not polluted" by these agents.

The proposed lawsuit asserts there are 1,405 active sites on LANL "from which pollutants are or may be discharged. These sites typically include old material and liquid disposal areas, hazardous waste landfills, old dilapidated structures, contamination areas, dumping grounds, explosive testing sites, storm drains, firing ranges, septic systems and seepage pits. Following rain or snow melting events contaminants from these sites can, and have, run off into the soils, surface water and shallow groundwater of LANL's seven watersheds and canyons eventually traveling down-gradient to the Rio Grande."

The discharge from these sites is currently regulated under a National Pollution Discharge Elimination System (NPDES) permit for multi-sector general use. However, the EPA has conceded that "the existing [permit] does not address all of the [sites], their specific pollutants, and the parameters to be monitored because of LANL's unique circumstances." As a consequence, the EPA and LANL have agreed "to establish a program and schedule of compliance for regulation of . . . discharges from all sites . . . until EPA issues an individual NPDES permit to regulate those discharges." Until such a permit is issued and LANL actually meets the standards set by that permit (which it clearly is going to do everything in its power to avoid), it is operating in violation of the Clean Water Act.

The coalition's lawyer, Matthew Bishop of the Western Environmental Law Center, says "the impending lawsuit is based on four specific violations of the Clean Water Act: failure to conduct adequate monitoring; failure to report violations; failure to have pollution controls in place; and making unauthorized discharges. The result of these failures is that toxic contaminants are migrating to the Rio Grande, the future source of drinking water for Albuquerque and Santa Fe." The coalition also notes that this contamination will affect food irrigated with the water, as well as fish and other wildlife that are dependent on it.

According to the coalition's press packet, the most pervasive contaminates are PCBs (Polychlorinated Biphenyls) and gross alpha. PCBs are a group of industrial chemicals used in electrical equipment. The manufacture of PCBs was banned in 1977 because they were proven to accumulate in the environment and cause adverse health effects including cancer, thyroid, stomach and liver damage, and impaired reproductive and immune systems. PCBs have been detected in LANL streams at levels that far exceed New Mexico water quality standards. Gross alpha is defined by a 2004 LANL report as "The total amount of measured alpha activity without identification of specific radionuclides." The same report defines alpha particle as "A positively charged particle . . . emitted during decay of certain radioactive atoms." Plutonium-239, the principle ingredient in nuclear warheads, is the "most hazardous alpha emitter . . . highly carcinogenic, chemically reactive and flammable."

Other contaminants detected in water drawn from LANL streams and test wells are known to cause thyroid damage, birth defects, cancer, gastrointestinal problems, respiratory problems, kidney and liver damage, as well as circulatory and nerve problems. Many of these contaminants have already been detected in the municipal wells that supply Los Alamos and White Rock.

LANL Water Watch says that the purpose of the proposed suit is five fold: 1) Make LANL clean up all 1,405 contaminated sites; 2) Eliminate all contaminants currently discharged from LANL and prevent discharge of contaminants in the future; 3) Make LANL monitor and implement a Best Management Practices plan for discharges and dumping; 4) Make federal and state regulators hold LANL accountable; 5) Make LANL pay fines for all prior and on-going violations (which could total more than a billion dollars) and apply that money to an independent monitoring and remediation program of the sites in question.

Amigos Bravos director Brian Shields underscored the importance of the proposed lawsuit in a recent op-ed piece stating, "LANL boasts a 2.2 billion dollar budget and a secure position as the darling of our Congressional delegation. LANL provides jobs. Our congressional delegates manage to procure almost as much money (4.11 billion dollars) for the Department of Energy's New Mexico facilities—which include LANL, Sandia National Laboratory, and the Waste Isolation Pilot Plant—[as] the State of New Mexico's entire operating budget (4.8 billion dollars). Moreover, with the highest concentration of PhDs and millionaires in the entire country, along with a small army of lawyers, LANL can throw its weight around and successfully squelch any effort by effected communities to hold it accountable for the threat it presently poses to New Mexico's future water supply."

After two years of diligently collecting data on the Lab's toxic discharges and bringing together a coalition of additional community organizations and individuals, the coalition, now named Communities for Clean Water (CCW) filed a suit against LANL on February 7, 2008 in U.S. District Court. At a press conference announcing the lawsuit CCW stated that because "regulators have been unable to get LANL to clean up its discharges it is time for citizens to take over that task." The suit claims that LANL has failed to comply with the terms and conditions of its storm water National Pollution Discharge Elimination System (NPDES) permit at 59 dump sites, where contaminated storm water is allowed to run off into the soils, surface water, and shallow groundwater of LANL's Los Alamos and Pueblo canyon watersheds, eventually traveling down-gradient to the Rio Grande.

The plaintiffs asked the court to issue a "declarative judgment" that LANL has violated the Clean Water Act; a mandatory injunction for cleanup and monitoring; and assess civil penalties to LANL for violating the terms of the NPDES permit. Joni Arends, director of Concerned Citizens for Nuclear Safety, a CCW member group, stated, "We want specificity of site cleanup at LANL."

PCBs from 59 sites in two canyons represent only a portion of the contamination LANL has produced for over 60 years. The New Mexico Environment Department estimates there are approximately 2,093 dump sites at LANL where toxic chemical and radioactive nuclide waste has been deposited (NMED secretary Ron Curry attended the press conference and stated that he welcomed the lawsuit as another tool to help keep our drinking water safe). Many of these contaminants were dumped directly into the seven canyon watersheds that extend like fingers from the Pajarito Plateau, where the Lab is situated, to the Rio Grande. While these contaminants have long been traveling in storm runoff towards the river, after the 2000 Cerro Grande Fire, which caused enormous erosion and soil loss, there has been an accelerated movement of contaminants.

The week before the lawsuit was filed, the Bush administration released its 2009 budget: funding for the design and construction of plutonium pit production facilities at LANL will be increased to nearly $3 billion, while the $164 million budgeted for cleanup falls far short of the $222 million necessary to keep up with cleanup benchmarks of the "Consent Order" LANL signed with NMED. Communities for Clean Water filed suit to not only hold LANL accountable but to emphasize that a change of mission there is imperative.

Twenty

Aamodt Adjudication and Top of the World Saga Continues

The initial proposal in the Aamodt Settlement agreement that stipulated non-pueblo residents would be required to hook up to a $280 million water delivery system met with huge opposition from that community. After the federal government announced it would not commit to underwriting the cost of the water delivery system in 2004, negotiators went back to the table and in May released a "draft conceptual proposal" that did not require non-pueblo residents to cap their domestic wells. Hook-ups would be voluntary and the amount of water production would be reduced to a negotiated amount (post-1980 wells were reduced from 3-acre feet to 1-acre foot). The conceptual proposal stated that a water delivery system serving non-pueblo water users "may be reduced . . . but will be adequate to enable water service to be extended to all areas in the Settlement Study as the County obtains future funding." The settlement also guaranteed the pueblos first priority water rights and future development rights of 2,500 acre feet per year (afy) that would be supplied by the pipeline to access imported water from the Rio Grande.

Despite this concession there remained strong opposition to the proposed settlement. The Rio Pojoaque Acequia and Well Water Users Association and the Pojoaque Basin Water Alliance represented the non-Indian water users in the settlement area. The former group participated in the settlement negotiations while the latter group was formed in opposition to the proposed settlement. After the two groups formed a blended board, several board members were allowed to participate in subsequent settlement negotiations. Taos attorney Fred Waltz was hired to represent the Alliance.

Attorney Mark Sheridan, who represented the Rio Pojoaque Acequia and Well Water Users Association, asserted that the proposed settlement represented an earnest effort to protect all existing non-Indian uses throughout the basin. He warned that litigating this suit could result in the federal court severely limiting those uses. Sheridan agreed, however, with

132

many Aamodt defendants who claimed that the court's strict application of the law of prior appropriation in this case was contrary to Spanish and Mexican law that the federal government vowed to uphold in the treaty of Guadalupe Hidalgo. He told *La Jicarita* that he had argued in the 1980s that the "custom and tradition" of water sharing within the stream systems throughout the basin should be factored into the court's decision, but the court rejected that argument. While Sheridan conceded that the proposed settlement still had room for improvement, he maintained that under the circumstances it represented a reasonable compromise that protected both the acequia and domestic uses of non-Indians.

The Pojoaque Basin Water Alliance continued to raise serious questions regarding the proposed settlement into 2006. The conceptual proposal guaranteed the pueblos 2,500 afy of water in addition to their current water rights. The amount of water provided to non-pueblo residents would be reduced from the 1,500 afy described in the initial proposed settlement to provide for only current water needs—750 afy. The additional 750 afy needed for future growth might or might not become available, depending upon the County of Santa Fe's ability to purchase water rights. People questioned the fairness—and wisdom—of guaranteeing future water rights for the pueblos to underwrite growth and development of casinos and golf courses while non-pueblo residents might receive no additional water for growth of any kind. Judge Nelson, who presided over the negotiations, was blunt in his answer to this concern: "We're not going to sugar coat this proposal. It provides protection of your existing use, period. If you don't accept it, the Pueblos have the right to make a priority call on your water. You could lose everything."

Where was the pipeline water coming from? Top of the World (TOW) water rights (588 afy) were still under protest. The Alliance asked Francis West, a retired hydrologist, to submit an opinion regarding the hydrogeology of the TOW water rights. According to West, the groundwater conditions in the Sunshine Valley, where Top of the World Farm is located, are "very complex" and "unusual hydrologic conditions exist." Therefore, the effects of a transfer of these rights cannot be determined using a "one size fits all" template devised by the Office of the State Engineer for the Rio Grande. West's report stated, "In the area of the TOW wells the aquifer varies from being perched to semi-perched and un-perched [perched water is groundwater that is unconfined and separated from an underlying main body of groundwater by an unsaturated zone]." Because of the complexity of this hydrology, West was of the opinion that there would "probably be a substantial increase in the time needed for the effects of pumping to hit the Rio [Grande] due to the perched nature of the aquifer. . . . The location of the move to 'well' makes the move tantamount to sucking the water directly out of the river. There has never been a philosophical problem of taking your surface water rights out of ground water, but turning a ground water right into a surface right has some scary implications." In other words, it is extremely difficult to calculate what the correlation is between the groundwater wells at TOW and the amount of water that would be pumped out of the Rio Grande for the water delivery system in the Aamodt settlement.

Cost sharing agreements and governance had yet to be negotiated. The Alliance felt strongly that they should pay only for services that benefited their community. None of the projected $280 million cost of the project was committed at this point. The state was expected to cover $20 million and Santa Fe County between $5 and $10 million, leaving the federal government with a substantial chunk of the bill. Alliance members wanted a full disclosure of costs and they also wanted a seat on the board of the Regional Water System, which would be controlled by the four pueblos and the Santa Fe County Water Utility. There was the danger of privatization of either of these entities and the Alliance wanted to be onboard to protect the interests of non-pueblo residents.

In mid-2005 Santa Fe County attorney John Utton told attorneys for the Top of the World water transfer protestants (remember, Mark and I were among the protestants) that he would recommend to the county that it commit to not piping TOW water south of the Otowi Gauge if protestants would drop their transfer protest. The 588 acre feet of consumptive water rights transferred from TOW would be used only for the water delivery system to non-Indians in the Pojoaque Basin as part of the Aamodt Settlement. The County was already negotiating for the purchase of additional Top of the World water rights to meet the settlement's promised 750 acre feet delivery to the non-pueblo users and a percentage of the 2,500 acre feet dedicated to the pueblos.

The city and county still reserved the right to construct a pipeline from a diversion north of the gauge to the Buckman Well Field to meet their growth and development demands. The settlement also allowed a transfer of up to 100 afy of the TOW water rights to offset surface water depletions in the upper basin Rio Tesuque caused by groundwater pumping in the Santa Fe basin, which is technically a transfer of water rights across Otowi Gauge.

In light of these unresolved issues, we were in no hurry to drop our protest. The county proceeded to acquire the remaining TOW land and attendant water rights and we didn't want to set a precedent that might affect a protest of the second transfer. At a previous status conference with the protestants in late 2004, Utton had already told us that if the second application was indeed protested, the pueblos in the Aamodt adjudication would attempt to acquire the San Juan/Chama water rights that were then designated for settlement of the Abeyta adjudication.

In a final settlement offer in November of 2006, drafted by Utton, the county agreed to three provisions:

1. The county would amend its application to limit the place of use to the upper Rio Grande Basin above Otowi Gauge.

2. The county would not acquire, transfer, or use water rights from community acequias in order to satisfy its obligation to acquire 750-acre feet per year of water rights under the Aamodt Settlement Agreement.

3. The county would limit the amount of upper Rio Grande Basin water that would be diverted to offset the upper basin Rio Tesuque to not more than 2-afy. When the county's regional water system reaches Tesuque Pueblo the county would not use any upper Rio Grande basin water rights to offset Rio Tesuque depletions by county wells in the Santa Fe basin.

While these were all important concessions, the protestants pointed out that the county claimed to have already acquired approximately 3,400 afy of the 4,000 afy it needed for the Aamodt settlement. This list included:

• 750 afy from domestic wells that would hook up to the water delivery system;

• 304 afy from Nambe Pueblo;

• 588 afy from the first Top of the World application;

- 1,164 afy from the second TOW application (the county estimated there would be an 18 percent evaporative loss of these rights);
- 800-1,000 afy of Cochiti Lake evaporative rights (this was highly speculative and percentages of evaporation were still being argued within the Aamodt Settlement negotiations).

It was unlikely that the county would try to transfer acequia water rights with or without our settlement agreement, as it would have political repercussions and would no doubt create an administrative nightmare: acequia transfer proposals would be small and piecemeal and would no doubt be protested. Many northern New Mexico acequias had already incorporated into their bylaws the 2003 state statute amendment that requires approval of the acequia commission for any proposed transfer within the acequia system. This provides added protection for acequia rights at the local level.

Santa Fe County was also assuming that once a water delivery or utility system was in place in 10 or 15 years the county would be able to divert San Juan/Chama Project water to offset upper Rio Grande depletions that resulted from its groundwater diversions and use it within the Rio Grande basin below Otowi Gauge. Of course, the Aamodt settlement had yet to be signed by the federal government, whose considerable financial resources were critical to building a water utility, and there was certainly no guarantee there would be a water utility anytime soon. And if the county was betting on acquiring additional San Juan/Chama water rights—it then had the use of 375 afy of San Juan/Chama water—it would have to fight the parties to the Abeyta adjudication in the Taos Valley.

The protestants to the TOW water transfer application believed that water should stay in its area of origin and purpose of use, and that the Office of the State Engineer should deny transfers that underwrite inherently inequitable adjudications, like the Aamodt, and that threaten the integrity of another region or sub-region's water resources. In May of 2006 the Taos County Commission passed a resolution that it "will support, and possibly join, any protestants to water rights being transferred from Taos County, to protect the traditional culture, communities, and the future growth of the county."

TAOS COUNTY Resolution No. 2006

A resolution to support the protestants to any transfer(s) of water from Taos County in order to preserve and retain the waters of the County within the Area of Origin.

WHEREAS, The historical cultures of the Taos Region—Native American and Hispanic—have revered water as the lifeblood of their communities; and

WHEREAS, the hydrology of ground and surface water is important to the viability of the acequias, Pueblos, and traditional communities; and

WHEREAS, the County seeks to protect the agricultural water rights that sustain the rural way of life within the County; and

WHEREAS, the long term growth and economic stability of the County depends upon adequate water supplies to sustain the vitality of the County.

NOW, THEREFORE, BE IT RESOLVED BY THE GOVERNING BODY OF TAOS COUNTY, NEW MEXICO, that the Taos County Board of Commissioners hereby, will support, and possibly join, any protestants to water rights being transferred from Taos County, to protect the traditional cultures, communities, and the future growth of the County.

PASSED, ADOPTED, AND APPROVED this 20th day of February 2006.

TAOS COUNTY BOARD OF COMMISSIONERS

Emanuel B. Pacheco, Chairman

Nicklos E. Jaramillo, Vice-Chairman

Virgil D. Martinez, Commissioner

Gabriel J. Romero, Commissioner

Don Francisco R. Trujillo II, Commissioner

While it was too late for Taos County to be a party to the extant TOW protest, when Santa Fe County applied to transfer the second tier of TOW water rights Taos County would be the likely protestant (as it turned out to be). In the meantime, Santa Fe County was contracting 450 afy of TOW rights in the Questa area and negotiating with the federal government to buy the second tier of rights to transfer directly to the pueblos in the Aamodt.

The protestants to the Top of the World (TOW) water transfer application officially rejected the county's settlement offer in early 2007. That supposedly meant the case would go to a hearing before the Office of the State Engineer, where the protestants intended to argue that the transfer was detrimental to the public welfare of New Mexico and contrary to sound conservation practice. But as ensuing chapters explain, that hearing never happened once Santa Fe County committed the TOW water rights to the Aamodt Settlement and combined the initial 588 afy transfer application with the second 1,164 afy transfer. Controversy over the settlement would drag on even after it was signed in 2010, and over 700 parties to the adjudication filed objections once the decree was issued. The story continues in a subsequent chapter.

Twenty-one

Acequias Once Again Confront Forest Service Over Access Rights

Camino Real District Ranger John Miera always introduced himself at community meetings as an acequia parciante and land grant heir, but after a three and a half hour meeting in April 2009 with local acequias on a cold, windy day at the Peñasco Community Center, parciantes came away with the impression that he was just another government bureaucrat, plain and simple.[31] If you recall, Miera was formerly the Española District Ranger who tangled with parciante Virgil Trujillo in Chapter Seven over access to his acequia. The issue of acequia pre-existing rights on federal lands arose this time on the Camino Real Ranger District, where Miera had been transferred in the mid-2000s.

The meeting was called by the Forest Service to address the acequia rehabilitation projects of five area acequias whose projects are located on national forest land (all former land grants). While most of the parciantes who attended the meeting wanted to focus on their concerns regarding the slowdown of their rehabilitation projects, which was jeopardizing their funding, Miera insisted that the Forest Service proceed with excruciatingly long presentations detailing the regulatory process it contended the acequias must undergo.

Miera was taking the position that acequia projects that require more work than he deemed simple "maintenance" are subject to analysis under the National Environmental Policy Act (NEPA) and have to obtain a special use permit from the Forest Service. Just what constitutes "maintenance" is open to interpretation, of course. Miera asserted that it only included removal of silt, reduction of erosion, maintaining water flows, and the replacement of a compuerta or presa that exactly replicated the structure being replaced. He claimed, for example, that replacing a presa made of logs and hay bales with gabions and cement, even in the same location as the previous dam, did not fall within regular maintenance. Acequias, on the other hand, asserted that work that was "essential" to the maintenance of their ditches and remained within their easements should not be subject to Forest Service regulation.

The regulatory process includes five steps: 1) submitting a SF 299 permit; 2) determining the "cost recovery," or administrative fees that the Forest Service charges to obtain necessary permits and monitor special uses for compliance; 3) conducting a NEPA analysis; 4) obtaining a special use permit; and 5) implementing and monitoring the project. The Forest Service was insisting that all acequia projects submit a SF 299 application so that the agency, not the acequia, could determine whether it was only a "maintenance" project or "beyond normal maintenance."

"Beyond normal maintenance" was the terminology used in a 2001 letter from then Regional Forester Eleanor Towns to David Benavides, attorney with New Mexico Legal Aid. Benavides had asked for clarification of Forest Service policy regarding acequia rehabilitation on federal lands for the Nacimiento Community Ditch Association on the Santa Fe National Forest (see Chapter Seven). In her letter to Benavides, Towns stated that a special-use authorization was required for activities "beyond normal maintenance or minor improvements . . . or outside the right-of-way; or which involve significant changes in location or alignment, significant increases in the area occupied, construction of new access roads, and enlargements and extensions that increase the capacity of the system."

Benavides believed that this policy statement "should have ended Forest Service badgering of parciantes to get special use permits and allow them to do what they've always done." But Miera, who has a history of interfering with acequia maintenance, seemed to think Towns's policy was subject to his interpretation. The commissioners of one of the five acequia projects chose not to attend the meeting because they asserted that the Forest Service did not have authority over acequia easements and they intended to proceed with their project.

Despite the fact that acequia easements pre-date Forest Service tenure, Miera insisted he had authority to regulate work within these easements. At the meeting in Peñasco, Miera did bring up the 1866 Congressional Act that acknowledges the validity of existing easements without the necessity of a permit or other authorization. The Act states: "Whenever, by priority of possession, rights to the use of water for mining, agricultural, manufacturing, or other purposes, have bested and accrued, and the same are recognized and acknowledged by the local customs, laws, and the decisions of courts, the possessors and owners of such vested rights shall be maintained and protected in the same; and the right of way for the construction of ditches and canals for the purposes of aforesaid is hereby acknowledged and confirmed."

Miera noted that this Act provides an alternative way for acequias to establish their pre-existing rights, but warned that the process required a claim to the Regional Office of the Forest Service, which necessitated copious documentation and placed the burden of proof on the acequias, rather than the Forest Service. He also cited the Federal Land Policy and Management Act (FLPMA) of 1976 that he claimed gives the Forest Service the right to "reasonably regulate" water rights and accompanying rights of way. At the meeting Benavides questioned whether FLPMA also recognized pre-existing water rights easements, which it does in the section regarding rights of way: "Nothing in this subsection [of the Act] shall be construed as effecting any grants made by any previous Act to the extent any such previous grant of right-of-way is a valid existing right, it shall remain in full force and effect."

Consensus among the parciantes, of course, was that everyone knows acequias pre-date the Forest Service and it is incumbent upon the Forest Service to recognize their pre-existing rights. A commissioner on one of the ditches that had been trying to implement its rehabilitation project since 2004 and had been dealing with Miera for two years (the commissioner complained that Miera was seldom in the office and often failed to return his phone calls) said, "We shouldn't have to prove our pre-existing rights. If we go through the permitting process we've already sold ourselves to the devil." Another parciante on the same acequia said to Miera, "Your position is insulting and degrading to the community."

Not long after this meeting John Miera was transferred to the Carson Supervisor's Office in Taos where he would serve in the Special Projects Division. In October of the same year the Supervisor's Office sent out a scoping letter on the proposed reconstruction of compuertas by four of the acequias in the Peñasco area that had been trying to improve their systems for several years. Acequias Chamisal y Ojito, Llano de San Juan Nepomuceno, Acequia Aguilar de El Valle, and Acequias de las Trampas ended up submitting their proposed projects to the Forest Service for NEPA review. The Forest Service scoping letter described the various projects. Chamisal y Ojito and Llano de San Juan Nepomuceno wanted to reconstruct their concrete compuerta on the Rio Santa Barbara to more efficiently divert water and replace the existing corrugated metal pipe drop structure. The Acequia Aguilar de El Valle is a private ditch in my village that wanted to replace its rock and log diversion with a cinder block head gate, and Acequias de Las Trampas wanted to replace its rock and log compuerta with a concrete structure. The Acequia de Ojo Sarco did not apply for special use permits from the Forest Service.

All the acequias had been under the gun to complete their projects or lose capital outlay funding from the state legislature. While all the acequias initially expressed reluctance to recognize Forest Service authority over maintenance and reconstruction of their headgates, during an on-site meeting at the Rio Santa Barbara project site that summer, Carson Forest Supervisor Kendall Clark offered to consult with the Regional Office about waiving fees associated with the NEPA review, acknowledging that in previous discussions with the acequias the issue of fees had not been raised. Acequias de las Trampas had already been assessed a cost share fee of $4,500. Subsequently, the Forest Service offered to waive both application and cost share fees.

According to Bonafacio Vasquez, one of the commissioners on the Llano San Juan ditch, the commissioners were "caught between a rock and a hard place." Unless they were able to proceed with the reconstruction of their compuerta that year the acequias would lose their funding from the state legislature. They went ahead and obtained a special use permit from the Forest Service but asked David Benavides of New Mexico Legal Aid to help them draft language to include in their special use permit request that stated their opposition to the Forest Service requirements.

This was a one-time fee-waiving offer by the Forest Service that put acequias on notice that they should factor in cost share fees when they make their capital outlay requests. This is not the solution to the controversy of access to acequias on public lands, however, and in a phone conversation with a Washington D.C. aid to Representative Ben Ray Lujan, *La Jicarita News* asked if the congressman's office was taking any steps to address the problem. According to the aid, the office at first pursued the idea, with both the Regional Forester and Secretary of Agriculture, of having acequia maintenance and construction projects classified as Categorical Exclusions, a NEPA category that would exempt them from full-fledged assessments and avoid fees and delays. This proposal was rejected. Lujan's aid told *La Jicarita News* that even though the four Peñasco area acequias were granted fee-waivers, the Forest Service continues to place an unfair burden on the acequia community and the solution to the problem lies with a legislative fix: exempt acequias from regulations such as the Federal Land Policy and Management Act (FLPMA), which the Forest Service cites as its authority to regulate acequia easements and require special use permits.

Twenty-two

Acequias de la Sierra

One of the Acequias de la Sierra ditches, which divert water from the west side of the Jicarita watershed (Peñasco) to the east side of the watershed (Mora), completed a new diversion in 2009, renewing parciantes' interest in the history of this unique trans-basin system.

According to a 1985 article by historian Anselmo F. Arellano, "Acequias de la Sierra and Early Agriculture of the Mora Valley," published by the Center for Land Grant Studies,[32] the Mora Valley was first colonized in the early part of the 19th century by a group of Indo-Hispano families who had formerly resided within the Pueblo of Picuris grant on the west side of the Jicarita watershed. In need of agricultural land to feed a growing population, the group of intrepid settlers, led by the soldier Antonio Olguín, made the journey over the mountain in 1816 into the remote but fertile valley.

Their efforts were initially successful, and by 1818 seventy-six families petitioned the church to establish an independent parish in San Antonio de lo de Mora. However, while the land in the valley was extremely fertile, the waters of the Mora River proved insufficient to meet the agricultural and domestic needs of the colony. As a result, Olguín (according to Arellano) "approached the Picurís Indians and successfully requested permission to take some pueblo water from the high mountain valleys and the crest of the Jicarilla [Jicarita] Mountain." Whether the Pueblo actually gave its permission for this diversion is questionable, and that issue will be addressed later in this chapter. Regardless of the politics involved, the engineering feat of diverting the waters of the middle tributary of the Rio Pueblo from the west side of the Jicarita watershed to the east side (to what is now the village of Cleveland), accomplished with only primitive tools, is staggering. Arellano speculates that the initial diversion canal was constructed before 1832, when it is known that the colony was abandoned due to the attacks of nomadic tribes.

The Mora Valley was subsequently resettled in 1835 and a formal grant

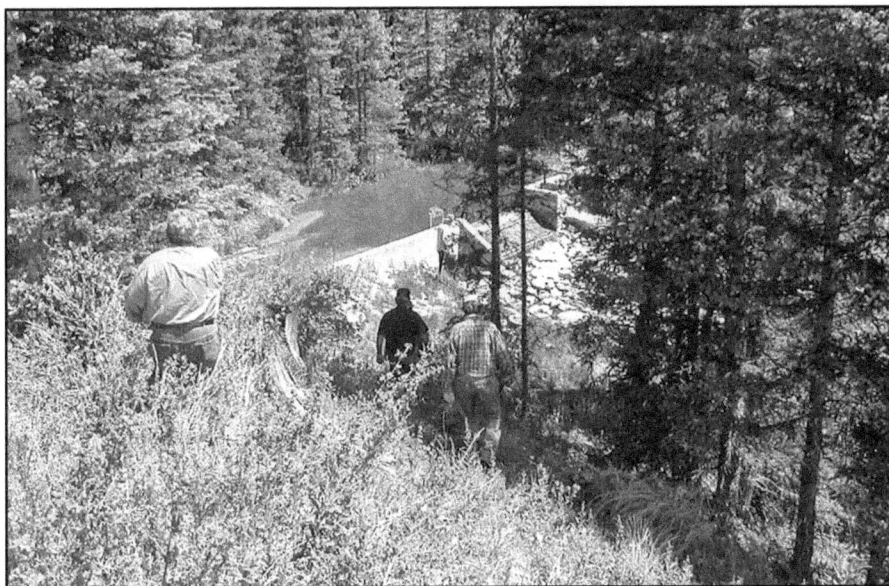

Headgate of one of the Acequias de la Sierra that flows to Chacon

was issued in October of that year by Mexican Governor Albino Pérez. Once again, the population burgeoned, spawning new settlements and placing increased demands on the limited water supply. In an effort to meet those needs, the residents of Chacón (north of the village of Mora) began construction of a second diversion from the northern branch of the Rio Pueblo that was completed in 1865. A third ditch, diverting the waters of the southern branch of the Rio Pueblo, was begun in 1879 and was delivering water to the community of Agua Negra (Holman) by 1882.

There is no mention in Arellano's article of permission being sought from or granted by the Pueblo of Picuris for either of these later diversions. While all three of these diversions are testament to the Mora Valley settlers' ingenuity and perspicacity, the question remains whether the diversions were legal. In point of fact, Picuris Governor Juan Pando, through the Pueblo's attorney S.M. Barnes, filed suit in New Mexico Territorial District Court in 1882 seeking a perpetual injunction to stop the diversion of water from the southern branch of the Rio Pueblo and naming twenty-three residents from the community of Agua Negra (Holman) as defendants.[33] In that suit Barnes asserted that pueblo members "have always been entitled to the full free and undisturbed possession of all the water of said streams and branches and said main stream the Rio Pueblo that naturally flowed to, through and upon their said land for domestic and all other uses in supplying their gardens and fields and for the purpose of sustaining their numerous animals . . . and they have enjoyed said water . . . as they had the lawful right to until the interferences hereinafter mentioned."

The suit not only sought to enjoin the diversion from the river's southern branch but went on to state: "that [for] many years since . . . the people of the County of Mora took and diverted the water from the middle branch of said Rio Pueblo and still continue to the use of the same and that they also some fifteen or twenty years ago took and converted the water from and of the northern branch of said Rio Pueblo to their own use contrary in both instances to law and good conscience." The suit noted that the two previous diversions had also been protested, but that the Pueblo's "objections were wholly disregarded," thus bringing into question Arellano's claim that Olguín received permission from the pueblo for the original diversion. Moreover, the suit claimed that the named defendants from Agua Negra "combined and confederated with others whose names . . . are unknown, but whose names, when discovered, your orators [Picuris Pueblo] pray that they may be at liberty to insert herein with apt words to charge them as parties, defendants hereto . . . ." The suit also asserted that the impairment of the Pueblo's water rights has "lessened the value of their said land grant and . . . diminished largely the amount of tillable land . . . used by them."

For unknown reasons, however, the Pueblo did not pursue the law suit and three years later in an ironic twist emblematic of New Mexico's schizophrenic colonialist history, the named defendants, now represented by Thomas B. Catron, the godfather of New Mexico's usurious land speculators, who by this time had secured an interest in the Mora Land Grant, successfully sought the dismissal of the suit "for want of prosecution." While the suit was dismissed, it was dismissed without prejudice, meaning the Pueblo was free to pursue its complaint in the future. As a result, the acequias of the Mora Valley continue to divert water from the Rio Pueblo, which in times of shortage may affect the amount of water available

146

to Picuris Pueblo and other Rio Pueblo/Rio Embudo dependent acequia communities.

In July of 2011 I went on a field trip to inspect the three trans-basin diversions with key players in water management from both sides of the mountain: Picuris Pueblo Governor Gerald Nailor and Lieutenant Governor J.D. Martinez; New Mexico Acequia Association director Paula Garcia and board members Antonio Medina, Harold Trujillo, and Estevan Arellano; Bureau of Indian Affairs (BIA) representatives; and acequia mayordomos and commissioners from the affected ditches. We had Carson National Forest to ourselves that day because of the forest-wide closure due to high fire danger (Las Conchas fire was burning the east side of the Jemez Mountains from south to north).

The mood of the field trip more than a hundred years after the apparently illegal diversions were made was conciliatory. Governor Nailor told the assembled group that the Pueblo wanted "an equal playing field" and that there needed to be gauges installed at the diversions that measure the amount of water agreed to by all the involved parties.

What we saw at the oldest diversion on the Alamitos (tributary of the Rio Pueblo), which delivers water to the Cañoncito y Encinal Acequias, was disturbing. The diversion was originally constructed out of logs, but the acequia commissions received capital outlay money from the state legislature to build a concrete headgate in 2007. Somehow the Texas branch of Trout Unlimited got involved in the project and added a fish barrier for native trout to the diversion. In July of 2010, however, floodwaters blocked the headgate with debris and washed away the embankment. The commissioners subsequently received $22,000 in FEMA funding (they also received $143,000 in stimulus funding in 2010 for other acequia rehabilitation) to return the acequia to its original condition. John Miera, at the Carson National Forest Supervisor's Office, was demanding that the acequias get special use permits to rebuild the project, just as he did on projects on the west side of the mountain (see previous chapter).

Just below the Cañoncito y Encinal headgate the Acequia de la Sierra de Holman crosses the Alamitos as it travels from the Jicarita Peak bowl (Horseshoe Lake), the headwaters of the Rito Angostura (tributary of the Rio Pueblo), to Holman. This is the acequia you cross when you climb

Governor Gerald Nailor (in black hat) and commissioners and mayordomos of the Acequias de la Sierra

Forest Trail 19 to Serpent Lake. During natural flows both ditches divert all the water from the Angostura and Alamitos, which serve as an overflow channel to the Rio Pueblo.

The Acequia del Rito Griego y la Sierra in La Junta Canyon feeds into two acequias in Chacon, Acequia La Joya and Rito Griego. If you drive into Chacon from the Mora Valley you can see its drop-off from the mountaintop to the acequias. The headgate for the new diversion was built in September of 2008. This is the ditch that seems to run uphill and defy gravity. It is testimony to the ingenuity and perseverance of its builders, but on the day we visited, during a year of drought, the water being diverted was not able to travel the three and a half miles to the drop-off. One of the BIA officials on the tour suggested the obvious: that when there is not enough water to make it to the acequias the diversion should be closed and the water allowed to travel down La Junta Canyon to the Rio Pueblo. When I asked how the acequia commissioners on the two Chacon ditches divide the water into shares, they responded that the headgate diverts half

148

to the Chacon acequias and the other half flows down La Junta Canyon to the Rio Pueblo. Again, Governor Nailor pointed out that there needs to be a gauge and an agreed upon formula for sharing the water.

At the end of the day Governor Nailor suggested that all the parties agree to meet again, at either the Pueblo or in the Mora Valley, to further discuss what they witnessed on the tour. Antonio Medina invited everyone to the Community Center in Mora whenever the Governor wanted to convene a meeting. Meetings continued sporadically over the next few years, but to my knowledge, no changes have been made to the system. Historian Malcolm Ebright, who lives in Guadalupita on the east side of the mountain, has written extensively on this trans-basin transfer; his article in the *New Mexico Historical Review* documents the long history up to the present day.

Twenty-three

The Pueblo of Picuris

The watershed coalition that was formed in 1994, the Rio Pueblo/ Rio Embudo Watershed Protection Coalition, was largely put together by the efforts of Carl "Cat" Tsosie at Picuris Pueblo. As members of the coalition and editors of *La Jicarita News* Mark and I have had a long time relationship with this tiny Pueblo in the heart of the watershed. Maintaining this relationship was not always easy, as various administrations—governors and tribal councils—were elected every two years and focused on different agendas, which rendered continuity difficult.

Located just west of Peñasco and Rio Lucio (a small community on the edge of Peñasco), the Pueblo of Picuris lies at the foot of Picuris Peak where the Rio Pueblo runs west towards the Rio Santa Barbara to become the Rio Embudo. A small cluster of administrative buildings and the church form the center of the pueblo (of approximately 300 people) with houses and fields scattered alongside the river.

The Pueblo took on many "big issues" throughout the 1990s and 2000s: the proposed expansion of a mica mine at the Pueblo's ancestral clay pit; development of a strip mine in the Copper Hill area; expansion of Sipapu Ski and Summer Resort beyond its permitted boundaries; and the implementation of water quality standards to protect the watershed.

In 1995 the Pueblo adopted a Water Quality Code consistent with the Federal Clean Water Act. The code sets standards for water quality that provide for the protection and propagation of fish, shellfish, wildlife, and recreation in and on the waters within the exterior boundaries of the Picuris Pueblo Indian Reservation and Grant Lands. The Code stipulates that all water uses, including agricultural, municipal and industrial, recharge of domestic water supply via surface waters, and irrigation shall not lower the quality of the water below these standards.

Those facilities upstream from Pueblo lands that are required to have a National Pollutant Discharge Elimination System (NPDES) permit would also have to adhere to these water standards. They were granted up to

Carl "Cat" Tsosie

three years, on a case by case basis, to make treatment modifications so that the resulting effluent met final permit requirements.

According to the All Indian Pueblo Council's Environmental Protection Division, non-point source pollution, such as that of septic tanks, would also have to be identified and mitigated to conform to the standards. Picuris Pueblo was committed to monitoring the Rio Pueblo to determine what entities might be contaminating the river, and work with the communities involved to establish compliance.

One of the first threats to water quality that arose in the watershed was the exploration drilling at the old Champion copper mine site west of Pueblo tribal lands on State Highway 75. If deemed profitable, the Denver based Summo Minerals would develop a strip mine utilizing the "heap leach" method of drizzling water and sulfuric acid to separate the copper. Apparently the Champion Mine, which was claimed a hundred years ago (on Bureau of Land Management (BLM) land), was never fully developed, due to a fire that burned the original smelter and the vicissitudes of the copper market. The inherent dangers of the mine included spills of sulfuric acid during transportation to the site, acid leakage from the bottom of the pits despite plastic liners, and contamination of groundwater from the heavy metals that also separate from the soil during the process. While the Mining Act of 1872, which sets minimal federal standards for the mining of hard rock minerals, is an anachronism, devised at the time as a tool to help colonize the western United States, state mining laws and regulations were stricter, requiring public hearings and various permits (including the acquisition of water rights) that might make the process difficult.

Led by tribal governor Gerald Nailor and lieutenant governor Cat Tsosie, community opposition to the possibility of a strip mine was overwhelming. At an October 23, 1996 meeting at the Pueblo 100 people showed up to meet the president and CEO of Summo Minerals, Gregory Hahn, who began his presentation by stating: "I am absolutely astounded at the turnout here." He stated that Summo had drilled 18 holes that year and planned to drill another 22 the following year; there appeared to be a 200 foot-thick belt of copper close to the surface. If the company decided to go ahead and apply for the necessary permits to mine the area, it would take at least four years for mining to begin.

He then gave a demonstration of the technology involved in mining for copper. He proceeded to pour a solution of water and sulfuric acid over a glassful of crushed rock containing copper. On the ground, this would happen on top of a plastic liner, where the copper comes out of the rock into the solution. Questions immediately erupted from the audience regarding the reliability of liners in preventing leaks of acid into the watershed. Someone then asked whose water the company was going to use in this process. Hahn responded that Summo would have to compute its water needs, but at its proposed copper mine in Utah, the company has asked for permission to pump 900 gallons of groundwater per minute. He stated: "I can almost categorically assure you we wouldn't use surface water here, unless there is no groundwater available. We would have to purchase water rights, as rights in this basin have already been prescribed." That elicited a response from Carol Miller, Picuris Health Planner, who stated: "I see that creating water rights [purchasing water rights] is in reality dividing our water rights." A resident of Dixon and mayordoma of her acequia, Marie Coburn, told Hahn that the area was already experiencing a drought, and any use of water, be it groundwater or surface water, would be opposed. Hahn responded by asking the community to "keep an open mind" until they had all the necessary information, and that he believed his company could design a facility that "doesn't impact any of you." He also stated that the project would be dead if they did not find sufficient water. He also stated that if Picuris Pueblo opposed the project, federal approval "will probably not happen." At the end of the meeting, Herman Agoyo, Picuris Pueblo Planner, summed up public sentiment by formally asking Hahn to "pack up and not come back. We'll save a little money and you'll save a lot."

Over the course of the next year many more meetings were held and a new group was formed, Taos/Rio Arriba Mining Reform Alliance (TRAM-RA), comprised of concerned citizens and members of other community and environmental groups such as Amigos Bravos, the Rio Pueblo/Rio Embudo Watershed Protection Coalition, and the Sierra Club. The new group, under the leadership of Michael Wildgoose and Robert Templeton, acted as a clearinghouse for information and coordinated efforts to stop the proposed mine. The Bureau of Land Management Albuquerque District Manager proposed that Summo Corporation relinquish all its mining claims in the Copper Hill area in return for title to BLM land in Lisbon Valley, Utah, where it also held claims (activists from the Lisbon Valley let the BLM know they didn't want New Mexico's problems dumped in their backyard). Rumors about the financial stability of Summo Corporation began to fly, but even if Summo lacked the resources to develop its claims, without mineral withdrawal the company could sell these claims to another developer.

Finally, in a press release dated July 27, 1998, Summo Minerals Corporation announced that it was abandoning its interests in the Champion Mine on Copper Hill as well as the Caslin mine in western Colorado. Citing a loss of $1.5 million for the first half of the year, the corporation claimed that the abandonment of these properties would allow the company to focus on its more promising enterprises (including the mine in Utah). In other words, Summo needed to cut its losses and invest in operations that could produce an immediate profit, using the Champion and Caslin mines as a tax write-off. Opponents of the Champion Mine were hopeful that this turn of events would lead to permanent withdrawal of this area from mineral extraction. On July 1 of 1999 the BLM officially withdrew 3,632.31 acres of public land from surface entry and mining and 1,148.19 acres of federally reserved mineral interests underlying private land for a period of 20 years.

Another big water issue the Pueblo faced concurrently with the proposed Summo Mine was the proposed expansion of Sipapu Ski and Summer Resort. I wrote about Sipapu in my other book *Culture Clash: Environmental Politics in New Mexico Forest Communities,*[34] and will write more extensively about ski areas' use of water in Chapter Twenty-six. The Sipapu proposal would expand the area boundary from 185 acres to 977 acres (with 220 skiable acres), build two new parking areas, two new lifts, and a 2,700 square foot restaurant/ski patrol building, including a well and septic system (in two phases) at the top of the lifts. New modular motel units, on private land, had already been shipped in, and a new wastewater treatment plant had been constructed to try to bring the area up to current standards. The Pueblo was especially concerned about the resort's application to transfer Rio Pueblo agricultural water rights for snowmaking. In a partial victory for opponents of the transfer, the Office of the State Engineer found that the resort had actually abandoned its water rights years before (by allowing the highway department to pave over the acequia on resort property) and denied the transfer. The resort owners then transferred other agricultural water rights they owned downstream to use for snowmaking. And while the Pueblo succeeded in forcing the United States Forest Service (the ski area is permitted on forest land) to withdraw its 1995 Environmental Impact Statement when the agency acknowledged it had failed to adequately consult the Pueblo on its historic and cultural properties in the area, the fight to stop the expansion dragged on for many more years until the early 2000s when the ski resort implemented a smaller expansion within its current boundaries and then sold majority interest to investors.

Yet another mine proposal came down the pipe in the early 2000s. This time, Oglebay Norton Specialty Minerals, owners of a mica mine on U.S. Hill between Peñasco and Taos, filed a Permit Revision Application in 2002 with the state's Mining and Minerals Division to expand its mining operation from 10 acres to 270 acres, including over 200 acres of U.S. Forest Service land. Its extant operation, on ancestral tribal lands that were erroneously incorporated into the public domain by the federal government and then patented by mining companies under the notorious 1872 federal mining law, had drawn severe criticism from the Pueblo, which contended the mine had destroyed the micaceous clay pits Pueblo potters had used for centuries. The Pueblo, along with other community members and environmental groups, has also been critical of the company's closeout plan, which it claimed did not do enough to address safety, wildlife, and erosion issues. The company's milling operation in Velarde, the Rio Grande community north of Española, had also drawn criticism from that community, which claimed its stockpiles were polluting the air, causing respiratory problems for residents, and fouling machinery.

The Pueblo and its supporters worked for four years *within* the system to oppose the mine expansion, filing appeals and lawsuits, and demonstrating *outside* the system with several physical blockades (with bodies) of the mine access road off State Highway 518. Finally, in February of 2004, Governor Gerald Nailor (several other interim governors, Red Eagle Rael and Richard Mermejo, also led the Pueblo during this struggle), in conjunction with the tribal council, clan mothers, religious leaders, tribal members, and a team of lawyers, filed an aboriginal land claim in state court. The suit sought to regain possession of approximately 200 acres of culturally significant land that had been decimated by nearly 40 years of mining. The suit also alleged that Oglebay Norton Specialty Minerals, the mine operator, as well as Franklin Industries and Preston Capital Corporation, previous owners of the claim, had trespassed on tribal lands, denied the tribe access to the clay, removed valuable minerals, polluted the area with mine waste, and caused loss of income for tribal members.

Then, in a scenario similar to that of the Summo copper mine, the mica mine operator suspended operation of the mine while it filed for bankruptcy in November of 2004. Less than a year later the 537-acre tract, which included 195 patented acres and 342 acres of unpatented mining claims, was transferred to the Pueblo under an agreement with Oglebay Norton Specialty Minerals. The agreement stipulated that the Pueblo dismiss all claims against the company in exchange for the patented and unpatented lands. The agreement also stipulated that the Pueblo would be responsible for reclamation of the property (the Pueblo received a grant from the Lannan Foundation to begin the restoration work).

Twenty-four

Take Me For a Walk in El Valle

I've often talked about the concept of "inhabited wilderness" in my
La Jicarita articles detailing norteño life. This refers to the role villages like
El Valle play in maintaining a landscape and way of life that have managed
to remain extant for many hundreds of years. As part of the Las Trampas
Land Grant, the people in the village used the common lands to sustain
their communities: harvesting trees for firewood or building materials;
grazing their livestock in the upland meadows; and utilizing the extensive system of acequias that descended from the high mountain lakes and
springs to water their fields and gardens and to provide drinking water as
well. To live sustainably in these high mountain villages requires a human
touch that maintains both people and the land. I love this quote from Bill
Bryson in *A Walk in the Woods*. He is talking about the Appalachian Trail,
but he could be talking about northern New Mexico:

"In America, alas, beauty has become something you drive to, and nature an either/or proposition—either you ruthlessly subjugate it . . . or you
deify it, treat it as something holy and remote, a thing apart, as along the
Appalachian Trail. Seldom would it occur to anyone on either side that
people and nature could coexist to their mutual benefit—that say, a more
graceful bridge across the Delaware River might actually set off the gran-
deur around it, or that the AT might be more interesting and rewarding
if it wasn't all wilderness, if from time to time it purposely took you past
grazing cows and tilled fields."

Every morning I walk with my dogs Paco and Benny (and sometimes
my neighbor's dog Sammy if she's in the mood) past grazing cows and
horses and hay fields. My route takes me up the road that crosses the Rio
de las Trampas and ascends the llano southwest of the village. This is
where many of the people in the village lived before the Forest Service
put in the road on my side of the river that is now the main access to El

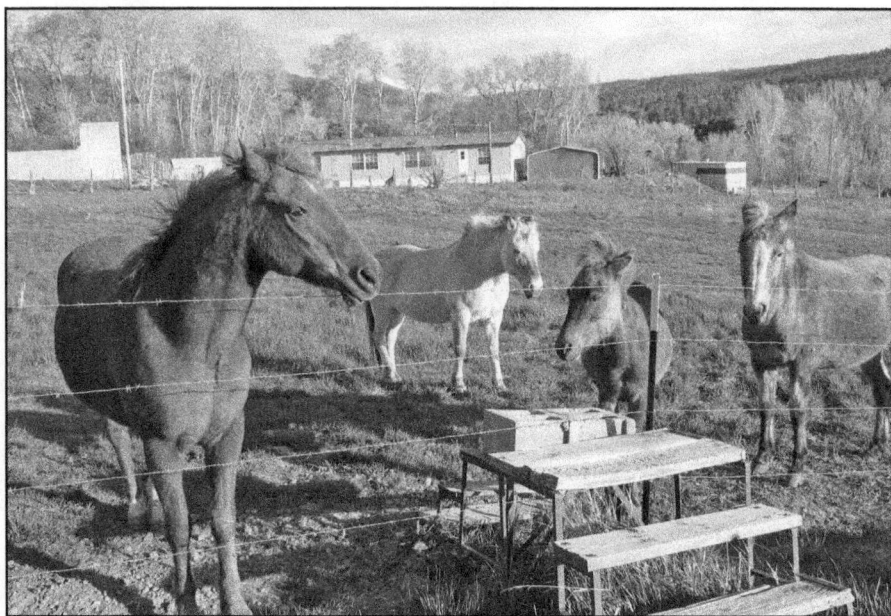

Valle from State Highway 76. This access road continues six miles up from the village to trails leading to the Pecos Wilderness, where I also walk and cross-country ski when I have the time.

Acequia de Arriba runs alongside the road on the first part of my walk and feeds everyone's property through culverts that run underneath the road. The first house I pass belongs to Debbie and George Romero, who moved to El Valle the same year Mark and I did, 1992. George was born and raised here and came back after taking early retirement from the mines in Nevada. I remember Debbie (who was raised in Chamisal) telling me that when George retired they asked their daughters if they would find it hard to leave the city (Las Vegas) and live in El Valle where you can't say, "Let's go to the movies," and then hop in the car. Both girls did OK I guess, as one now lives in Albuquerque and the other one recently moved back to El Valle and lives in her grandmother's old house (she works at LANL). They use the water to irrigate Debbie's beautiful gardens of black-eyed Susans, their orchard, and lower field, where occasionally a neighbor's horses graze.

The next house belongs to the commissioner on both the Acequia de Arriba and Acequia de Abajo and his fields are always green and lush (this is a not so subtle way of saying that commissioners' fields usually are). He's retired now and still runs a few head of cattle that he rotates among his fields, his brothers' fields (they don't live in the village), and a field he manages for another woman who lives in Albuquerque. This is becoming more and more common up here in el norte; more and more folks leave the villages and those who are left end up taking care of their fields and putting their water rights to beneficial use. It's not an ideal situation, as it puts power into the hands of fewer and fewer people, but it's better than losing the water rights to forfeiture (after four years of nonuse the owner is notified by the OSE that he or she could lose their water rights if they don't start using them).

The Lucero family compound is next. The matriarch, Corina, died recently and it was a loss for us all. She was a sweet, kind woman whose children all remained in El Valle and helped take care of her as she aged. On Halloween, when my kids were little, we'd walk through the village knowing that at Corina's house we'd be expected to sit down and talk about how the family was doing, what was in the news, who had died or given birth, etc., etc. She always wanted to know everything about my kids and told me everything about her growing brood of grandchildren. Her daughter Eliza grows beautiful Maximilian sunflowers (she retired from her job as the high school secretary several years ago) and Corina's son Albert irrigates their field for his horse.

The house on the corner where I turn up the road to the llano belonged to Orlando and Priscilla Montoya. Orlando was Tomás's brother and died several years ago after serving many years as the mayordomo on the Acequia de Abajo. Like many men in the village he worked in the mines of Colorado while Priscilla (who was from Ojo Sarco) raised the kids and took care of the garden and fields. She died a few years after Orlando and the house now belongs to their son Jake, the only Montoya brother who doesn't live in El Valle (he works at LANL). Below what is now Jake's house is his brother Nelson's trailer and the pens full of chickens, turkeys, ducks, and geese that he loves to raise now that he, too, is retired (he also worked at LANL as a subcontractor). Nelson only moved back to the village after he retired; he raised his kids in Rio Lucio, where his wife Teresita still lives (they have an interesting relationship where each maintains a home but still do many things together much more harmoniously than they did when they only maintained one home). Nelson inherited most of his parent's land and irrigates one field from the Acequia de Arriba and one field from the Acequia de Abajo, which cuts midway through his property. His brother Miguel, who lives farther up the main road, periodically utilizes Nelson's pastures for his cattle.

Nelson is a buen vecino. He'll do just about anything to help anyone, including me. He gets my machinery going when I can't (weed whacker, log splitter, etc.); he puts air in my tires when they're low; he stops by and picks up my trash on his way to the dump; and he provides me with a steady supply of eggs (I gave him my chickens a couple of years ago when I decided to quit raising them but the trade has been in my favor for quite a while now). He is also kind to the animal world. Besides his chickens and ducks, he takes in any lost or injured animal—cats, dogs, chicks, geese—and either takes care of them himself or finds them a home.

Past Nelson's house I walk by the Acequia de Abajo that Tomás, Mark and I ran for many years, and it makes me feel good to remember the hard work we all did to rebuild the presa and keep the waters flowing. At the bottom of the valley I cross the Rio de las Trampas, which originates at the 11,000 foot Trampas Lakes and supplies the acequias in the villages of El Valle, Las Trampas, and Vallecito before making its way to the Rio Grande. The road ascends the llano from the river, past a spur road that leads to large fields that used to be watered by the Acequia del Llano but haven't been utilized for many years as their owners live in Santa Fe and Albuquerque. Recently, the owners sold some of the property to the kids of one of the commissioners on the other acequias, keeping it in the village family.

An "S" curve brings me up to the top of the llano with views of the stunning high mountain peaks: the Truchas Peaks, Sheep's Head, Leonardo Peak, Trampas Peak, and Jicarita Peak define the horizon. Here more open fields that also belong to folks who don't live in the village anymore line the road, some of which are actively for sale. Irrigated land isn't cheap; someone told me the family is asking $20,000 an acre, which restricts the pool of potential buyers along with the road that sometimes requires chains in the winter to ascend.

And finally, at the top of the road is the Buechley house. Nancy and Larry have lived in El Valle for 40 years, transplants from Indiana who came to these norteño villages like so many others to adopt a life on the land. They raised three kids along with chickens, goats, horses, a donkey (shared by my family), and llamas, which are currently grazing their lower field irrigated by the Acequia del Llano. They also own an upper field that surrounds their woodworking studio where they make beautiful bentwood laminated furniture. This field was also irrigated by the Acequia del Llano but when the families moved across the river many of these fields were left fallow. The remains of the Romero house sits across the road from the Buechleys, but Gerson and Adrian Romero, father and son, continue to irrigate the fields above the house for their cattle. Over the years a few other Anglo families bought pieces of land from absentee owners near the Buechleys where they sometimes come stay for the weekend. When we first moved to El Valle there were no second home owners in the village; now there are a handful, owned by folks who live in Albuquerque or Placitas, a few who live in Texas, and several who plan on retiring here.

When Mark and I moved to El Valle in 1992, most of the men who had retired and moved back to the village, or those folks who managed to remain in El Valle and scam together a living with numerous jobs, were in their sixties, the age I am now. As they reached their seventies and eighties illness and incapacity began to catch up with them. The first, and biggest loss, was Tomás, who died just before his birthday in December of 2009. He'd been sick with diabetes, a stroke, and cancer and was more than ready to go, but his death signified a fundamental change in the nature of the village, which I alluded to in Chapter Two. The younger men who had moved back to the village had been challenging Tomás's authority since the early 2000s, and with his death they took over the administration of all the acequias, which they strove to run more "efficiently," meaning they hired crews to clean them instead of the parciantes and ran them "by the book," meaning that whatever they deemed was the right way to do things was not open to question.

I delivered the eulogy at Tomás funeral. This is what I said about what is lost by attending to only efficiency and business as usual:

"It was Tomás's example of community spirit and sense of place that is the indicator of our collective health. Those of us who live here now, and those whose families have lived here for centuries must be able to make a living that defines us as caretakers of the land, the community, and the soul of this wonderful place. Tomás knew that required working the land and knowing what is necessary to take care of it. In our small corner of the world, as in many rural areas around the world, Tomás knew it was important to hold onto the jobs that do just that: growing gardens and hay fields; raising animals; cutting vigas and latillas as well as firewood; and building our houses.

"These jobs ensure a connectedness to each other as well. I can sit in front of my computer all day, turning out words and thoughts on all kinds of things, many of which may be meaningless to anybody but me. But when it's time to go get a load of firewood, get some manure for my garden, or fix the fence, I go to Tomás and Fred [his son] for help. And it is that sense of community that makes all of our lives in El Valle so much richer for having known our buen vecino, Tomás."

My personal life was forever changed when Mark died of pancreatic cancer the following year, in November of 2010. He had already been

given a terminal diagnosis when Tomás died, so for almost three years, as they both suffered with cancer and Tomás lost a leg to diabetes and his speech to a stroke, I struggled to stay strong enough to care for them both. Amazingly, though, Mark was also able to pay considerable attention to his intellectual work. For many months during his illness he edited and serialized in *La Jicarita News* an article he had written concerning the adjudication of land grants in New Mexico. The article was intended to be the introduction to a book dealing with this sordid period in New Mexico's history, where indigenous people were dispossessed of millions of acres of land that had been granted them by the Spanish and Mexican governments. Titled "A Brief History of American Imperialism" it chronicled early American expansionism, Manifest Destiny, the Mexican-American War, the Treaty of Guadalupe Hidalgo, and racism in the New Mexico Territory.

Not only that, but he spent two or three hours several days a week spread out on the floor of the bedroom finishing the article that evaluated George W. Julian's tenure as Surveyor General of the New Mexico Territory (1885-1889). He had received a grant from the New Mexico Historical Records Advisory Board to do the research and writing in 2009, and he finished the work by the spring of 2010.

Now, as I look down over the fields and houses of the village I hope that if our kids don't come back to farm or take care of the land that there's new blood out there ready to make use of this invaluable resource to which Tomás and Mark were both so attached. If we price them off the land, this magnificent green corridor will be brown and the waters will be that "instream flow" that sounds so right but in my mind, at least, remains so wrong.

Twenty-five

Aamodt Again

New Mexico senators Jeff Bingaman and Pete Domenici introduced federal legislation to authorize and fund the Aamodt and Abeyta settlements in July of 2008. Congress approved these two Indian settlements, along with the Navajo, in 2010. But all three settlements were far from being "settled," as financial, legal, and grassroots opposition continued for many more years.

Federal funding requests to settle Indian water rights lawsuits in the Southwest have been staggering: the Navajo Nation, $800 million; the Ute tribes in southern Colorado, $360 million; the Aamodt adjudication in the Pojoaque Basin, $150 million; and the Abeyta adjudication in the Taos Valley, $120 million. The numbers of acre feet of water (afy) at stake are also astonishing: 600,000 afy for the Navajos; 132,000 for the Utes; 18,000 for the Aamodt, and 50,600 for the Abeyta (these figures have been adjusted both up and down over the years and reflect both existing and imported water rights).

Most of these enormous costs are for dams and water delivery pipelines for irrigation projects, domestic water supply, and commercial development for both Indian and non-Indian water users. Most of the water necessary to meet these needs is San Juan Basin water. And in this time of drought, all this "paper" water—what is contracted on paper versus what actually may come through the the delivery pipelines—may not even be wet enough to cool down a dog on a hot afternoon. All of these adjudications have been litigated individually and are now being settled individually as well, but they are all interconnected, particularly via the question: Where is the water coming from?

As of 2010 the state of New Mexico had set aside only one-tenth of the funding required for the purchase of water rights and development of infrastructure associated with the Aamodt settlement. At that time, the federal government was due to pay $106.4 million (in 2006 dollars); the state of New Mexico, $49.5 million; and Santa Fe County, $21.4 million. The cost of hooking up the maximum number of customers to the water delivery system over the life of the project was $18 million. Other costs included water rights acquisitions (the federal government paid for 1,100 afy of the Top of the World water rights and the County for 600 afy for a total of $5.4 million), operation and management ($37.5 million), an impairment fund (part of the negotiated settlement, $500,000), rehabilitation of existing pueblo infrastructure ($15 million), and free initial hook-ups to the water system ($4 million).

We need to remember that the federal court decision by Judge Edwin Mechem in the Aamodt adjudication, upheld in 2001, ordered that the pueblos were entitled to domestic water rights equal to the actual water they used between 1846, after the Mexican-American War when the area became part of the United States, and 1924, when the Pueblo Lands Act quieted title to all rights developed prior to that time. As Mechem quoted in his decision, "The effect of this Congressional act was to fix pueblo rights, that is, it terminated their right to develop further future water uses with aboriginal priority." If that decision had been the final court order, pueblo development activity would have been severely limited and perhaps the second tier of TOW water rights (1,141 afy) would have stayed in their area of origin.

Santa Fe County was not only brokering TOW water rights for the Aamodt Settlement, it was also dramatically increasing the number of water rights transferred from the Middle Rio Grande Basin to the county. In March of 2007 the county filed eight applications to transfer 110.22 acre feet of in-basin water rights to 19 wells throughout the county. The move-to wells were spread out from South 14, through the community college area and Agua Fria Village, to NM 599 near the intersection of CR 62. According to the county, it needed these wells to supplement the Buckman Well Field and the Buckman Direct Diversion that accesses Rio Grande and San Juan/Chama project water (two citizen groups appealed the diversion citing possible radionuclide contamination from LANL but lost the appeal[35]), which would serve utility customers in the growing areas south and west of Santa Fe. The proposed transfer rights belonged to developers who were required to provide water to the county utility before getting approval for their building projects.

There remained extensive opposition to the Aamodt Settlement. A survey revealed that 59 percent of Pojoaque Valley water rights owners said they had "negative feelings" regarding the settlement. In response, Santa Fe County paid the Utton Center at the University of New Mexico Law School to hold a series of community meetings throughout the Pojoaque Valley "to discuss the Aamodt water rights settlement and what it means to Pojoaque Valley residents." According to Melanie Stansbury of the Utton Center, who had been meeting with various parties in the Aamodt case for two years, people who continued to question the settlement "seem to have some legitimate concerns over how the settlement was reached and how they were or were not represented. There seems to have been a real disconnect between people doing the negotiations and trying to resolve problems, and the people who are raising questions."

Darcy Bushnell of the Joe M. Stell Ombudsman Program at the Utton Center, who chaired the meetings, said that the primary concern of many attendees was whether or not they should give up their domestic wells and sign on to the water delivery system, what the water delivery rates would be, and if they would be protected against a priority call by the pueblos. She also said people had complained that they felt the settlement was dividing the pueblo and non-pueblo communities, a complaint that had come up numerous times at previous meetings during settlement negotiations. People also questioned where the water for the settlement was coming from, and if the settlement would impact native Rio Grande water supplies.

Then, in 2011, the federal government declared the terms of the settlements were unacceptable, that they were inconsistent with the legislation that was written for implementation. An Implementation Committee, comprised of five federal agencies, started meeting to revise the agreements.

The folks of the Pojoaque Basin Water Alliance were asking, how could this be? How could a settlement agreement that was negotiated by the parties involved in the adjudication, including representatives of the pertinent federal agencies (Department of Justice, Department of the Interior) be rewritten after the fact by lawyers and bureaucrats to fit legislation? There was plenty of complaining at the time that many of those who should have been at the negotiating table were left out, so you can imagine how they felt when it was "deja vu all over again." The answer was that the settlement agreements for the Aamodt, Abeyta, Navajo, and several other Colorado adjudications that Congress approved in December of 2010 and appropriated billions of dollars to implement, were signed only by local governmental agencies, not the Department of the Interior, and now the settlements were being altered to fit the legislation that has been written by the powers that be in Washington. Concurrently, the Cost Sharing and System Integration Agreement had to also be revised. It was in the Implementation Committee that the 300 afy was taken from Taos Pueblo in the Abeyta Settlement to supplement Aamodt water rights. The total delivery to the pueblos, as stated in the revised settlement, was "at least 2,381 afy" (this reflects conveyance loss from the original 2,500 afy), and the delivery to the non-pueblos was reduced from 750 afy to 611 afy.

Several other issues had to be resolved as well. One, would non-pueblo residents serve on the Water Authority Board, which would administer the water delivery system, along with representatives from the four pueblos and Santa Fe County? Two, what size non-pueblo delivery system would the county build? The settlement terms committed the county to deliver 611 afy for landowners without wells or water rights who want to hook up to the water delivery system and up to 750 afy for those who retire their wells and dedicate that water to the system, but no decision had been made as to how big or how small the system would be.

As I continued to report on the status of the settlement, I'd periodically call John Utton to see what progress the Implementation Committee was making. I ended up calling him for two years until 2013 when Secretary of the Interior Ken Salazar came to New Mexico and signed the settlement on March 14. The district court entered a Partial Final Decree quantifying the pueblo water rights and an Interim Administrative Order, which allows the OSE to administer water rights in the basin according to the terms of the settlement. The next step was for the court to adjudicate all the non-pueblo water rights consistent with the settlement agreement. Over 700 water rights holders objected to these orders, which I will discuss in more detail in Chapter Thirty-five.

Twenty-six

Ski Area Expansions in the Southwest

Ski areas in New Mexico are usually described as "not in the same league" as those in neighboring Colorado, where resorts like Vail and Aspen cater to an elite clientele that can afford to pay a hundred bucks for a daily lift ticket. As "skier days"—the number of skiers per day—decline as the baby boom generation ages, those ticket prices are only going to increase. And as climate change impacts water resources, particularly in the West, ski areas are going to continue to expand to compete for a shrinking skier population, buy up water rights to compensate for a dearth of natural snow, and raise ticket prices to pay for all of it—risky measures that may or may not maintain their viability. Their enabler, the United States Forest Service (USFS), upon whose lands many of the ski areas are situated, seems to have never seen a ski area expansion it didn't like.

While ski areas in New Mexico generally draw from a more middle income clientele, there's been no lack of controversy over ski expansion proposals that also include increased snow making capacity to cover those new ski slopes. USFS Environmental Impact Statements rarely take into account the potential secondary impacts of transferring water out of agricultural use into commercial use for snowmaking. These could include: taking land out of agricultural use and making it available for development; impairing an acequia's ability to divert enough water to have the hydrological power to reach all of its parciantes' fields; impairing an acequia's ability to maintain the membership necessary for maintenance and repair work; and impairing groundwater recharge upon which plant, wildlife, and human communities depend. Neither do they address the induced development that is associated with ski area growth: second homes, condos, restaurants, and outfitters. Environmental assessments don't assess the impact this kind of growth has on the social fabric and infrastructure of rural communities.

Sipapu Ski Area and Summer Resort

As I mentioned previously, in 1995 Carson National Forest issued a Final Environmental Impact Statement (FEIS) that approved a large expansion at Sipapu Ski Area, the small, family resort located just east of Peñasco on the Rio Pueblo. The proposal included expansion of the ski area boundary from 185 to 977 acres (with 220 skiable acres); two new parking areas; two new lifts; and an additional 2,700 square foot restaurant/ski patrol building, including a well and septic system, at the top of the mountain. The FEIS was appealed by local citizen groups that questioned Forest Service analysis of the expansion's impact on water quality, quantity, and traditional cultural properties—and the ski area's economic needs used to justify the expansion on public land. The Forest Service also neglected to look into the fact that the ski area didn't actually have the water rights it wanted to transfer to commercial use for snow making, claiming that was the purview of the Office of the State Engineer (OSE). The OSE indeed found that the resort had abandoned its water rights (because the acequia had been filled in), and the Forest Service withdrew the FEIS because it had failed to consult with Picuris Pueblo regarding traditional cultural properties that might be affected by the expansion.

While the ski area failed to achieve this initial expansion, it continued its development march in more incremental phases. On July 3, 2000, Bruce Bolander, then owner of the ski area (Sipapu was subsequently sold to out of state investors), wrote a half-page letter to Camino Real District Ranger Cecilia Seesholtz briefly outlining work the ski area proposed to undertake within its permitted boundaries as part of a plan to expand its facilities. This letter contained no site-specific work plan, no work schedule, and most importantly, no mention of environmental assessments. On July 12 Seesholtz wrote a three-sentence response to this letter concluding, "We have received your summer operation plan and have found it within the parameters of your special use permit."

As a result, several areas were clearcut, others selectively cut, and at least 125 cords of wood and saw timber were removed. The tree removal increased the area's skiable terrain from 34 acres to approximately 65 acres. The ski area also purchased a new chair lift and other equipment necessary to implement this expansion. Ironically, on the very day Seesholtz signed off on the summer work plan she met with more than 20 community members and representatives from the Rio Pueblo/Rio Embudo Watershed Protection Coalition, the New Mexico Acequia Association, and the Santa Fe Group of the Sierra Club to hear their concerns about the ski area's expansion plans. During that meeting she was asked to inform the group of any proposed actions on Forest Service land associated with Sipapu. She failed to make any mention of the "Summer Work Plan."

It was not until November of 2000, as a result of ski area advertisements in *The Taos News* and on the radio, that everyone became aware of the expansion work. Folks immediately contacted Seesholtz to ask how this work could have been permitted without necessary assessments and public input. She responded that assessments had been done years ago, which gave her the authority to permit the work. The coalition members asked to see those assessments. Seesholtz said she would find them. Two days later she called and claimed she had been misled by members of her staff: there were no assessments in place, and she had ordered the ski area to stop all work and seal off the affected area.

The ski area sued the Forest Service for injunctive relief. On September 4, 2001, Federal Judge Bruce Black granted a hearing on Sipapu's claim that it would suffer irreparable financial harm if it were not allowed to proceed with the project. On September 11, Judge Black issued a preliminary injunction granting the ski area the right to proceed with the project as outlined in the summer work letter and ordering it to post a $100,000 bond against possible environmental degradation. He also directed ski area owners to work with the Forest Service to plan and undertake environmental assessments.

To comply with the judge's order concerning environmental assessments, the Forest Service sent out a scoping letter in the fall. It was at this point coalition members learned that the ski area had trespassed on approximately 30 acres outside its permitted boundaries. The Forest Service continually refused to acknowledge this trespass and said only that it sought to "modify the previous boundary by approximately 30 acres to incorporate the new improvements." The agency, however, clearly did not have the authority to do this because the July 3, 2000 letter regarding the "Summer Work Plan," which was the subject of the injunction, states: "All work to be done is within our current permit area." In addition, the trespass impacted an area protected by the Roadless Initiative.

More than 50 community members and environmental groups commented on the scoping letter, expressing concerns that ranged from the document's numerous procedural violations and self-contradictory statements to impacts on cultural and historical properties, water quality and quantity, fish and wildlife habitat, community infrastructure, and induced development. Once again the Forest Service ignored or glossed over these concerns when it issued its Environmental Assessment in December and then again when it issued its Finding of No Significant Impact in August of the following year. The development proceeded.

Santa Fe Ski Basin

Sipapu isn't alone in its dependence upon the Forest Service to write blank checks for development. Several decades ago the Santa Fe Ski Basin implemented an expansion that raised enormous opposition from the public. In the mid 1990s opposition to the proposed expansion of ski terrain into the Big Tesuque, south of the ski area and sacred site of Tesuque and Nambe pueblos, resulted in a plethora of bumper stickers around Santa Fe saying NO! Despite overwhelming opposition to the proposal (including both the city and county of Santa Fe), the Santa Fe National Forest initially promulgated a preferred alternative in its Draft Environmental Impact Statement that supported a 75-acre expansion into the Big Tesuque area but ruled out building a chairlift. But then, in the Final Environmental Impact Statement, the forest supervisor approved an expansion from 585 to 891 acres with three new chairlifts, including the controversial Big Tesuque lift, and an 800-space parking lot. Opponents appealed the decision and in 1996 the regional forester ordered the forest supervisor to reconsider the decision based on Native American concerns and the availability of water rights. The Big Tesuque chairlift was never built (although the parking lot was).

Then, in 2001, the ski area again faced strong opposition to a proposal to expand its facilities. The Santa Fe Ski Area Containment Coalition, a group of downstream parciantes, environmental groups, Tesuque Pueblo, and other concerned local citizens that fought the previous expansion, was joined by the Santa Fe County Commission in its opposition to the project. The proposal called for clear cutting 1,800 trees (1,630 on slopes over 30 percent) to allow the ski area to install a new, mile long triple chairlift to the summit of Deception Peak and extend three ski trails, which would be serviced by the new lift.

The county became involved because county land use regulations prohibit tree removal and development on slopes that exceed 30 percent. The commission claimed that the ski area must apply to the county for a variance in order to proceed, but the owners of the ski area and the Forest Service (which had already completed an Environmental Impact Statement (EIS) granting approval for the project) claimed county land use regulations did not apply to federally owned lands. A county attorney and the attorney for the containment coalition, however, countered that a California case, which was heard by the United States Supreme Court, ruled that local governments could enforce their own standards on federal land. It had also been demonstrated that the Forest Service EIS neglected to include a portion of the area that would be affected by the development.

The ski area proposal prevailed, but in 2005 Tesuque Pueblo filed a lawsuit in federal district court charging the Santa Fe National Forest with unlawfully permitting the expansion of the Santa Fe Ski Area into the Lake Peak/Deception Peak area. The lawsuit cited three reasons for this action: 1) The Forest Service's approval of this project would substantially impair the Tribe's ability to carry out religious and ceremonial practices in and near the ski area; 2) The Forest Service expanded the special use permit boundary and uses for the ski area without following the procedures for permit amendments required by federal and internal Forest Service regulations; and 3) The Forest Service's approval of changes to the lift design violated the procedural requirements of the National Environmental Policy Act (NEPA).

The Santa Fe Ski Area had already begun work on a new triple chairlift that would extend over 5,500 feet into the Lake Peak/Deception Peak area to an elevation of 12,074 feet and have a capacity of 1,800 passengers per hour. The lawsuit asked the Court to enjoin the construction and/or operation of the new lift, declare the Forest Service decision to permit the work unlawful, and remand the decision.

With regard to impairing its ability to exercise its religion, the suit asserted the project would impact the Pueblo's right to make pilgrimages to Deception Peak to fulfill religious obligations and communicate with the spirit world and flood the area with a surfeit of skiers, snowboarders, and hikers. The suit sought relief for this complaint under the Religious Freedom Restoration Act of 1993.

The suit went on to note that the Forest Service signed a "Memorandum of Agreement" to "continue consultation with the pueblos of Tesuque and Nambe . . . about development and operation of the Santa Fe Ski Area." Under the terms of this memorandum the Forest Service is also obligated to carry out a number of specific mitigation measures "to provide for the management and preservation of traditional cultural resources concerns." The lawsuit asserted that the Forest Service failed both to consult with the Pueblo and to undertake the mitigation measures outlined in the agreement.

As anyone who's visited the ski area lately knows, there is indeed a chairlift up Deception Peak.

Wolf Creek Ski Area

Wolf Creek Ski Area, in the San Juan Mountains of southern Colorado, would be more at home in New Mexico (in fact, it's owned by a New Mexican family) with its low key atmosphere and lack of supporting condo and hotel infrastructure. This area, too, has been the focus of controversy over a proposal to develop "Wolf Creek Village" to bring that infrastructure to its base. In October of 2006 La Jicarita News reprinted an article, "Are Some Strings Being Pulled to Develop Wolf Creek Village?" by Allen Best from Colorado Central Magazine that detailed the battle at Wolf Creek, which is still going on today.[36]

In the article Best introduced us to Billy Joe "Red" McCombs, the billionaire from Texas who is intent on building a "part-time city" at Wolf Creek Pass. To access this proposed "city" the Forest Service, claiming that federal law left "no option but to allow access to the inholding," gave McCombs a permit in early April of 2006 to build a 750-foot road across Forest Service land connecting Highway 160 with his private land, which he obtained 20 years ago in a land exchange. The agency also gave him authority to extend a road from the Wolf Creek Ski Area for 250 feet, although this latter road could be used only for shuttles and emergency vehicles during ski season. McCombs, one of the richest men in the U.S., planned to build approximately 400 single-family homes and 1,800 weekly time-share units on his 237 acre parcel.

The thrust of Best's article dealt with allegations that the Forest Service decision approving the access road was influenced by political pressure emanating from the George Bush administration. Best quotes Peter Clark, Supervisor of the Rio Grande National Forest, from a letter sent to *The Denver Post*: "At no time during this process did I receive direction, influence or pressure from higher levels on how or what decision to make."

This is Best's analysis of the allegations:

"[Clark's] insistence flew in the face of claims by critics, who for many months had been saying that McCombs had unethically gained influence over Bush appointees who oversee the Forest Service. In March, *The Denver Post* presented evidence that circumstantially supported them. McCombs had given generously to candidates for Congress, mostly Republicans from Texas. In turn, he had lobbied for the appointment of Mark Rey, a former timber industry representative, to the position of undersecretary of agriculture in charge of the Forest Service. The Post also found that Mc-Combs representatives had met with Rey — although Rey, in a letter to the editor, curtly noted that he had also met with opponents.

"Far more damning was the allegation by recently retired Forest Service employee Ed Ryberg. Ryberg, who had overseen ski areas in Colorado for many years, said that Dave Tenny, an assistant to Mark Rey, had intervened with regional officials, indicating he wanted 'movement' on the road case at Wolf Creek. Ryberg told The Post that 'it's not often you get a deputy undersecretary involved in an easement issue.' In this case, a conference telephone call was held, and 'we were basically told by Tenny to help these guys and address their issues,' said Ryberg. He added: 'The ski area was being obstinate, and they needed to be able to demonstrate they already had access so the project could move along.' Ryberg also argued that the environmental impact statement was flawed, because of an implausible no-action alternative."

Known as a Forest Service company man, Ryberg's statements were given considerable credence. And ironically, he was standing up for the owners of Wolf Creek, who had been fighting McCombs over development of the village ever since they disagreed on its size. Owner Kingsbury Pitcher, who was involved in the development of Ski Apache and the Santa Fe Ski Basin, wanted a much smaller real estate development and contested McCombs's large scale plans in federal court. The Pitcher family also disputes McCombs's claim that there is sufficient water in dry years to support this kind of development.

A local environmental group, Colorado Wild (now Rocky Mountain Wild) filed a lawsuit against the Forest Service in 2006, in which the judge found evidence that the Environmental Impact Statement (EIS) process was illegally influenced by the developer and issued an injunction preventing the Forest Service from using the EIS. The Forest Service was forced to issue a new EIS that would supposedly be transparent and unbiased, but the November 2014 issuance of the new EIS opted to grant a land exchange that would trade approximately 205 acres of federal land for 177 acres of private land. This land exchange would connect McComb's private land to U.S. Highway 160, negating the need for a Forest Service easement and allowing for greater development of the private inholding. The Friends of Wolf Creek Coalition filed another lawsuit, and in a hearing in October of 2015 another judge found that the Forest Service had withheld thousands of documents pertaining to its decision and ordered the agency to release them through the Freedom of Information Act.

And finally, on May 19, 2017, a federal judge in the case invalidated the U.S. Forest Service's decision to approve the land exchange that would have essentially brought McComb's proposed Village at Wolf Creek to fruition. "What NEPA requires is that before taking any major action a federal agency must stop and take a careful look to determine the environmental impact of that decision, and listen to the public before taking action," Judge Matsch wrote in his decision. "The Forest Service failed to do that in the Record of Decision. The duty of this Court is to set it aside." (On October 16, 2017 McComb's Joint Venture filed an appeal of the federal judge's ruling and on November 9 the Forest Service joined the appeal. The fight goes on.)

Davey Pitcher, who now runs the ski area and was the family member who was responsible for fighting McComb's development, is, ironically, engaged in a "bigger is better" proposal himself. He wants to expand the ski area onto the backside of the mountain with new lifts and a tram, which would double the area's size. He claims the 20-year expansion plan would not significantly boost skier visits and he remains opposed to any destination resort development. The environmental groups that are celebrating the decision in the McComb's case are disappointed with Pitcher's proposal ("the timing really stinks").

Taos Ski Valley

And finally, Taos Ski Valley (TSV) got the go ahead from Carson National Forest in 2012 to implement its expansion: an increase of its expert terrain by 60 percent with two new lifts accessing high-alpine areas currently accessible only to hikers; upgrades to three other lifts; thinning of trees to expand two new glade areas for advanced intermediate to expert skiers; construction of a permanent tubing facility; a snowshoe trail system; and a lift-served mountain bike trail for summer visitors. It also plans to upgrade its water treatment facility, which will require a permit from the New Mexico Environment Department. Immediately after approval the founders of the ski area, the Blake family, sold it to billionaire investor Louis Bacon, who has the money to actually implement these expansions.

Bacon, a billionaire hedge fund manager, has even greater designs for the ski area. A *Wall Street Journal* article[37] revealed how Bacon and his fellow investors plan to make Taos Ski Valley into an "elite" ski area where skiers will want to "invest" in the ski valley rather than the town of Taos. The article quotes Jerome de Bontin, a French-born businessman, who with several partners plans to redevelop three parcels of land in the base area: "Now that so many good things are happening at Taos Ski Valley, the challenge is to convince people to buy here, as opposed to the town of Taos."

When word first circulated that Bacon intended to buy TSV from the Blake family in late December of 2013, most newspaper articles[38] touted him as an environmentalist who had established conservation easements on his ranches in Colorado. But as *The Denver Post*[39] also reported, the easement placed on his 171,400 acre Trinchera and Blanca ranches (in southern Colorado near Fort Garland) was the result of his fight against

176

Xcel Energy's plan to run solar transmission lines across the property. As the paper described it: "One side of the environmental clash paints the 54-year-old hedge-fund-managing land baron and conservationist as a natural-resource champion protecting one of the state's last unspoiled ranches. The other sees a deep-pocketed NIMBY guarding his own private Eden and thwarting Colorado's pioneering push for statewide solar energy." He's the recipient of millions of dollars of tax breaks on not only his properties in Colorado but also in New York, North Carolina, and the Bahamas.

His business dealings don't reflect well on his reputation. In August of 2013 Bacon's primary business, Moore Capital, agreed to pay $48.4 million to settle a class action lawsuit alleging that the hedge fund manipulated platinum and palladium prices. More recently, in March of 2015, Julian Rifat, a former senior executive trader at Moore Capital, described by U.S. prosecutors as "the face of Moore Capital" in London, was sentenced to 19 months in prison after pleading guilty to a £285,000 insider-trading scam. He earned more than £700,000 a year and was paid approximately £1.4 million in severance pay between his arrest in 2010 and his sentencing.

Bacon's purchase of Taos Ski Valley coincides with the proposed expansion of the Taos airport that will accommodate larger types of planes, such as turbo-prop jets carrying up to 100 passengers, a boon to business in the ski valley. Airport expansion opponents have long argued that the new runway will not benefit the town of Taos economically and is unnecessary, incompatible with the neighborhood, and may compromise the safety of local residents. As I write this chapter, they have filed an appeal of Taos County's approval of the expansion.

Addendum: As this book goes to press I've just come back from a meeting of "stakeholders" with the mountain manager of Sipapu Ski and Summer Resort as the area amends its outdated management plan to resubmit to the USFS. The area plans to submit an expansion plan that largely resembles the 1995 plan to increase its boundary to 977 acres with new lifts, trails, and a restaurant at the top of the mountain.

Twenty-seven

The Mother of All Water Rights Adjudications?

In 2009 I began covering the Lower Rio Grande (LRG) Adjudication, which has turned out to be even more complicated that the Aamodt and Abeyta adjudications despite there being no Indian pueblo involved. This adjudication, heard in the Third Judicial District Court in Doña Ana County, had the potential to force a profound change in the way the State of New Mexico manages the Rio Grande. The initial judge assigned to the case, Jerald Valentine, ordered the state and the U.S. Government to reach settlement on the issue of the Rio Grande Project, or Elephant Butte Irrigation District (EBID), with regard to the amount of water rights the federal government actually owns. Scott Boyd, whose great-grandfather Nathan Boyd originally owned the Rio Grande Project, is also a party in the case along with Doña Ana County farmers, El Paso County Water Improvement District1 (EPCWID), New Mexico State University, and many others.

One hundred years ago the federal government seized Nathan Boyd's Rio Grande Dam and Irrigation Company, including all rights of way, the dam he had constructed to serve the irrigation needs of Lower Rio Grande irrigators, and the water rights the farmers had already turned over to the company. It took this action under what is referred to as Application 8, citing the War Powers Act to make the claim that the Rio Grande was a navigable river above El Paso and Boyd's dam interfered with ship travel. This seizure allowed the Bureau of Reclamation to proceed with construction of Elephant Butte Dam and the administration of Lower Rio Grande water rights. Those water rights, as stated in Application 8, were "all unappropriated water of the Rio Grande," obviously not including senior, or prior appropriation water rights. After the takeover of Boyd's company, the State of New Mexico filed an application so that the Office of the State Engineer (OSE) could begin permitting these water rights, essentially commingling the senior and subsequent junior water rights. The OSE set a universal senior priority date of 1906, the date of Application 8.

Elephant Butte Reservoir

Scott Boyd, who represents the Boyd estate, believes the federal government illegally acquired Rio Grande Project water rights and that the adjudication of these federal rights may now involve the determination of prior appropriation rights and how they will be managed by the OSE. Any changes in priority dates with regard to these rights could potentially impact both water rights allocations and transfers throughout the Rio Grande.

Nathan Boyd was the driving force behind the Rio Grande Dam and Irrigation Company, which acquired Mesilla Valley water rights from farmers to build the Leasburg Dam at Ft. Seldon, a diversion dam for irrigation, and a dam and reservoir at Elephant Butte. Boyd, who was a medical practitioner before he married into money and became an investor, had convinced bankers from London to finance the Rio Grande Dam and Irrigation Company. He had initially been brought to New Mexico by the infamous law officer Pat Garrett to look at the possibility of a dam on the Pecos River, which didn't work out, and was subsequently contacted by farmers from Las Cruces. Whether his motives were altruistic, as his great-grandson Scott Boyd believes, or whether he just saw the dam projects as a good investment, he acquired 40,000 acres of Mesilla Valley land and as much as two-thirds of mesa land at a very small cost. Many farmers conveyed one half of their land for water rights to the other half. The plan was also to supply cities, industries, and other uses.

In order to understand how his projects affect the current adjudication of the Lower Rio Grande, they need to be put in historical context. In the late 1880s, before New Mexico became a state, Texas, Mexico, and El Paso area farmers were jockeying for control of the Rio Grande. Investors were looking at building reservoirs on the river because of a lack of sustainable water supply in the Mesilla Valley and El Paso-Juarez Valley. Texas was concerned about getting its allotted supply, and in 1890 the U.S. and

179

Mexico signed an agreement that outlined guidelines for equitable river management. El Paso wanted a dam built three miles above the city (the U.S. Geological Service, under John Wesley Powell, initially endorsed this project), but that would flood Mesilla Valley farmlands. When Boyd's Rio Grande Dam and Irrigation Company got the right of way to build a dam and reservoir at Elephant Butte and an irrigation dam at Ft. Seldon, the city of Juarez protested its permit, claiming it would prevent the building of a dam closer to El Paso and Juarez, thereby robbing citizens of their international waters. While this protest was working its way through the courts, another tactic was used to fight Rio Grande Dam and Irrigation Company's projects. The U.S. Secretary of State, under the auspices of the War Powers Act and under pressure from Texas and Mexican speculators (and according to some accounts, President Teddy Roosevelt) who wanted to control the fertile agricultural lands in the area, declared the Rio Grande a "navigable river" and an injunction was imposed, stopping any of the Rio Grande Company's work. This declaration was made in spite of the fact that the Army Corps of Engineers had declared that the Rio Grande was only irrigable, not navigable. This case also worked its way through the court system, twice reaching the U.S. Supreme Court.

Initially, the New Mexico Territorial Government defended the Rio Grande Company because it saw the issue as a power struggle between Texas, Mexico, and the federal government, and its position was to protect water for New Mexicans. Nathan Boyd, as head of the company, had already agreed that in return for an annual payment of $225,000 over 20 years his company would deliver water to Mexican irrigators for $1.50 per acre foot.

The Territory's defense of the company evaporated, however, once the U.S. Reclamation Act was passed and the Bureau of Reclamation recommended building a dam at Elephant Butte, below the Rio Grande Company's site, with sufficient water for southern New Mexico and the El Paso-Juarez Valley. The government demanded forfeiture of the Company's franchise in 1903 because of non-use of water rights, which Boyd declared was due to the injunctions imposed on the company because of the lawsuits (by the city of Juarez and the U.S. Secretary of State). The Bureau of Reclamation built Elephant Butte Dam, its first major project, and established the Elephant Butte Irrigation District, which administers Lower Rio Grande water rights. Nathan Boyd fought this takeover for 30 years, and now his great-grandson Scott is a party to the current LRG adjudication that has been dragging on for more than 10 years, to finally determine the federal government's water rights.

A quiet title suit initiated by the United States in 1997 triggered this long, complicated adjudication. At that time the federal government sued in federal court asking title to virtually all the waters of the Lower Rio Grande, 2,638,860 acre feet of storage water, to meet various uses: irrigation, municipal, and industrial within the Project boundaries in New Mexico and Texas; water delivery to Mexico as stipulated in the 1906 Treaty between the U.S. and Mexico; and flood control, hydroelectric power generation, and water storage in Elephant Butte and Caballo reservoirs to meet the terms of the Rio Grande Compact (which determines water deliveries to Texas). Opposing parties to the suit were successful in convincing the federal court to abstain from hearing the case and move it to state district court as an adjudication. The 10th Circuit Court of Appeals upheld that ruling.

Initially, four Stream System Issues were heard in the Third Judicial Court (Judge Valentine was replaced by Judge James Wechsler), or issues that affect the interests of all or most of the parties to the adjudication. The first three issues deal with Consumptive Irrigation Requirements/ Farm Delivery Requirements, Elephant Butte Irrigation District groundwater claims, and domestic wells. The fourth issue, Stream System Issue SS-97 104, will determine the federal government's water rights, which gets at the heart of Scott Boyd's claim that it illegally seized his great-grandfather's Rio Grande Company to construct the Elephant Butte Dam to supply irrigation water to LRG farmers, and that those water rights have to be quantified and validated as part of this process. Under Stream System 104 the determination of groundwater rights that were part of the Rio Grande Project will be connected to surface water rights as well.

In February of 2011 the court approved a fifth Stream Issue that addressed the water right claims of the Estate of Nathan Boyd, as well as any related claims by Scott Boyd, as an *inter se* (between themselves) proceeding. This issue was subsequently dismissed and was appealed to the

New Mexico Court of Appeals, where it was again dismissed. Boyd then appealed to the U.S. 10th Circuit Court of Appeals, where he lost again in 2016.

In 2013 six pre-1906 senior water rights claimants asked the court to hear their case as Stream System Issue 106 as a "global" issue or one that affects the interest of all or most of the parties to the adjudication. These landowners, whose lands would have been irrigated by the Rio Grande Project, some 90,000 acres, have a priority date of 1894, not 1906, when the Project was seized. Essentially, the senior water rights claimants want their claims to be heard first in court, which they believe will also benefit the adjudication process by focusing on the Rio Grande Dam and Irrigation Company Project's historical diversions and infrastructures that predated the takeover by the federal government. The court denied their motion, saying the pre-1906 rights would be heard sub-file by sub-file, i.e., on a case by case basis, after the other stream system issues are addressed.

There is good reason why the court and the other parties to the adjudication don't want the pre-1906 senior water rights claimants at the table. The attorney for the claimants makes it quite clear just what could be at stake if the court was forced to recognize their priority: "If the pre-1906 Claimants are correct, that their appropriation of all the flood waters of the Rio Grande has a priority date of 1893, then all persons claiming later rights are affected by this adjudication, including water rights claimants with later priority dates throughout the entire stretch of the Rio Grande. This Court probably cannot meet its obligation to adjudicate all the rights of the claimants without considering all priority claims on the river."

As the LRG negotiations continued into 2012 and 2013 the extended drought in New Mexico made terms of the settlement seem more like a fantasy than a realistic quantification of water rights. With the drought in mind, reading through all the responses to the court's decision regarding the amounts of water that would be available through the various Rio Grande dams in the adjudication was like reading the fairy tale Rumpelstiltskin where the miller's daughter is supposed to spin straw into gold. The parties to the suit—the State, El Paso Water Improvement District, the Elephant Butte Irrigation District, and others—quibbled over the wording regarding the maximum amount of water the dams can hold and release and over the wording "the U.S. has an unlimited right to divert surface water from the Percha, Leasburg and Mesilla diversion dams." What water, pray tell? The irrigation district shut down in mid July of 2013 because irrigators ran out of stored lake water months earlier than in non-drought years. Elephant Butte's end-of-irrigation-season low was at three percent full, Caballo at two percent. Even with the unanticipated rains in September Elephant Butte held 122,700 acre feet of water. The full capacity of all the dams is 2,638,860 acre feet.

The six landowners claiming pre-1906 water rights filed another motion in 2013 asking the court to reconsider their case as Stream System 106, and responded to the on-the-ground dire circumstances: "The recent drought conditions and the over appropriations of the Rio Grande have shown that those who have prior appropriated rights (pre 1906 or pre federal rights) cannot rely upon EBID [Elephant Butte Irrigation District], OSE [Office of the State Engineer] or the U.S. to defend their rights for the full delivery of their prior appropriated allotments of water. . . . [and] will leave the farmers once again, as it did one hundred years ago, without a current legal remedy to protect themselves and once again place them in economic peril. . . . If justice delayed is justice denied, this is a classic example."

The response also laid out what a resolution of their priority rights should look like:

• The federal government will negotiate with the representatives of the Boyd family to acquire the project rights for the entire LRG irrigation system, which they illegally seized.

• The court will take evidence of the date of first use of the pre-1906 claimants either individually or communally based on the creation of a community ditch or acequia.

• Claimants who first used water after 1893 will have a priority date of 1893 because they were part of the irrigation system that was served by the Rio Grande Project initiated on this date.

• Each claimant will be delivered the water they are entitled to based upon their historic use of water. If there is a shortfall on delivery of water due to lack of available water, then the federal government, OSE and EBID [Elephant Butte Irrigation District] will need to make a call on junior water rights holders' water up and down the river in order to meet the his-

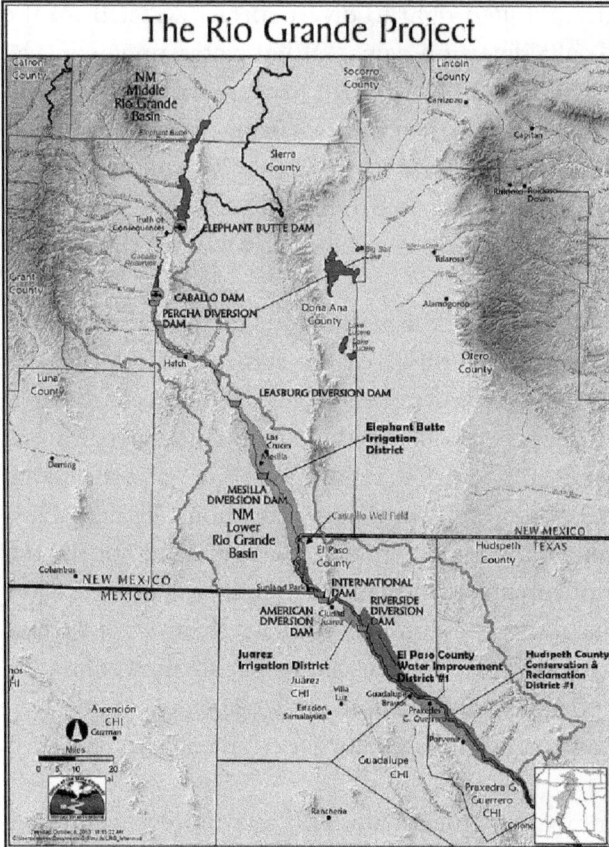

The Rio Grande Project

toric delivery amount to each farmer and claimant in the LRG is entitled to.

In February of 2014 the district court granted summary judgment to the United States, giving the State of New Mexico and the City of Las Cruces maximum storage capacity in Elephant Butte Reservoir of 2,638,860 acre feet of water. It granted a normal annual release of 790,000 afy. It granted the United States the right to divert Project water "without limitation" at the Percha, Leasburg, and Mesilla diversion dams.

What it didn't grant was summary judgment for the pre-1906 claimants regarding their priority dates and the ownership of the Rio Grande Project water rights. The February decision was appealed by the pre-1906 claimants on March 12; in anticipation of this, they filed a motion to stay further proceedings in the Stream System Issue 104, which will determine the amount of the federal government's water rights in the adjudication, "until such time as it is finally decided whether the U.S. or the Boyd interests with the Pre-1906 Claimants hold the vested appropriated rights to the project and diversion rights."

They also made another attempt to incorporate the Lower Rio Grande adjudication into the larger picture of water management on the entire Rio

184

Grande. The motion objects that the February decision grants an amount of water in Elephant Butte Reservoir that "exceeds the amount of claims to beneficial uses that could ever be historically proven by landowners below EBID and thus interferes with upstream users. Thus upstream claimants need to be joined in parties to this adjudication because their rights are being affected."

In the spring of 2016 the pre-1906 claimants again filed motions to clarify their rights derivative of the Rio Grande Dam and Irrigation Company.[40] On the New Mexico State Water Plan Yahoo Group (NMStateWaterPlan@yahoogroups.com) that circulates among an eclectic group of folks following water issues in New Mexico, the e-mails were flying fast and furiously: misrepresentation and "illegality" in the Lower Rio Grande Adjudication; the unfairness and "illegality" of water adjudication settlements in general; the need to adjudicate the Middle Rio Grande, which will affect every water source along the river; why the state won't enforce priority administration and why some folks like it that way; the failure of adjudication settlements to factor in drought and climate change; and the nefariousness of water lawyers, one of whom wrote in to defend her profession. Sig Silber, who has long been following the LRG adjudication, had this to say: ". . . watching this case unfold [is] even more interesting than the NFL since although there are occasional errors by the officials in pro football, you generally at least know who is allowed to be on the field and participate in the game. With the law, especially in New Mexico, it is not clear who is allowed to participate."

In March of 2017, Scott Boyd filed another appeal to be allowed to present his evidence concerning the Rio Grande Dam and Irrigation Company in trial. Many of the farmers' cases are being heard as subfiles, with some agreeing to a settlement of their water rights. In September of 2017 the court ordered a six-month stay: Boyd's appeals are apparently the only thing holding up the movement towards a decree. He continues to argue that all the pre-1906 water rights were vested; everything else that's being claimed are junior water rights that are part of a political ball game run by the OSE and the federal government. In my last conversation with him he said: "We have a connection to the land and water from the people who first settled here and established their water systems under prior appropriation and self rule. We believe in due process and local rules and customs."

Twenty-eight

The Drought Hits Home in El Valle

This is what I wrote in my blog, *Unf*#!ing Believable*, on June 28, 2011, in the first year of a four year drought that plunged much of the west into severe water shortage:

"I'm here in El Valle and it's 90 degrees outside but I've closed all my doors and windows and have every fan I own running full blast (I only have two) so that I can breathe without coughing. The smoke from the Las Conchas fire above Los Alamos has settled over our valley for two days now, so thick it's almost impossible to differentiate between smoke and cloud, except for the orange striations that spread across the plumes along the entire southern horizon. Ash particles so minute that sometimes the only way they are visible is when they're caught in cobwebs (or as my neighbor told me, on her white skirt) rain upon our downwind communities. So here we are, eleven years after the Cerro Grande Fire that burned 47,000 acres in two weeks throughout the Los Alamos area, watching and breathing a fire that has burned 61,000 acres in 36 hours.

"The town of Los Alamos has been evacuated as the fire approaches from the south and west towards the mesa canyons full of legacy waste and the active Los Alamos National Laboratory technical areas that store nuclear weapons and waste. I've made an arbitrary decision that if the fire reaches Tech Area G, where waste containers sit in nylon tents waiting shipment to the Waste Isolation Pilot Plant in southern New Mexico, I will load up my dogs and leave for Albuquerque to move in with my son Jakob and his wife Casey. But really it's just an excuse to stay here in El Valle as long as possible (I pity the poor Los Alamos residents who had to leave their homes as I curse those complicit in this nuclear madness) because I know I've already been contaminated by the radionuclides, PCBs, and other toxins that reside in the ponderosa pine, piñon pine, and mixed conifer forests that are now exploding fire balls, desiccated by years of drought and federal agency mismanagement.

Las Conchas Fire   *Photo by Jakob Schiller*

"I say 'load up my dogs,' but this means somehow getting a seventy pound, 14 year old dog who can barely walk and a 10 year old cocker spaniel who is deaf and almost blind into my car and transporting them in 100 degree heat to Albuquerque. I already asked my neighbor, a former Los Alamos construction manager, if he will take my chickens and put them in with his brood. But why should he stick around to take care of my chickens when he should be getting the hell out of Dodge with his parents, of whom he is the caretaker. The only place they might go is Española, where his brother lives, but as we saw in the Cerro Grande Fire, that town will no doubt be a smoke-filled hellhole as well.

"When I venture out in the smoke to feed the chickens I see that a little water is coming down the acequia into my orchard, which I'm struggling to keep alive between a long rotation of 22 parciantes in a summer of drought the likes of which I've never before seen. I'd asked the mayordomo to let a little water come down from an irrigator up the valley, and his response was, "Go ask them." I didn't, but for some reason the water is there, so with a wet bandana across my face I manage to at least wet down my trees before the water disappears several hours later. As my former vecino Jacobo Romero said (in William deBuys book, *River of Traps*), 'never give holiday to the water.' Even if the fires are raging, get out there and irrigate."

Although El Valle is at the top of the watershed, we were not immune to the exigencies of the drought. The most glaring example, for me at least, was the pathetically patchy growth in my two hay fields, which, in the good years had produced many bales of hay that Tomás and his son Fred bailed for us. Now, dependent upon my skill to guide the acequia waters that had to compensate for little or no rain, there were many "Saharas" barren of grass hay but full of weeds. For three years, 2012 to 2014, I didn't cut the hay but put my horse, and some of my neighbors' horses and mules, into the pastures to graze.

I worried each of those years that the acequias would dry up as well, but the water continued to flow, enough to keep my orchard and garden alive and well, and enough for most of my neighbors to get at least one hay crop per season (the ones who somehow know how to get the water to the Saharas). I also expected that El Valle would have to resort to the repartimiento agreement we have with the village of Las Trampas, directly below us on the river, which we had done in previously dry years. When this occurs, each village is allocated certain days of the week, three or four to El Valle, the other days to Trampas. Parciantes have to regulate their rotation within this regimen, meaning, of course, that we get the water less frequently and in smaller amounts as we wait for rain. But we managed to make it through this most recent drought without having to instigate the water sharing system.

The Las Conchas fire was finally contained—or burned itself out, depending on your point of view—but the threat of catastrophic fire, particularly in the Jemez Mountains surrounding Los Alamos, continues. In 2012 the Santa Fe National Forest began the scoping process for the Southwest Jemez Mountains Restoration Project (SJMRP). The SJMRP was among ten nationwide projects selected by the United States Department of Agriculture (the United States Forest Service is part of the USDA) in 2010

188

for funding under the Collaborative Forest Landscape Restoration Program (CFLRP). The project proposes to thin trees on 90,000 acres and use prescribed fire on 76,000 acres within the Jemez Ranger District and the Valles Caldera Preserve. Portions of Bandelier National Monument, Santa Clara Pueblo, and Jemez Pueblo are also included. Most of the thinning is proposed for the ponderosa pine forests, but mixed conifer, piñon/juniper, and aspen are also slated for treatment. Site-specific methods will be used: chainsaws, mechanized equipment, or whole-tree mastication. Wood removal techniques will also be site specific: firewood sales, commercial harvest, and prescribed burning.

Theoretically, considering what's happened to the Jemez Mountains over the past few decades it's hard to understand why anyone would oppose a rigorous management plan of thinning, prescribed burning, and watershed restoration, which is what the SJMRP proposes. In practice, of course, it was a prescribed burn at Bandelier National Monument that started the 2000 Cerro Grande fire. You can also question United States Forest Service (USFS) policies of total fire suppression that helped create monolithic tinderboxes like the Jemez, and why the agency is now dependent upon special funding to do the work that local loggers could have done to keep their businesses alive. Instead we have a long history of crown fires that have burned through this range and threatened Los Alamos National Laboratory: the 1954 Water Canyon fire of approximately 5,000 acres that forced the first evacuation of Los Alamos; the 1977, 15,000-acre La Mesa fire; the 1996, 16,000-acre Dome fire; the 2000 Cerro Grande fire, which burned 47,000 acres and forced another evacuation; and the 156,000-acre Las Conchas fire, the then largest fire to date that also forced evacuations at Los Alamos and Santa Clara Pueblo.

Craig Allen, research ecologist with the U.S. Geological Survey, is the go-to guy on anything to do with Jemez Mountain forestry. On an NPR show on mega-fires, drought, and climate change he spoke about the 1,000-year history of ponderosa pines in the Jemez Mountains and what he and other scientists call the "new normal," or the reality that climate change is exaggerating the normal swings in weather: droughts will be more intense and periods of wetter weather will decline. Drought has already destroyed 95 percent of the mature piñon pine at Bandelier; the ponderosa may be

189

next. As with the USFS fire policies, we've come full circle with trees: first there was piñon/juniper, mixed conifer, and ponderosa, then there was ponderosa, now there is no ponderosa.

In June of 2013 I saw smoke come up over the El Valle ridge just where the Borrego Fire appeared in 2002 to threaten the villages of Córdova, Truchas, and conceivably El Valle. My first thought was, "Here we go again," but my second thought was, "Maybe it will burn into the Borrego scar and run out of fuel." Which is a sad commentary on what we think of as fire management these days: a former conflagration is the only way to put out a current conflagration. But the Jaroso Fire burned further east than the Borrego Fire, in the Pecos Wilderness in steep, mixed conifer terrain near Pecos Baldy. It's not easily accessed country, frequented mostly by backpackers and folks from the surrounding villages who've been riding their horses into the backcountry for generations. After the USFS closed the wilderness it started to rain, in the middle of June, which it never does. So nothing is as it has been, there is no "normal," and no one really knows what to expect—except that whether it's climate change, extended drought, or both, it's only going to get worse.

Twenty-nine

How Not To Manage Water in a Drought

A February, 2013 National Resources Conservation Services (NRCS) report predicted that Elephant Butte Irrigation District would have 38 percent of its normal spring run-off flows during the year and wouldn't even begin the irrigation season until June; it "normally" begins in February. The report also said, "While it is painful to contemplate, there is also the possibility that, if the spring runoff fails, we may not have enough water to make any release, allotment or delivery in 2013. Being so dry for so long, the river will have very high conveyance losses, and those losses occur before any diversion or delivery. A zero release season has never occurred in Project history, and we certainly hope it will not occur this year, but we are in hydrologic new territory, and we must consider the worst."

This information compounded the fact that the previous two calendar years (2011 and 2012) had been the driest and warmest two-year period on record for New Mexico. According to the NRCS, only 1956 was drier in New Mexico: "In light of these desiccating facts, it is no surprise that New Mexico reservoir storage is well below normal in the Rio Grande Basin, Canadian Basin, and Pecos Basin."

These figures were all over the news reports and a hot topic of conversation on the NM State Water Plan listserv (NMStateWaterPlan@yahoogroups.com) that I referred to previously. Everyone had a different idea of how to deal with these extreme circumstances. Lynn Montgomery articulated his ideas in an article for the *Sandoval Signpost*.[41] He wants the State to do its job and implement priority administration through the Lower Rio Grande adjudication. He also wants us to recognize that we are "desert dwellers" and implement meaningful water conservation. A water broker wants us to use free market forces to move water around to the "highest and best use." Others exchange information on cloud seeding in Utah and Colorado and want New Mexico to seriously consider trying it. And Las Cruces State Senator Joseph Cervantes introduced Senate Bill

440 asking for an appropriation of $120 million from the general fund to protect the senior water rights of the Lower Rio Grande Basin through the "importation" of water, the conservation of water, and "acquiring" and/or "retiring" water rights. In a video interview with *Watchdog New Mexico* Cervantes explained his reasoning: We're trying to bring growth and development here in New Mexico and that requires water.

Unless your idea of how to address current and impending drought in New Mexico includes building pipelines, dams, and tunnels to move water around and spending lots of money buying water rights you're not likely to be hired by a water management bureaucracy in New Mexico or get elected to the legislature (except maybe Peter Wirth or Michael Sanchez). There are consequences to these practices.

Rio Grande Compact issues:

The state of Texas filed a lawsuit in the U.S. Supreme Court in January of 2013 alleging that New Mexico has failed to comply with the Rio Grande Compact. The suit claims that because of groundwater pumping below Elephant Butte Reservoir Texas isn't getting its required water delivery. As I mentioned above, Rio Grande flows in Elephant Butte had been way below normal for two years, and with the dire warning issued by the NRCS regarding 2013's flows, there was going to be even more pumping of groundwater by the farmers in the irrigation district—and these are big-time farmers who are already involved in the litigation of the Lower Rio Grande Adjudication. One of the Stream System issues being heard in this case is the connection of ground and surface waters, which has to be factored into the final decree determining everyone's water rights. In an earlier agreement between Texas and New Mexico it was agreed that New Mexico would deliver more surface water to offset its groundwater pumping, but that deal fell apart and Texas took the case to the Supreme Court. In a third year of drought, without adequate surface irrigation water, farmers and ranchers were going to continue to pump groundwater to meet their needs. In 2016, a special master assigned by the U.S. Supreme Court recommended the rejection of a motion by New Mexico to dismiss the case, meaning it could move forward as long as the high court agreed. In early 2017 the case headed to the Supreme Court, and in January of 2018 oral arguments were heard over whether the federal government could intervene in the case. The feds believe that because the New Mexico farmers have been over pumping groundwater, the Bureau of Reclamation may fail to deliver the amount of water from Elephant Butte Reservoir that is required by the Rio Grande Compact and the international treaty with Mexico. In February of 2018 the Supreme Court ruled that the federal government could intervene in the lawsuit. The decision was based on "treaty obligations to Mexico" and doesn't look good for New Mexico, as some believe it will allow the feds to support Texas's compact arguments.

This is not the first time the two states have been in court over water allocation; the first time it was over the Pecos River. Em Hall, former UNM law professor, wrote an entire book about it, *High and Dry: The Texas-New Mexico Struggle for the Pecos River.*[42] In this case, which lingered in court from 1974 to 1988 during the infamous New Mexico State Engineer Steve Reynolds' tenure, Texas also claimed that New Mexico failed to deliver required water under the terms of the Pecos River Compact. This compact differed from the Rio Grande Compact in that it included a provision stating that New Mexico could not deplete "by man's activities" the 1947 condition of the Pecos River, which didn't obligate the state to deliver a set amount of water to Texas but to curtail human uses of the river to meet that 1947 condition. Ultimately, however, instead of complying with the condition by enforcing the state's priority system, which would have required acknowledging Carlsbad Irrigation District's senior water rights by shutting off Roswell area junior wells to get water to the Texas state line, the New Mexico state legislature bought and retired enough water rights to meet the Texas water demand. It cost $100 million.

Priority Calls:

Also during this critical year of 2013 the Carlsbad Irrigation District (CID) issued a priority call on the Pecos River against the Pecos Valley Artesian Conservancy District (PVACD).

The CID has late 1800 senior surface water rights as opposed to the Roswell area farmers in the conservancy district with junior groundwater rights that, as the CID claimed, were being pumped while the irrigation ditches went dry. The attorney for the CID seemed to think that this time around the Office of the State Engineer, instead of the state legislature, was going to come to the rescue. That's because of the Active Water Resource Management (AWRM) rules (recently upheld in a decision by the New Mexico Supreme Court), which allow an appointed water master to implement an administrative priority cut-off date. All water rights holders whose priority date is later than the administrative date must stop using the water. This would, of course, cut off water to the PVACD, just as enforcement of the priority system would require, except that AWRM would enforce it more expeditiously and also allow the PVACD to file a replacement plan: the junior water right holder could temporarily use other senior water rights that aren't being used, assuming it's hydrologically viable. (A settlement was reached but the problems of priority administration remain.)

When AWRM was first promulgated in 2004, as I discussed in Chapter Fourteen, many expressed concern that replacement plans denied the due process of formal water transfer protests and hearings and that it expedited the marketing and leasing of water (acequias and community ditches are expressly exempted from expedited marketing and leasing provisions). According to the OSE, replacement plans "do not adjudicate your water rights but are only an interim determination for administration and can be superseded by the courts." Replacement plans would be limited to two years, which the OSE claimed would prevent developers from transferring water rights without a full public hearing.

So while the state moved further away from priority administration the worsening drought continued to count coup on all efforts at water management and distribution. According to the NRCS, the April stream flows remained dismal. The Rio Grande Basin stream flows ranged from 57 percent of normal for the Rio Lucero near Arroyo Seco, to 11 percent of normal for the Jemez River below Jemez Canyon Dam. At Otowi Bridge, flows were forecast at 30 percent of normal, or 192,000 acre feet, and San Marcial was also 11 percent of normal or 53,000 acre feet. March precipitation was 32 percent of normal, drier than 2012. Year to date precipitation was at 60 percent, also lower than the previous year at the same time. While snowpack was below average at 55 percent, a little better than the previous year, much of the low to mid elevation snowpack had already melted, much earlier than average. Total reservoir storage in the basin was

614,300 afy, down from the previous year's 974,400 afy.

Native American Adjudication Settlements:

The water rights settlements for the Navajo Nation (San Juan Basin), the pueblos of Pojoaque, San Ildefonso, Nambe, and Tesuque pueblos (Aamodt), and Taos Pueblo (Abeyta) were signed by the federal government and the state of New Mexico in the late 2000s, ending years of litigation (more than 50 years for the Aamodt). The Colorado Ute Indian Water Rights settlement, which also affects water flows in New Mexico, was signed in 1988 (then resigned in 2000) and set the standard for costs: originally slated to run at over $500 million, the amount of dams, reservoirs, and hundreds of miles of pipeline and canals were eventually reduced, but only fractionally. The New Mexico settlements continue to rely on massive spending and movement of water.

The Navajo Nation was awarded 600,000 acre feet per year or 55 percent of San Juan Basin water rights. This settlement also entails several massive projects, the Navajo Irrigation Project (begun over 40 years ago and still not completed) and the Navajo-Gallup Water Supply Project, and would cost the federal government $800 million. It immediately generated controversy from Indians and non-Indians alike. Former Navajo Nation chairman Peter McDonald argued that the Indians should take their case back to court, under the Winters Doctrine (remember, the Doctrine declares that when Congress reserved land for Indian reservations it also reserved water, both present and future, to fulfill the purpose of the reservation), to better protect their senior water rights and take whatever water the tribe deems it needed. Senator Pete Domenici chimed in saying that "legislation authorizing the Navajo settlement will be very difficult to fund given the huge budget deficit confronting the nation." The Citizens Progressive Alliance, based in Farmington, claimed it allowed "special interests to promote speculation and unrestrained growth at the expense of the common good," and that it allowed the Navajos to market the water. As I mentioned previously, in a letter to the *Albuquerque Journal*, Elouise Brown, President of Dooda Desert Rock (the Navajo organization opposed to the proposed Desert Rock coal fired power plant on the reservation), wrote that "The proposed diversion across hundreds of miles of desert smacks

195

more of the white man's predisposition toward resource exploitation than it does of traditional Native American values of cautious use of resources." And the Ute Mountain Ute tribe issued a priority call on San Juan River water, claiming a priority date of March 2, 1868 (as opposed to the Navajo priority date of June 1, 1868) for 7,300-9,300 acre feet per year of water. The tribe notified the New Mexico Office of the State Engineer of this claim before the state had signed the Navajo Nation Water Rights Settlement, but was apparently ignored. At the time, the state claimed a hydrographic study, not yet completed, would show that there would be enough water for everyone concerned.

I've already discussed in detail the Aamodt and Abeyta settlements that govern the Pojoaque Valley pueblos and Taos Pueblo, whose hotels, golf courses, and casinos have made them big-time players in the economic development game. Pojoaque Pueblo, in particular, has become one of the main power brokers, and the guarantee of water rights for future development in the Aamodt settlement reflects that. Santa Fe County and the feds argued before the Office of the State Engineer that by shutting down the Top of the World irrigation wells the aquifer water will migrate to the Rio Grande and flow downhill to the diversion dam where it will be diverted into the multimillion dollar water delivery system to Pueblo and non-Pueblo residents who pay to hook up to it. If and when this water will reach the Rio Grande is open to debate, and everyone involved had their own hydrologic study to back up their claims.

The Abeyta Adjudication relies on San Juan/Chama water rights of 2,690 acre feet per year. San Juan/Chama water is not included in the Navajo Nation settlement's 55 percent of San Juan Basin water rights but, if the terms of the Navajo Nation settlement are not achieved, the tribe would assert a Winters Doctrine claim to the San Juan River, threatening supply for the San Juan/Chama Project. The Ute Mountain Ute Winters Doctrine claim could also impact the San Juan/Chama supply. If there is insufficient snowpack and rainfall in the San Juan Basin there will be very little San Juan River water for the Colorado tribes or San/Juan Chama water for Taos Pueblo or any of the downstream contractors: in 2002, only 6,000 afy of project water came through the Azotea Tunnel into Heron Lake. Additional terms of the settlement revealed in 2013 that several water transfers from outside the Taos Valley would be needed to offset pumping from the mitigation wells (to be discussed in the next chapter).

Government institutions continue to manage water resources as a commodity and those who "doth protest too much" face bureaucratic and legalistic impediments in the narrow window of opportunity they have to challenge that management. If at this point in the game the repartimiento, or sharing of water, can only be achieved on a very small scale within community water systems, at the very least water adjudications must be completed to protect senior water rights and serious conservation measures must be implemented to avoid all the political machinations that are promoted as solutions—the pipelines, the dams, the groundwater pumping, and the money—lots of it.

Thirty

Taos County Public Welfare Committee:
Abeyta Movidas Revealed

The Taos County Advisory and Informational Committee on Public Welfare Impacts of Water Appropriations and Changes in Point of Diversion, Place of Use, or Purpose of Use (whew, what a title; from here on out I will simply refer to it as the Public Welfare Committee) had its first meeting on January 31, 2011 at the Taos County Commission Chamber. The Committee is comprised of nine members selected by the Commission to represent the sub-regions in Taos County that were defined in the Taos Regional Water Plan. Interested citizens submitted letters to the Commissioners and members of the Regional Water Plan's Public Welfare subcommittee recommended other potential candidates.

The members chosen by the County were: Glorianna Dominguez Atencio, an acequia commissioner from Arroyo Hondo; Milton Cisneros, a commissioner from Cerro; Ron Gardiner from Questa; Joe Torres from El Salto; Norman Quenzler from Taos; Arthur Coca, a commissioner from Ranchos de Taos; Bob Romero, board member of El Valle Water and Sanitation District from Ranchos de Taos; Tanya Leherissey, a mayordoma from Llano San Juan; and myself, a commissioner from El Valle.

Simeon Herskovits, the Taos County contract attorney who helped draft the Public Welfare Ordinance, presented draft bylaws for the Committee to review, and discussion at this first meeting centered around the nuts and bolts of how the committee would fulfill our obligation to review transfer applications from or within the county. We would decide whether to establish a *de minimis* amount of water in a transfer application, perhaps five acre feet per year or less, that would not require review by the committee, or whether to look at every proposed transfer on a case by case basis. We also discussed the need to convene the committee in a timely fashion once a transfer application was filed with the County Clerk, as required in the Public Welfare Ordinance, to ensure adequate time to review and recommend to the County as to whether it should protest the application.

Before the meeting I called Santa Fe County Attorney John Utton to get an update on the Top of the World (TOW) water rights transfer. According to Utton, the Department of the Interior, along with Santa Fe County, would likely make an application that year, 2011, for 1,711 acre feet per year (afy), the total amount of water rights at TOW. The Department of the Interior would ask for the 1,141 afy that it purchased from Santa Fe County as part of the Aamodt settlement agreement, on behalf of Pojoaque, Nambe, Tesuque, and San Ildefonso pueblos, while the county would be applying for 611 afy of non-pueblo water rights. Utton reiterated to me that Santa Fe County had offered to trade TOW water rights to the Abeyta settlement parties for San Juan/Chama water, but Taos Pueblo was not interested in the trade because it intends to market some of the San Juan/Chama water. The TOW application would of course come before the Public Welfare Committee for review.

At the second meeting of the Advisory Committee I was elected chair, and the committee was off to the races as numerous water transfers came before our review, particularly those involved in the Abeyta Adjudication. We soon discovered that on November 24, 2010, two days before the Taos County Public Welfare Ordinance went into effect, El Prado Water and Sanitation District, a party to the adjudication, had filed eight applications with the Office of the State Engineer (OSE) for the following purposes: 1) to appropriate underground water; 2) to combine and commingle underground water; 3) to change the location of well and place and /or purpose of use of underground water; 4) to add points of diversion and expand place and/or purpose of use of underground water; and 5) to change purpose of use from surface to groundwater.

These applications lingered in the OSE until the first two applications, to appropriate underground water and to combine and commingle underground water, were published in the June 16-22, 2011 *Taos News* legal section. The Committee met as quickly and frequently as possible to assess these two applications. Under the auspices of the Abeyta Settlement, El Prado Water and Sanitation District sought to increase its water rights from its then current amount of 25 afy to 575 afy. According to district manager John Painter, this would bring the District in line with its actual consumer use and the projected 40-year water plan the District was required to promulgate to meet the terms of the Settlement. The District had been pumping more than its allotted number of water rights (100 to 130 afy) for many years and owed the state of New Mexico almost 800 afy of water rights. The Abeyta Settlement also stipulated that the District limit pumping from the three existing wells that were located in the immediate vicinity of the Taos Pueblo Buffalo Pasture and dig two new, deep wells (1,000 feet) tapping into the Rio Grande in the area along U.S. 64 towards the Gorge Bridge.

The first of the two applications the committee reviewed was for a new appropriation of water in the amount of 549.53 afy that would be pumped from its three existing wells (Overland Sheepskin Well, Las Colonias Well, El Torreon Well) and the two proposed wells (Rio Grande Well and Midway Well) for domestic, livestock, irrigation, municipal, industrial, and commercial purposes. This would allow the District to beneficially use 575 afy. The second July application was for a permit to "Combine and Comingle Underground Water." This would allow the District to use its existing wells and the two proposed wells together.

The Committee invited John Painter to attend a July 6 meeting to provide additional information regarding the applications and to answer the Committee's questions. At the meeting Painter informed members of the Committee that El Prado Water and Sanitation District believed it was not required to file notice of its OSE applications with the Taos County Clerk, as stipulated in the Public Welfare Ordinance, because its initial filing date of November 24 came two days before the Ordinance took effect, and also because it believed that parties to the Abeyta are exempt from the Ordinance. The committee rebutted the first claim, pointing out that the applications appeared in the legal section of the paper long after the Ordinance went into effect, thus requiring notification of the Taos County Clerk. The second claim, that parties to the Abeyta are exempt from the Ordinance, was patently false: all such transfers would be reviewed by the OSE as well as our committee.

The committee raised very valid questions about the effects the two deep Rio Grande wells might have on both the river itself and the shallow water aquifer that supports area wells and surface water. It questioned the

OSE hydrologic model that the Abeyta parties used to support the concept of these deep wells might be oversimplified, particularly in an area like Taos where the geology and geohydrology are extraordinarily complex. The proposed deep aquifer wells are separated from shallow water aquifers in the Taos Valley by severe fault lines where not enough data has been accumulated to tell us whether these faults will influence the amount of water that will be available from the wells. Also, there can be a 50-year "residence" time in underground stream flows from tributaries to the Rio Grande.

Based on the information provided in the applications and by Painter, the Committee decided to recommend to the Board of County Commissioners that it protest the two El Prado Water and Sanitation District applications. Unfortunately, we ran out of time due to El Prado's failure to notify the County Clerk that the applications had been submitted to the OSE back in November of 2010 and the constraints of getting our recommendation before the regularly scheduled meetings of the County Commission (protests of proposed water transfers must be submitted to the OSE within 10 days of the last required publication of the proposal in the legal section of a local newspaper). Several individual members of the Committee (including me), as well as other concerned citizens of Taos County, filed individual protests of the two applications. The results of these protests will be discussed in Chapter Thirty-two.

The next three El Prado applications were published in February of 2012 to transfer water rights from northern Taos County to the District's five wells in El Prado. They included a transfer of 245 afy from land owned or leased by the District, called the Gallagher Farm; 17 afy from land owned or leased by the District at Top of the World; and 22 afy from land owned or leased by the District, also at Top of the World. The combined 284 afy were to be used for irrigation and to offset groundwater pumping effects from the new deep wells on the main stem of the Rio Grande.

Once again the advisory committee recommended that the county protest the El Prado water transfer applications, and this time the 2012 commission voted to file a protest. The committee pointed out that the water rights from TOW—groundwater rights—that would be transferred as offsets for the drilling of the wells were "paper" water rights, meaning no one really knew if the underground water from the TOW farms would be providing real, "wet" water to the Rio Grande to compensate for additional pumping. In its protest the county would have the opportunity to argue its case based on the public welfare criteria where the issues of mining groundwater and offsetting it with paper water, transferring agricultural water to a more urban area, and the lack of transparency within the settlement agreement could be heard.

Then, to no one's surprise, when newly elected county commissioner Tom Blankenhorn, whose district includes El Prado Water and Sanitation District, took office in 2013 he asked that the county commission "revisit" its decision to protest the El Prado water transfer applications. Blankenhorn, a former county attorney, made it clear in his public statements and cross examination of the committee that he, too, like John Painter, believed the Abeyta settlement shouldn't be messed with, and if all the El Prado water applications were part of that agreement, then so be it. He also requested the insertion of new language into the amended Public Welfare Ordinance that says: "Taos County recognizes the impact of the Abeyta Settlement on resolving disputes with regard to water rights within the County and watershed and that the transfer of water rights between entities within the County is a necessary mechanism for the implementation of the settlement."

The Public Welfare Advisory Committee was called in on two different occasions before the commission to explain its reasoning to recommend that the county protest the water transfers. As I expressed to Commissioner Blankenhorn, the committee did its job to the best of its ability and if the commission wanted to take another vote that was its job, not ours. It's an interesting irony that while the committee has no real power—we could only recommend that the county protest a transfer—and the county in turn has no power to stop a transfer—that's in the hands of the OSE—so much time was spent to block its inclusion in the regional water plan by the Abeyta parties and to reverse its recommendation to protest the El Prado transfers.

But as usual, there were plenty of political movidas that helped explain why. Blankenhorn and John Painter's relationship with development interests was at the time on the front page: the county and El Prado Water and

Sanitation District were co-litigants in a lawsuit to prevent the Town of Taos from annexing the New Mexico State Highway 64 corridor through El Prado to the Taos airport, where an expansion proposal was currently being litigated. The water district wanted to retain development opportunities along the highway corridor and was actually involved in negotiations to provide the water for the airport expansion.

Adding to the general accusation of lack of transparency in the movement of all this water was Painter's involvement in previous and current water transactions. As far back as the mid-1990s he helped negotiate the proposed water transfer to Las Sierras, a huge resort and development in the El Prado area that was proposed by real estate developers and fought by the community. The criteria of Public Welfare was raised by the State Engineer at the time, who denied the water transfer based on the fact that the developers failed to present exact figures on how they were going to meet the resort's water needs. The proposed development never came to fruition.

Painter is also an employee of the Cerro San Cristobal Ranch, whose owner Alfred Keller has long been involved in water markets and is the owner of 17 afy of TOW water rights that El Prado applied to purchase for $340,000 ($20,000 per acre foot). El Prado was guaranteed $2 million from the state to buy water rights as part of the Abeyta Settlement, but the Interstate Stream Commission (ISC), which manages the funding, claimed that price was above market value. Both sides hired "experts" to determine current market value of water rights. El Prado hired Paul Saavedra, former head of the OSE Water Rights Division, who is now a consultant (a revolving door there?). This is what he concluded: "It appears to me that there are no other water rights offered to El Prado from Alfred Keller. Since there are no other recent transactions to my knowledge in this area, this particular offer of water rights for $20,000 per acre foot of consumptive use, is setting the fair market value at this time, and therefore is at the fair market value." The ISC got an estimate value of $7,250 per acre foot from Southwest Water Consultants. El Prado sued the agency and settlement talks ensued: the water rights were eventually assessed at $18,000 and the ISC paid $16,000 per acre foot. Additional moneys were raised to pay the rest.

Yet another Abeyta-related water transfer came before the Public Welfare Committee. Once again the 2013 Commission failed to hear the Committee's recommendation to protest an application to transfer approximately 100 acre feet per year from a Questa acequia to acequias in the Taos Valley. As part of the settlement agreement, Palemon Martinez, president of the Taos Valley Acequia Association, negotiated a transfer from the Llano Community Ditch in Questa to compensate the Acequia Madre del Rio Lucero y del Arroyo Seco, an association of 12 acequias in the El Salto and Arroyo Seco area of Taos Valley, for a "taking" of water rights on the Rio Lucero by Taos Pueblo in 1935. The Questa water rights belong to the estate of Bernabe Ortega and were severed from the land in the 1960s.

Who was buying the water rights was ambiguous. The Acequia Madre del Rio Lucero y del Arroyo Seco is a member of the Taos Valley Acequia Association. Palemon Martinez is the chairman of the board of the TVAA and was then secretary of the Acequia Madre. According to the contract with the Ortega estate that Martinez signed, the federal government and the state of New Mexico would pay up to a half a million dollars for these rights to compensate the ditch for the loss of water rights to the Pueblo. The water would be transferred to two Aquifer Storage and Recovery (ASR) wells that would augment the Acequia Madre's irrigation. The water would be diverted from the Rio Lucero in the winter, stored in ASR wells until spring, then pumped from the wells and transported via pipeline to the acequias.

No one outside the parties to the Abeyta Settlement knew of this agreement, including the parciantes on the Acequia Madre del Rio Lucero y del Arroyo Seco. As word got out, many of them showed up at commission hearings and told the commission that they didn't want to take water rights from another acequia and that this deal was made without the consent of the Acequia Madre parciantes. This opposition would eventually lead to the ouster of Palemon Martinez from the Acequia's commission in 2015.

The Public Welfare Committee voted six to two to recommend that the Board of County Commissioners protest this application based upon our evaluation of its impact on the public welfare of Taos citizens. One of the committee members who voted against the recommendation, Joe Torres, represented the Arroyo Seco subregion and is a parciante on the Acequia

Madre in El Salto (his house and land are right at the headgate where the Rio Lucero merges with the Rio Seco to form the Acequia Madre), but also based his decision on the fact that the Llano Community Ditch never officially leased the Ortega water rights and therefore could not claim the transfer would impair the ditch. The other member who voted against the transfer also cited this fact as well as the need to fulfill the terms of the Abeyta Settlement.

The County Commission cancelled the special meeting scheduled to hear our recommendation to protest and never reconvened before the protest period was up. The Llano Community Ditch and its neighboring acequia association the Cabresto Irrigation District both appealed the transfer.

The parties to the Abeyta Settlement fought against the establishment of the Public Welfare Advisory Committee because they wanted unfettered access to water wherever they could find it. The provisions to import water and to also pump water from deep aquifers to meet present and future water supply demands are both controversial components that should have public hearings before of Office of the State Engineer. The folks in the move-from watersheds were not at the negotiating table; they deserved a seat at this table.

Thirty-one

Backlash

New Mexico communities have maintained—not preserved—their commons in ways that remain part of our everyday lives: parciantes irrigating crops and fields with acequias; extant land grants managing their forest resources communally; grazing associations forming to collectively raise cattle on private and public lands; and farmers saving seed to reproduce crops regionally grown for hundreds of years.

State and market forces continually threaten all of these practices. Mark and I and our contributors have written extensively in *La Jicarita* on the history and impact of public land management agencies such as the United States Forest Service (USFS) that was the beneficiary of a generation of land grant dispossession and that denied communities access to needed resources—timber, pasture, and acequia infrastructure. We've written about how locally managed water is being transferred to underwrite urban, recreational, and industrial use despite the priority system that is supposed to protect traditional communities. We've written about the oil and gas and mining industries that continue to pollute our common aquifers and abrogate local sovereignty.

We've also written about how these forces continue to be challenged. The Vallecitos Federal Sustained Unit Association fought back against both the USFS and the timber companies to reduce unsustainable timber cuts in the Carson National Forest.[43] We've written about the 2003 state statute that allows acequias to incorporate into their bylaws the power to deny water transfers from their ditches if they would prove harmful to the integrity of the system.[44] And we've written about how communities have galvanized to enact regulations to protect their land and water resources from oil and gas development.[45]

The agenda for a meeting that took place in the Taos County Commission chamber on Monday, October 28, 2013 called for a conversation about the Taos County Public Welfare Statement and Public Welfare Advisory Committee's role in reviewing water transfer applications. I thought about getting up and talking theory, but I think most folks at the meeting understood that the conversation was about the contested terrain between the commons and free market capitalism. Those who believe in the integrity of the commons work to keep water in its area of origin and not transferred to underwrite future development in different watersheds or out of the region. Those who believe that market forces should dictate the movement of water, which has been defined by the state as private property, don't want any regulatory or public oversight to get in the way of development. Allowing natural resources to help determine sustainable growth and development patterns is not the way things work in a market economy.

And so we see the breakdown between the concept of the commons versus the state and market. But several folks at the meeting also raised an important argument that put the issue in more practical terms. When the county, under Blankenhorn's leadership, takes the position that the Abeyta Settlement is sacrosanct, it weakens the county's position to protest the impending Aamodt Settlement transfer of 1,170 acre feet per year of water from Top of the World in northern Taos County. Bill Whaley, editor and publisher of the online *Taos Friction* put it well in one of his columns:[46]

"If the County wants to protest against water rights transfers, like Top of the World water rights being sold to Santa Fe to support the Aamodt Settlement downstream, then the County must also vet and publish its record of decision re: intra-County transfers re: El Prado and the Rio Lucero [Arroyo Seco] purchases of water rights from northern Taos County or it will be challenged in court about making exceptions that smack of 'special' or 'political' decisions that undermine its own criteria. In other words Commissioners must balance special and general interests but make sure transfer decisions are consistent and well-argued so they can stand up to potential legal challenges from downstream municipalities and governmental entities."

As Ron Gardiner, one of the Advisory Committee members, also pointed out, Taos was the last region to draft its Public Welfare Statement and was motivated to provide as much protection as possible for its water resources that other regions are or will be attempting to transfer to meet their own needs. The OSE has a long history of rubber-stamping water transfers that if scrutinized under a Public Welfare Statement the agency would be hard pressed to defend.

It was up to the County Commissioners how they would define the future role of the Advisory Committee, and they weren't getting any help from county staff. The staff proposed changes to the Advisory Committee that would "broaden" its responsibilities to include a more general role in water planning and narrow its role in assessing water transfers under the Public Welfare Ordinance. It wanted to make the Committee a more "in-house" function of the Planning Department and diminish its role as an informational conduit to the public (the Public Welfare Ordinance states that one of the purposes of the Committee is "To inform residents of the County about proposed appropriations and changes in point of diversion, place of use or purpose of use of water from and within Taos County"). Proposed changes to the Committee's bylaws, which were formulated by staff and hadn't been reviewed by the Committee, reflected this position.

I saw the writing on the wall. I resigned a few weeks after the Commission meeting where I was forced to defend the Public Welfare Committee's mission. Then Deputy County Manager Rick Bellis wrote me that the Advisory Committee had "gotten away from the general concern of the Commission and intent of the ordinance to monitor water rights to minimize or prevent them leaving the county or watershed." I wrote Bellis back pointing out that the Public Welfare Ordinance stipulates that the Advisory Committee "evaluate the public welfare and conservation of proposed water appropriations and changes in point of diversion, place of use or purpose of use of water from and *within* Taos County (emphasis added)."

But it was an interesting three-year ride. While the outspokenness of many of the committee members who believe in the commons may have resulted in this backlash from the county, the fact that we had this discussion before the County Commission, as obtuse as it may be to some, and as obvious as it was to others, was actually encouraging: we knew where we each stood in the divide. It put the powers that be on notice that the decisions they make will have real and lasting consequences and that those affected by these decisions will be there, up close and personal.

Thirty-two

How Far Can a Lawyerless Protestant Get?

As I've touched on previously, pursuing a protest is like participating in a trial: there is a pre-hearing conference to set a schedule; both protestants and applicants must provide a witness list, proceed with discovery, call witnesses, etc.; and finally there's a hearing before a hearing examiner of the Office of the State Engineer (OSE), the agency that approves or disapproves transfers. You can represent yourself, just as you can in a court of law, but it isn't easy. As a protestant to two of the Taos area water transfer applications I decided to see how far I could get without official representation. (Disclaimer: I solicited the advice of some of my favorite water lawyers who never work for the dark side.)

As I discussed in Chapter Twenty-nine, El Prado Water and Sanitation District sought to increase its water rights from 25 to 575 acre feet per year from two deep wells that would be drilled near U.S. 64 and the Gorge Bridge. The District submitted two applications to the OSE: one, to appropriate water from these new wells; and two, to transfer water rights from the Top of the World (TOW) area to offset the pumping.

When the Taos County Advisory Committee recommended to the Taos County Commission that it protest El Prado's applications, I also protested as an individual. Several other folks also filed protests with me, but in the end decided that without legal representation it would be too difficult to pursue their protests. Taos County was initially a co-protestant on the transfer of water from the TOW area (as I discussed previously, the Taos County Commission ultimately voted not to continue as a protestant under the direction of Tom Blankenhorn, the commissioner whose district includes El Prado) but I was the lone protestant on the application to appropriate underground water from the wells.

In October of 2014 I participated in two pre-conference hearings with the applicant El Prado, its lawyer Jim Brockman, the OSE lawyer Brett Olsen, folks from the OSE water rights division, the OSE hearing examininer, Taos County Attorney Bob Malone, and I'm not quite sure who else because they let me participate by phone. Brockman explained the terms of each application, Bob Malone and I explained our opposition to the applications, and then we spent almost an hour discussing the schedule for each hearing. The hearing dates were set for June of 2015.

As I participated in these phone calls it became distressingly clear how difficult it is for an individual to devote the time and study necessary to come up with a list of witnesses to help defend her position, interview them, take their statements, appear at oral hearings, etc. That's what Brockman and his staff get paid to do. That's what Brett Olsen, the OSE attorney, and his vast OSE staff, get paid to do.

At the end of one of the pre-hearing conferences Brockman announced that El Prado was going to challenge my standing as a protestant. Which they did in a formal motion, claiming under state statute I didn't meet the criteria of being "substantially and specifically affected by the granting of this application."

I was challenged to show how the application would "substantially and specifically" impact me. Am I the public in the concept of public welfare? In my response to El Prado's motion to strike me as a protestant (I had 15 days to deliver my response upon receipt of their motion), I laid out how I, as an individual, would be affected under the criteria included in the public welfare ordinance. For example, I argued that the transfer of agricultural rights to underwrite development along the El Prado corridor would threaten both the traditional agricultural communities and the natural resources that make the Taos area, including the village of El Valle where I live, so unique and valuable.

But I also argued that as a citizen of Taos County I am affected by any water transfer application that is deemed detrimental to the public welfare of Taos County as defined in the Taos Regional Water Plan and Taos County Public Welfare Ordinance 2010-4. This particularly applies to the water transfers from the TOW region, where the water rights in question could be better put to use in their area of origin. The village of Questa needs to acquire additional water rights; the TOW rights owned by Santa Fe County that will be transferred to the Aamodt Settlement could be leased to Questa.

There were no surprises in El Prado's response to my response regarding my standing to protest. Brockman argued that as an individual I couldn't prove I had a "personal stake in the outcome of the case that would establish standing." Instead, he implied that because my "real motivation" was to support the Public Welfare Advisory Committee's recommendation that El Prado's applications are contrary to the public welfare of the citizens of Taos County, my protest was underhanded and without merit. He also spent a portion of the response arguing that I couldn't prove impairment of my water rights, despite the fact that I raised only the issue of public welfare, not impairment, in my protest. The OSE would make a decision whether to schedule oral arguments on this motion.

In January of 2015 I was given the opportunity to defend my right to protest at an oral hearing before the Hearing Examiner and the OSE Water Rights Division. The only ones in the room who weren't lawyers were the administrative assistant who was recording the proceeding, Candyce O'Donnell, the newly elected Taos County Commissioner from my district, John Painter, the head of El Prado Water and Sanitation District, and me. I was the only non-lawyer who got to talk, however.

After Jim Brockman, lawyer for El Prado, reiterated his claim that under state statute I didn't meet the criteria of being "substantially and specifically affected by the granting of this application," I presented my case. Again, a water transfer protest is evaluated on three criteria: that the transfer/appropriation would impair someone else's water rights; that it is contrary to the conservation of water; or that it's contrary to public welfare. My protest was based on the public welfare argument that has been defined by the Taos County Public Welfare Ordinance. I wasn't claiming that the drilling of the two new wells or the transfer of the TOW water would impair my water rights (I have water rights on two acequias in El Valle). I was arguing that as a citizen of Taos County the two applications are detrimental to the public welfare of all county citizens.

As I've discussed previously, public welfare has never actually been legally defined in case law in a water rights decision. I was pursuing my protest so that we could move towards a definition of what constitutes the public welfare regarding the movement of water.

Interestingly enough, at the oral hearing both El Prado and the OSE seemed more interested in whether I could legally argue that my water rights would be impaired by the applications. Brockman brought a map showing that my water rights in El Valle are not in the same watershed as the transfer and appropriation. The OSE water rights lawyers responded that the water El Prado wants to move isn't in the same watershed as the move-to wells, either, and that "water is being moved up and down the Rio Grande all the time from one watershed to another." The issue of impairment is often addressed in those hearings. I distinctly got the feeling that neither El Prado nor the OSE wanted to open the door to a public welfare argument, which actually might set a precedent.

Several weeks later we received the hearing examiner's decision: I was granted standing and the right to proceed with my protest. Reflecting the impression I had at the hearing, the OSE's decision addressed the issue of impairment—that I provided a "minimal amount of information" required for my continued participation pursuant to state statute: "An OSE analysis of the effects of granting an Application for Permit must incorporate all State Engineer permits and water rights including the water rights that Matthews allegedly owns." The only mention of public welfare was that El Prado based its motion to strike me as a protestant solely on the grounds of public welfare and conservation of water within the state.

But alas, ten days later Brockman filed another motion with the OSE— 14 pages this time—asking the State Engineer to reconsider the decision to allow me standing. Many of the pages reiterated the original argument that I hadn't proved I would be "substantially and specifically affected by the granting of this application," regarding either impairment or public welfare, and that the Hearing Examiner's decision created a "very expansive standard that assures that nearly every protestant will be able to withstand a challenge to his or her standing." Brockman also claimed that my protest would extend what could have been a hearing process of several months to one and a half to three years and cost each applicant $150,000 to $750,000 (how he came up with these figures I don't know). He also said that a decision by the hearing examiner on standing couldn't be appealed to district court until the case went through the entire hearing process. He went on to say that, comparatively, I had limited costs in time and resources. Au contraire, Mr. Brockman. While I wasn't planning on spending much (any) money, I was spending a lot of my time, and unlike him and the rest of the lawyers around the hearing table, I wasn't getting paid.

Ultimately, I struck out. A week or so later the OSE, at the behest of El Prado Water and Sanitation District, once again declined to hear a protest based on the concept of public welfare. The folks whose special interests have been met by the terms of the Abeyta Settlement don't want any scrutiny of those transactions, and bureaucracies like the OSE don't want to open the flood gates (pardon the pun) to protests that might define what public welfare means when it comes to moving water around the state.

The Water Rights Division (WRD) of the OSE wrote the 13-page response to El Prado's request to dismiss me. They didn't bother to consider my arguments that drilling new wells to meet El Prado's enormous increase in water use, and transferring water from northern Taos County to offset the pumping of those wells, is not in the best interests of the citizens of Taos County. Instead, they linked the concept of public welfare to that of impairment. The WRD insisted that had I proved I own a valid water right I might have met the evidentiary burden to show I would be "substantially and specifically impacted" by the appropriation and transfer, the statutory requirement for standing on impairment.

I repeatedly stated in my protest, and during oral arguments that I was not basing my protest on impairment, even though I am a valid water rights owner, but on the criteria of public welfare. It is also the requirement for standing on that issue to prove that I would be "substantially and specifically impacted," but they didn't consider any of the evidence I presented in my protest or in my oral hearing. The WRD denied me standing saying that the hearing examiner's previous decision to grant me standing on impairment because I proved a "minimal amount of information" regarding my ownership of water rights didn't meet the standard of "substantial and specific" impact.

Confused? So was I. As far as I could figure, the WRD was using a Catch 22 to get rid of me: because I failed to prove I have water rights, even though I wasn't arguing impairment, I didn't have standing to argue public welfare.

However convoluted this entire process was, the intent was very clear: El Prado and the other parties to the Abeyta Settlement don't want any oversight on the behind-closed-door deals they made and the state doesn't want anyone messing around in the settlement either. But there was also some good news in the WRD response. The agency seemed to be just as annoyed with El Prado and Jim Brockman as the rest of us are. In Brockman's motion to reconsider my standing, he accused the hearing examiner of departing from historical OSE practices on standing determinations, claiming that protestants have to prove their standing in their written protests. The WRD letter refuted that assertion, citing state statute and saying it would "raise due process issues." In a revealing footnote the response states: "El Prado's contention that the WRD and Hearing Examiner have departed from longstanding agency positions is inaccurate. Instead, El Prado is making the same arguments for changing OSE practices as have been presented by El Prado's counsel [Jim Brockman] in other cases in which they represent water rights applicants."

Brockman also complained in his motion for reconsideration that my protest had placed an undue burden on El Prado. The WRD reminded him that the burden of proof in any protest lies upon the applicant. Whether or not the protest goes forward it is incumbent upon any applicant to "prepare for and present evidence . . . on all statutory bases" before the OSE before the application can be granted.

So that ended my tenure as a water rights transfer protestant. There would be no argument based on public welfare and no chance for the establishment of case law on the concept of public welfare. We would have to wait and see how Taos County's protest of the Top of the World water transfer to Santa Fe County played out, the subject of Chapter Thirty-eight.

Thirty-three

Dam the Gila River?

In 2014 the Interstate Stream Commission (ISC) was charged with making a decision by the end of the year whether to move forward with a billion dollar diversion project under the Arizona Water Settlements Act on the Gila River, in southwestern New Mexico, the last major undammed river in the state.

Under the terms of the 2004 Arizona Water Settlements Act, New Mexico was allotted 14,000 acre feet per year (afy) of Gila River water in exchange for Central Arizona Project water for the Gila Tribe in Arizona. New Mexico is entitled to $6.6 million a year for 10 years for non-diversion water projects; if the ISC went ahead with a diversion project the federal government would grant additional funds up to $62 million.

Opponents of the proposed diversion claimed the commission has never provided sufficient evidence to prove the diversion is fundamentally feasible or that it would produce enough water to justify the cost. The project would store water in reservoirs and pump it to southwestern municipalities, although it's unclear who will actually get the water and how much it will cost. The largest irrigable landowner in the Cliff-Gila Valley happens to be the giant gold and copper mining corporation Freeport Mc-MoRan, a likely candidate for the diverted water. Opponents also claimed that the ISC has vastly under estimated the price tag of the diversion, which they say would cost more than $1 billion.

Former ISC director Norm Gaume, who served from 1997 to 2002, claims the ISC has been misled by staff over the potential cost of the project and its feasibility. In testimony and in a report presented to the ISC at its monthly meeting in Tucumcari on April 30, 2014, Gaume told commissioners that the Gila River diversion proposal under consideration "would produce little or no water but with major waste of money, time and effort."[47]

Not only did he question the fundamental foundation of the project, he also sued the commission over violations of the Open Meetings Act in a petition for a temporary restraining order and injunction. The suit claimed that the commission's Gila subcommittee had met regularly since 2010 without issuing public notice or opening the meetings to citizens.

A State District Court judge issued a temporary restraining order barring the ISC from taking any action on the Gila diversion until an October 30th hearing when both sides presented their cases. The judge kept the restraining order in place but allowed the ISC to schedule its regular meeting for Monday, November 10. Another hearing regarding the restraining order was held on November 12.

The ISC staff recommended to the commission that 90 percent of the available funding be used for the diversion while 10 percent, or $7.85 million, be allocated for non-diversion alternatives. The restraining order, filed by Gaume, was lifted on November 20 but no decision was made regarding his Open Meetings Act violation lawsuit. On November 24, the ISC voted to move forward with the Gila River diversion. Adding insult to injury, the ISC countersued Gaume in January of 2015, claiming he needed to pay the ISC back—$100,000 worth—for the time and expense (these are state employees paid by taxpayer monies) of defending the agency. This kind of action looks just like a SLAPP suit, or strategic lawsuit against public participation, that puts citizens at risk of being sued for challenging their government (the New Mexico legislature adopted an anti-SLAPP law in 2001). The ACLU defended Gaume: "People in our country have a fundamental right to petition their government concerning matters of public importance. When the ISC files a lawsuit seeking exorbitant amounts of money in retaliation for the simple act of speaking out, it has a chilling effect on the ability of citizens to participate in public processes." (Statement by Daniel Yohalem, a Santa Fe civil rights attorney working with the ACLU.)

The groups fighting this plan—Gila Conservation Coalition, Sierra Club, Audubon Society—and the many individuals, including Gaume, made substantive arguments against it. There is ample evidence, which the ISC has ignored, that the amount of water will be less than half the 14,000 acre foot yield that is allocated in the settlement. After Gaume obtained the model spreadsheet used to calculate water availability (under the Inspection of Public Records Act), he was able to calculate that the model results show an annual quantity of available diversion water at 8,000 afy, not 14,000 afy. In testimony before the state legislature in October of 2014 Gaume claimed the "fatally flawed" engineering report on the proposed diversion was reviewed by a consultant hired by the ISC in March of 2014 that found "The expected [reservoir] seepage, when combined with evaporation loses, could easily equal or succeed the planned minimum annual diversion of 10,000 afy, which would result in no available usable water from the project."

Taxpayers would have to supplement the $66 million funding provided under the Arizona Water Settlement Act to meet the projected diversion cost of over a billion dollars. In his report Gaume also showed evidence that rates for project beneficiaries would more than double and that operational and energy costs (water will have to be pumped across the Continental Divide) have not been factored into the process.

The proposed diversion would also hugely impact the headwaters of the Gila River, habitat for federally listed endangered birds, fish, and snakes. Proposed reservoirs would reduce small floods and high-flow pulses that are important for the plant and animal life in this riparian corridor.[48]

With still no final design or exact location for the diversion, but having already spent millions, the ISC may fail to make the 2019 deadline for receiving the full federal subsidy.

Thirty-four

Acequia Madre Objects to the Terms of the Abeyta

In 2015 the Abeyta Adjudication Settlement had been signed and sealed but not yet delivered, and the parciantes on the Acequia Madre del Rio Lucero y del Arroyo Seco were trying to keep it that way. As I've discussed previously, the settlement agreement called for transferring water rights from a Questa acequia to two Aquifer Storage and Recovery (ASR) wells that would augment the Acequia Madre's irrigation. The water would be diverted from the Rio Lucero in the winter, stored in ASR wells until spring, then pumped from the wells and transported via pipeline to the acequias. The majority of the parciantes were saying this is a bad idea.

The communities of El Salto and Arroyo Seco, that the Acequia Madre serves, are two of the most beautiful in the Taos Valley. Nestled at the foot of Taos Mountain, just north of Taos Pueblo, you see their verdant pastures as you travel SH 150 towards the Taos Ski Valley. But like the Arroyo Hondo and Valdez communities, they, too, have seen residential development where the rich men's houses divvy up the fields and raise land prices commensurate with the already inflated properties in Taos. The communities remain diverse, however, a mixture of Anglo and Hispano, both of whom object to the wells.

One might ask why, at this late stage of the game—the settlement was signed in 2010—were the parciantes objecting to what would appear to be a beneficial project? Because, according to the parciantes, the water transfer was unnecessary, an abrogation of another community's water, a financial burden on the acequia (in maintaining the ASR wells), and a scheme that was never endorsed by the members of the acequia. Fundamentally, it was an issue of the lack of transparency in the Abeyta Settlement.

Palemon Martinez is chairman of the board of the TVAA and former secretary of the Acequia Madre del Rio Lucero y del Arroyo Seco. Remember, unbeknownst to most of the parciantes on the Acequia Madre, Martinez negotiated a water transfer to the acequia, paid for by the federal government and the state of New Mexico, to compensate the ditch for a "taking" from the Rio Lucero by Taos Pueblo in 1935. The transfer is from the Llano Community Ditch in Questa. Martinez contracted with Lawrence Ortega of Questa, as far back as 2005, to transfer 91.592 acre feet of water rights from his father Bernabe Ortega's estate that were severed from the land in the 1960s. The Interstate Stream Commission (ISC), which controls the funding, distributed $350,000 to the Acequia Madre in 2008 for the purchase of the water rights.

No one outside of the negotiating team knew about this proposed transfer and contract, including parciantes on the Acequia Madre, until 2013 when Martinez filed an application with the Office of the State Engineer (OSE) to transfer the water. In August of that year I chaired a meeting of the Taos County Public Welfare Advisory Committee to review the proposed transfer. The three-hour long August meeting was contentious, to say the least. Martinez was at the meeting with TVAA lawyer Rebecca Dempsey (Cuddy & McCarthy law firm) to present his case. Alfred Trujillo, who was one of the founders of the TVAA, was there to debate Martinez over the history of the Acequia Madre (he claims the Arroyo Seco area has the most junior water rights in the Valley) and object to the transfer. Jeannie Masters, a commissioner on the Llano Community Ditch, was there to say the proposed transfer would impair the other parciantes on her ditch who have been sharing the water rights for many years. She also had a letter signed by other members of the Ortega family contesting Lawrence Ortega's claim that as the personal representative of his father's estate he owns all the water rights. Lawrence Ortega was there to claim his father had previously offered the water rights to the village of Questa but it turned him down. Joe Cisneros from Questa was there to point out that the molybdenum mine is using all of Questa's water and the area cannot afford to lose any more. Former district judge Peggy Nelson, who lives in San Cristobal, was there to say that during a time of terrible drought water needs to stay in its area of origin. Tony Trujillo of La Llama was there to remind us that this was all paper water we were talking about: for several previous years the acequias hadn't been able to deliver their allotted water to parciantes in the Taos Valley or in Questa.

The Public Welfare Committee voted six to two to recommend that the Board of County Commissioners protest this application based upon our evaluation of its impact on the public welfare of Taos citizens. One of the committee members who voted against the recommendation represented the Arroyo Seco subregion and is a parciante on the Acequia Madre, and the other member who voted against the transfer cited the need to fulfill the terms of the Abeyta Settlement. At the Advisory Committee meeting one of the members asked Martinez, "How do you feel about taking water rights from another acequia?" He responded, "They're private rights."

The county commission and staff caved into the power brokers behind the Abeyta Adjudication Settlement and failed to schedule a hearing to consider the Public Welfare Advisory Committee's recommendation that it protest Martinez's application. The Llano Community Ditch, along with the Cabresto Irrigation District, filed protests of the transfer to the OSE. Several individual protests were filed as well but were either deemed untimely or dismissed for lack of standing.

While all of this was transpiring at the county administrative level, the parciantes of the Acequia Madre del Rio Lucero y del Arroyo Seco were educating themselves about the terms of the Abeyta Settlement and taking a more proactive role in the acequia's management. In March of 2015 the parciantes ousted Martinez as a commissioner and treasurer Fermin Torres resigned. Leo Valencia and Chris Pieper were elected to replace them. The new commissioners began the process of updating the acequia bylaws and investigating the ditch's fiscal management. One parciante raised the issue of a conflict of interest regarding Martinez: as chair of the TVAA he negotiated the state funding to facilitate the Questa water rights transfer to the ditch on which he served as commission secretary.

Over the course of 2015 there were confrontations between the new commission and Martinez and Dempsey, who continued to push for the new commission's approval of the Ortega transfer. Contract documents with the Ortega estate needed to be executed and a Trust established for payments for both the water rights purchase and to pay Dempsey's law firm for her services by December 31 of 2015 or the funding would revert to the state. The contract wasn't executed until June of 2016 but the funding remained in two Acequia Madre accounts. The commissioners accused Martinez and Dempsey of proceeding without the approval or necessary signatures of the commissioners. Complicating all of this was the fact that while Dempsey officially represented the TVAA, she didn't have a separate contract with the Acequia Madre del Rio Lucero y del Arroyo Seco.

In August of 2015 new acequia bylaws were approved that include the 2003 state statutes that allow acequia commissions to deny transfers of water rights from the acequia if they are deemed detrimental to the acequia and its members and to set up a water bank to temporarily re-allocate water for beneficial use within the acequia.

In March of 2016 the Llano Community Ditch and Cabresto Irrigation District, which also serves the Questa community, reached a settlement on their protest of the Ortega water transfer and the OSE approved the transfer, although the amount of water that the OSE deemed transferrable was reduced from the original application of 91.952 afy to 23.917 afy. Final payment for these rights was set at $250,000, which comes to almost $10,500 per acre foot.

According to Esther Garcia of the Cabresto Irrigation District, the OSE put pressure on her commission to drop its protest as it "wasn't their fight, it was Llano's fight," even though the Llano Ditch is dependent upon Cabresto water availability. The OSE argued that the small amount of transferred water realistically won't affect the amount of wet water that Cabresto can rely on and that the Llano Community Ditch's protest was "hypothetical" in that the land appurtenant to the transferred water had been dried up for decades and again, the amount of wet water Llano would get would probably not be impacted by the loss of the 23.917 afy of water in the transfer. Llano agreed to settle and was awarded $27,764 to cover the loss of ditch fees that the Ortegas would have paid over the years.

In a letter to OSE attorney Arianne Singer, and cc'd to various local officials, Acequia Madre Commissioner Pieper laid out these objections to the Abeyta Settlement wells:

• The costs of the ASR operation are way beyond the capability of our acequia. Schlumberger Engineering in Florida that specializes in ASR wells gave us a generic estimate based on the proposed well depths and GPM of over $100,000 a year. Our yearly budget is a fraction of that. The Abeyta Settlement provides 'up to' $121,000 for well assistance.

• The 90'x140' metal building that will house the treatment equipment for the injection well will dramatically affect the visual landscape of our small rural community.

• The injection water will be chlorinated and chemically treated to adjust its pH to match the ground water. Our community does not want chemically treated water injected into our aquifer.

• Our bylaws specifically state that acequia water is gravity fed stream water only. We cannot allow ground water to be pumped into our acequia – period.

• There is a strong possibility that water pumped from 1,000 ft will contain uranium and other toxins. It is not known how chlorinated, oxygenated water will react with ground water at that depth."

The letter also objected to the settlement alternative of a reservoir should the ASR wells prove unfeasible, and the fact that both storage options "call for the historic Rio Lucero ditch to be replaced with a 6,500 foot plastic culvert pipe. The Rio Lucero ditch was hand dug in 1759 and is a testament to our history with Taos Pueblo. It is also a living stream

Mayordomo Arnold Quintana and commissioner Chris Pieper on the historic Rio Lucero acequia. Photo by Anwar Kaelin

222

system supporting a healthy riparian habitat."

Pieper asked that the commission "meet with the State Engineers Office to pursue the return of these water rights to the state and investigate other options to protect acequia water."

When I spoke with Pieper he gave me a copy of a 2002 letter from Taos Pueblo Governor Vincent Lujan to Acequia Madre del Rio Lucero y del Arroyo Seco Commissioner Fermin Torres. The letter was in response to a request from the Acequia that the Pueblo allocate additional water to fill the acequia parciantes' livestock ponds because of drought conditions and to maintain a continuous flow of water in the acequia. The letter says, "in the spirit of cooperation and good will and our desire to help you minimize the hardship that this drought has placed on all of us, we agreed that we could divert additional flows into the Acequia Madre del Rio Lucero for two days out of the week without affecting our people." Pieper lamented that this, the traditional custom of repartimiento, could have obviated priority administration adjudications and settlements that call in the lawyers and engineers to move water out of watersheds and run up the big bucks. But that's not how it works anymore.

Thirty-five

Top of the World Transfer Application Finally Filed

Unbeknownst to anyone in Taos County, Santa Fe County and the Bureau of Indian Affairs (BIA) filed an application with the Office of the State Engineer (OSE) on January 12, 2015 to transfer 1,752 acre feet of water rights from Top of the World Farm (TOW) in northern Taos County to the Pojoaque Valley to meet the terms of the Aamodt Settlement. The BIA, under the Department of the Interior, was the applicant for the 1,141 afy that it purchased from Santa Fe on behalf of Pojoaque, Nambe, Tesuque, and San Ildefonso pueblos, while the county applied for 611 afy of non-pueblo water rights.

The Taos County Public Welfare Ordinance, passed in November of 2010, requires any entity that files an application with the OSE to transfer water within or from Taos County to concurrently file a copy of the application with the Taos County Clerk. This notification allows the Public Welfare Advisory Committee, established under the auspices of the Ordinance, to then start the process of analyzing the application using the Ordinance's public welfare criteria to determine whether the transfer is in the best interest of the citizens of Taos County. Neither Santa Fe County nor the BIA filed their application with the Taos County Clerk, and I only found out that the application had been filed after *Santa Fe New Mexican* reporter Staci Matlock told me in March.[49] I called Santa Fe County attorney John Utton to verify that the county and the BIA never filed the application with the clerk's office, which he confirmed. He was unaware of the Ordinance and indicated that it was not his responsibility to address the fact that Santa Fe County and the BIA were in violation of the Taos County Public Welfare Ordinance.

So three months transpired during which the Public Welfare Advisory Committee could have been doing due diligence on the TOW transfer application. There were many questions to ask and much information to gather regarding the hydrological basis of this transfer. The Aamodt Settlement's rationale for the transfer, based on OSE modeling, was that

224

because the deep irrigation wells at the Top of the World Farm would be shut down—the area has been farmed over many years, by many different owners—the water in the underground aquifer would migrate to the Rio Grande and flow downstream to the takeout on San Ildefonso Pueblo to supply the water deliver system to the pueblos and non-pueblo parties in the Pojoaque Valley. Over 700 of the non-pueblo water rights owners, referred to as "defendants" in the Aamodt adjudication process, filed objections to the settlement, many of which concerned the water delivery system. One hundred and ninety of those defendants also filed a lawsuit against the Aamodt settlement in May of 2014.

According to the settlement, the water for the delivery system will be taken from the Rio Grande at San Ildefonso Pueblo, by either diverting the surface water into a side intake structure or by collecting groundwater that is hydrologically connected to the river through the use of horizontal collector wells or infiltration gallery. This idea of a collector was first put forward back in the late 1990s when Santa Fe County proposed that a Ranney Collector be used to divert Top of the World water rights to the Buckman Well Field, the city and county's main water source, to offset over pumping and allow for future development.

The diverted water would be treated at a water treatment facility and transmitted to Aquifer Storage and Recovery wells (ASR). This concept has become more common in the last 10 to 15 years, largely because of its economic benefits—as opposed to the capital outlay for a reservoir or storage tanks—and because of already depleted aquifers that the injected water can help restore. The Bureau of Reclamation, charged with promulgating the Environmental Impact Statement for the regional water system, would have to prove the feasibility of the proposed ASR system by drilling wells to make sure the contained system won't mix with other aquifers (as it turned out, the ASR wells proved to be unviable and another storage system had to be developed).

All of this was going to cost a lot of money, of course, and the bill for the Pojoaque Basin Regional Water System grew steadily, climbing from the original $163 million (as stated on the Santa Fe County web site) in 2006 dollars to over $200 million in 2015. While cost increase indexes are factored into the settlement legislation, many of the original estimates for various components of the project, including the ASR wells, may be well below actual costs. Another major concern was that as the drought continued the imported water slated for the settlement—both San Juan/Chama and TOW—might end up being paper, not wet water. And members of the Pojoaque Basin Water Alliance (PBWA), the group of non-pueblo valley residents who have consistently opposed the water delivery system to non-pueblos residents, were wondering if Santa Fe County, which would be responsible for operating the water system for the first 10 years, has the capacity to enforce the terms of the agreement. The settlement stipulated that the terms of the settlement must be fulfilled by September 15, 2017.

The Public Welfare Advisory Committee recommended to the Taos County Commission that it protest the application to transfer TOW water rights, which it did unanimously at its April 21, 2015 meeting. The County would argue that the transfer is not in the public interest of the citizens of Taos County, based on the recommendation of the Public Welfare Advisory Committee. Actually *winning* a case based on a public welfare argument would be an uphill battle, particularly in light of the fact that the OSE has been a partner in the settling of both the Pojoaque Valley Aamodt Adjudication and the Taos Valley Abeyta Adjudication and is the agency through which state funding to pay for these settlements is funneled. As I discussed previously, the Taos County Commission failed to protest watershed transfers within the Abeyta Settlement that the Public Welfare Advisory Committee also recommended be protested. The following editorial that I wrote for the *Taos News* (April 23-29) explains why people urged the County to protest water transfers in both adjudication settlements:

"In the April 12 online *Taos News* article 'Taos County farm transfer a paper-water loss, but a wet-water gain,' J.R. Logan quotes New Mexico Tech hydrologist Peggy Johnson on the pending water rights transfer from Top of the World (TOW) to the Pojoaque Valley: 'I've never really understood what the drama was over transferring those water rights out of the county . . . it ultimately goes back in the river, it just means a healthier river corridor.' This statement begs a response that addresses the larger issues that are in play: local autonomy; the commodification and marketing of water; and the integrity of the commons.

As a journalist I've covered the promulgation of both the Aamodt Adjudication Settlement in the Pojoaque Valley and the Taos Valley Abeyta Adjudication Settlement. Initially, I thought the Abeyta the better of the two agreements, as it seemed to adhere to a philosophy that with proper management Taos Valley could meet its present and future water needs without the movement of water from watershed to watershed. The Aamodt, on the other hand, proposed to move 1,700 acre feet of water from TOW to the Pojoaque Valley for a water delivery system that many of its parties—there are over 700 Objectors to the terms of the settlement—didn't want in the first place.

Then we found out about the back-room deals that propose to move water from watersheds that were not parties to the Abeyta, outside the Taos Valley, to watersheds within the valley and into the hands of the water brokers who have leveraged millions of dollars from the state of New Mexico to underwrite this movement of water. It's not only a sweet deal for Taos Pueblo, whose first priority standing has largely dictated the terms of the settlement, but for the longtime power brokers in the Valley who will determine how these waters are put to beneficial use: to lease downstream; to underwrite the expansion of the Taos Airport; to support policies that encourage the growth of more houses, more resorts, and more amenities whose economic contribution to the community is poor paying service jobs and ultimately more people whose inherited wealth does not trickle down.

As far back as 2004 Santa Fe County told the protestants of the county's original application to transfer 588 acre feet of TOW water that if the second application to transfer the remaining 1,100 afy was protested, the county would try to acquire the San Juan/Chama water rights that were slated for the Abeyta Settlement. As Logan reported in the *Taos News*, when Santa Fe County proposed trading TOW water rights for the San Juan/Chama water rights, the Abeyta water brokers turned it down. Why? San Juan/Chama water is more marketable, particularly below Otowi Gauge (which separates the upper Rio Grande basin from the middle and lower basins), and Taos Pueblo, along with the other Abeyta parties, want to be able to market the water. Santa Fe County's interests are really no different; in the late 1990s, when it acquired the first installment of TOW water, the plan was to pipe it across the Otowi Gauge directly to the city and county of Santa Fe.

The Water Advisory Committee did its due diligence at the April 6 hearing and unanimously recommended that the county commission protest the proposed transfer of the TOW water rights based on criteria that help define the public welfare of the citizens of Taos County."

The BIA and County of Santa Fe published the required notice of the TOW water transfer application in June of 2015 and in July Taos County and several other parties filed protests with the OSE.

Taos County's protest claimed that the county has standing as a political subdivision of the state and that the Taos County Public Welfare Ordinance and Taos County Regional Water Plan both call upon the OSE to use local input to evaluate the impact of an application on water conservation and the public welfare. The county officially protested that the transfer is detrimental to the public welfare, contrary to the conservation of water, impairs existing water rights, and fails to comply with the New Mexico State Constitution and OSE regulations.

Several individuals who live in the Pojoaque Valley and are parties to the Aamodt Adjudication filed protests that the transfer would impair water rights and is contrary to public welfare. They are members of an organization called Northern New Mexicans Protecting Land, Water, and Rights (NNMProtects) that opposes the terms of the Aamodt Adjudication Settlement. Specifically, they pointed out that because the type and point of diversion at the move-to area on the Rio Grande had yet to be identified, the OSE could not adequately assess or identify any impairments "that will ultimately reduce the available surface water in the Rio Grande via the Pojoaque Basin Regional Water System." Public welfare arguments were also based on the reduction of Rio Grande surface water and the fact that other Aamodt Settlement agreements have not been executed.

Another protest from long time Questa activist Juan Montes argued that the transfer was detrimental to the public welfare and would impair water rights. Montes claimed that divorcing water from the land and selling it outside of its watershed is detrimental to the public welfare, that reducing the flow of the Rio Grande will impair other water rights, and that the beneficial use of the water by Santa Fe County had not been substantiated.

Over a year would pass before the actual hearing before the OSE took place. I will discuss the outcome in a subsequent chapter.

Thirty-six

San Augustin Plains Water Grab

Another water transfer case has lingered in the Office of the State Engineer (OSE), this one since 2007. More preposterous than Top of the World, and more frightening, is the proposed Plains of San Augustin water grab that would see 54,000 acre feet of water transferred from west-central New Mexico, between Socorro and Datil, to . . . where? That's the 64,000-dollar question and why this case has had a life span of nine years. The applicant, Augustin Plains Ranch LLC, wants to pump these thousands of acre feet of water from 37 wells to a location the applicant has failed to identify but would obviously be the more populated areas of the state along the Rio Grande corridor: Albuquerque, Rio Rancho, Belen, Socorro and other municipalities.

Augustin Plains Ranch LLC first filed the transfer application in 2007, which was protested by approximately 80 individuals and groups represented by the New Mexico Environmental Law Center. The OSE denied the application on March 30, 2012, basing its decision on state law that requires dismissal of any application that fails to specify any particular purpose or place of use of water or end user. The Ranch appealed the OSE's decision in 2012 in the Catron County Seventh Judicial District Court, but the Court granted the protestants' motion for summary judgment (Memorandum Decision) and on January 3, 2013 denied the Ranch's appeal of the OSE decision to deny the water transfer. The Ranch then appealed this decision to the State Court of Appeals but also filed an amended application to the OSE in 2014 (in fact two applications, in July and December) while the case was still pending in court. Then the Ranch withdrew its appeal and made a motion to the Catron County Court that it remand the matter back to the OSE. The Court denied that motion on February 8, 2016, and closed the case. The 2014 amended applications were almost identical to the 2007 application and again failed to specify where the water would be transferred.

The most recent "Corrected" application was filed on April 28, 2016 and published September 7, 2016. Once again the application failed to specify where or to whom the water will go. This is as specific as it gets: "for municipal purposes, including, but not limited to the following municipal entities and their service areas; the Village of Magdalena, the City of Socorro, the City of Belen, the Village of Los Lunas, the Albuquerque Bernalillo County Water Utility Authority and the City of Rio Rancho, and commercial bulk water sales in parts of Catron, Sierra, Socorro, Valencia, Bernalillo, Sandoval and Santa Fe Counties, limited to those portions that lie within the geographic boundaries of the Rio Grande Basin, including various municipal and investor owned utilities, commercial enterprises, and state and federal government agencies, including the U.S. Bureau of Reclamation and the New Mexico Interstate Stream Commission whereby groundwater would be directly discharged to the Rio Grande."

The New Mexico Environmental Law Center again represented the protestants, and on September 12, 2016, submitted a motion to the Catron County Seventh Judicial District Court that the Court re-open its 2012 Memorandum Decision (denying the Ranch's appeal of the OSE's rejection of the water transfer) so that the Court could order the OSE to reject the Ranch's amended 2016 application, which includes the same defects that caused the OSE to deny the application in the first place.

The OSE appeared to regard all of these applications as one. They all have the same filing number, RG-89943, and the agency determined that any protests filed in response to the original 2007 application "are considered timely for this corrected application and notice of publication."

Many of the Datil-area protestants believe that if the water transfer is approved, the Ranch, which owns 17,000 acres, will mine their rural water resources to supply the more populated areas of the state at great profit. The Ranch, on its website,[50] boasts that the "proposed Augustin Plains Ranch water pipeline project, much like the San Juan/Chama River Project before it, has tremendous potential to supply New Mexico's middle Rio Grande Valley with an abundance of water for centuries to come." It also states that it will "take advantage of the ranch's unique location to enhance recharge and replace all of the pumped water with rain water and snowmelt currently being lost to evaporation. No water mining would occur." How it plans to do this, at least from the information posted on the website, is unclear. A statement in the amended December 2014 application doesn't provide any more detail: "Applicant also intends to construct enhanced recharge facilities which will collect runoff that would otherwise evaporate in the Plains of Augustin. This water will augment the groundwater in the aquifer and offset the amount that is pumped from the Applicant's wells. Applicant requests that offset be recognized for these enhanced recharge projects in an amount to be determined at the hearing [before the OSE]."

In the summer of 2017 the Catron County Seventh Judicial District Court rejected the Law Center's motion that the Court re-open its 2012 Memorandum Decision denying the Ranch's appeal of the OSE's rejection of the water transfer. The case is now once again being heard before the OSE Hearing Officer. On a positive note, at a hearing at the Court in December of 2017 Chris Lindeen, deputy general counsel at the OSE, stated that while the application is complete and the OSE is required to hold a hearing, in his opinion the San Augustin Plains Ranch application is speculative and violates the prior appropriation doctrine. "So, the water rights division recommends that the State Engineer dismiss or deny the application based on speculation."

Just as this book went to press in August of 2018 the State Engineer accepted this recommendation and once again denied the transfer as "speculative."

Thirty-seven

Maintaining Traditional Acequia Systems in a World of Technological Fixes

Back in 2012 when *La Jicarita* first went online I wrote an essay called "The Political Economy of Acequias: From Democratic Communalism to Business as Usual?"[51] In it I lamented the "internecine bickering and demographic changes" within the communities of el norte that were elevating the concept of "efficiency" over that of traditional management: "Ditch banks are cleared of all vegetation and more and bigger culverts carry the water more 'efficiently' despite the loss of riparian habitat and groundwater recharge. Ditch fees rise every year due to increased payments for cleaning, maintenance, and improvements that are decided and implemented by the commissioners, often without the approval or oversight of the rest of the parciantes."

In 2016 several acequia projects were contested by their parciantes, indicative of this situation. As I discussed in Chapter Thirty, controversy arose over the proposed transfer of acequia water rights from Questa to the Taos Valley under the auspices of the Abeyta Settlement. One hundred acre feet of water from the Llano Community Ditch in Questa would be transferred to two Aquifer Storage and Recovery (ASR) wells to augment the Acequia Madre del Rio Lucero y del Arroyo Seco's irrigation. The water would be diverted from the Rio Lucero in the winter, stored in ARS wells until spring, then pumped from the wells and transported via pipeline to the acequia. The parciantes on the receiving end of the transfer, which has been approved by the Office of the State Engineer, have declared that the water transfer is unnecessary, an abrogation of another community's water, a financial burden on the acequia, and a scheme that was never endorsed by the members of the acequia.

Another contested situation involved the community of Llano, near Peñasco, where a former commissioner of the Acequia del Llano de San Juan Nepomuceno promulgated a $2.5 million dollar pipeline project on the upper feeder section of the ditch called the Acequia Madre Cañon.

The Army Corps of Engineers conducted a draft environmental assessment and funding through the Interstate Stream Commission (17.5 percent of the project) and Army Corps of Engineers (75 percent) was generated, with an acequia commitment of 7.5 percent. Approximately 220 parciantes on the ditch would share this debt. Parciantes objected to the project as a "boondoggle" and "overkill," suggesting that a much less costly project could help maintain the earthen ditch rather than replacing it with a pipe three quarters of a mile long.

Unfortunately, both of these controversial projects illustrate that the accumulation of power into the hands of a few disenfranchises the rest of the community. Whether this accumulation is due to internecine quarrels that discourage acequia participation, or due to the changing demographics of the community—an older generation of parciantes, the migration of the next generation to the cities, second homeowners—it diminishes their democratic nature. As I discussed previously, in the case of the Acequia Madre del Rio Lucero y del Arroyo Seco, the president of the board of the Taos Valley Acequia Association, Palemon Martinez, negotiated the concept of the ASR wells behind closed doors as a party to the Abeyta Settlement. As both president of the TVAA and a commissioner on the Acequia Madre he was able to sign off on the settlement without the knowledge and/or approval of the parciantes on the acequia.

In the case of the Llano de San Juan acequia, a previous commission, led by Bonafacio Vasquez, first began pursuing funding for repair of the Acequia Madre Cañon in the mid 2000s. Llano de San Juan stretches several miles long above the Peñasco Valley and below the looming Jicarita Peak on the Rio Chiquito. It's home to the former Hog Farm commune and several thriving vegetable farms that utilize its extensive acequia system. According to several parciantes *La Jicarita* spoke with, Jean Nichols, Tanya Leherissey (mayordoma of one section of the San Juan acequia), and Pablo Tafoya (mayordomo of the other section), the original proposal that was voted on by the parciantes back in 2009 called for a short section of replacement cement pipe in an area of the ditch that needed shoring up. As the years dragged on and Vasquez continued to pursue funding, the proposed project became much larger and more costly and, according to these same parciantes, little information trickled down. Tafoya told

La Jicarita that any time a change was made in the scope of the project it was the duty of the commission to inform the parciantes and obtain approval (Vasquez was a commissioner until October of 2015). The parciantes claimed that Vasquez exaggerated the need for extensive repairs in his reports to the Corps that the rest of the community never saw. They stressed that previous maintenance work with a track-a-hoe had adequately addressed any problems on the Acequia Madre Cañon.

Vasquez was present at many of the meetings in the Peñasco area that were held in 2009 to object to the position of the Untied States Forest Service that acequias must obtain a special use permit to conduct rehabilitation projects that lie within the boundaries of the national forest. He acceded to the USFS demands and obtained a special use permit to avoid losing the acequia's funding, which he claimed was vulnerable to any delay.

The Army Corps of Engineers issued a draft environmental assessment in late 2015 and many parciantes submitted comments questioning the project. Before a final EA was released, however, some of the property owners whose lands the pipeline would cross (none of whom are parciantes on the acequia) objected to the project and several hired an attorney to represent their concerns. They didn't want to see the acequia habitat negatively impacted or want a construction and maintenance road bulldozed through their property. There was also contention over how wide the acequia easement is for maintenance, which was raised at an acequia meeting where parciantes came prepared with proxies to vote up or down on the project. Representatives of the Corps told the parciantes that it was the parciantes responsibility to resolve the easement issues and that the project would be tabled in the meantime. When I called Patty Phillips, the Army Corps of Engineers project director, she told me that the acequia documents submitted by Vasquez, which stipulate a 36 foot maintenance easement, were approved by Taos District Attorney Donald Gallegos and that the Corps would go ahead and release the final EA.

There are other unresolved issues that pertain to these kinds of improvement projects. What are the safety and maintenance regulations surrounding pipelines or ASR wells? Who will conduct the maintenance and what is the overall cost? What are the consequences of defaulting on the loans—loss of water rights? How would the acequias assign the individual

Acequia Madre Cañon.   *Photo by Jean Nichols*

costs to each parciante—by individual or by water right?

In March of 2004[52] I reported on New Mexico State University's Sustainable Agriculture Science Center's project to document the relationship of acequia water to groundwater recharge and the rate of return of acequia water to its parent river. The research, conducted by Sam Fernald, estimates that the rate of return is close to 50 percent, which is the credit the Office of the State Engineer allows, and that acequias raise the level of the groundwater table, create riparian environments, and remediate groundwater as well. This study underwrites the value of maintaining our traditional acequia systems to keep farmland in agricultural production and improve both water quality and quantity through aquifer recharge. Technologies that are intended to conserve water don't address the fact that there's a key connection between surface and groundwater supplies.

When acequia commissions apply for funding for maintenance and rehabilitation projects through the ISC or the Army Corps of Engineers they become beholden to bureaucratic requirements. While some of these projects are vitally necessary for the integrity of the acequia, too many others burden the acequia with debt, create dry zones in former wetlands, increase maintenance requirements, compromise safety, and perhaps eventuate a reduction in water rights as conserved water becomes easier to transfer. Efficiency becomes loss.

Finally, in September of 2016 the Acequia del Llano de San Juan Nepomuceno parciantes voted overwhelmingly, 75 to 23, to cancel the three-quarter mile long, five-foot wide plastic pipe slated to replace their earthen Acequia Madre Cañon. While it was a victory for a small community, engaged in small-scale agriculture, the ramifications are much larger: traditional acequia systems can be maintained through active parciante participation despite changing demographics that often propel acequias to accept overbuilt solutions that burden them with debt and destroy riparian habitat and aquifer recharge.

On the heels of the decision in Llano San Juan to cancel its costly acequia rehab project, the communities of Chamisal and Ojito voted to also stop their $2.7 million project with the Corps for many of the same reasons. The two projects originate from the same presa, or headgate on the Santa Barbara River, near Hodges Campground, and both utilize feeder acequias that lead to their communities. The communities of Chamisal and Ojito, located on SH 76 west of Peñasco, lie even further away from the Santa Barbara headgate than Llano de San Juan. It was these feeder ditches that were slated to be replaced by large diameter plastic pipe for over a mile each.

The Acequias de Chamisal y Ojito parciantes, like those in Llano, were concerned about incurring debt, the maintenance requirements of the pipe, and the drastic restructuring of an earthen ditch. According to Commission Chair Samuel Lopez, in an interview[53] with Taos radio station Cultural Energy the day before a meeting to vote on the project, it was first proposed in 2005 to address problems in the Acequia Cañon and in 2006 a committee was approved to seek funding through the Interstate Stream Commission. In 2008 an initial survey by the Army Corps of Engineers estimated a project to replace the ditch with plastic pipe would cost approximately $1.9 million. The project remained in abeyance, however, because there was no funding available.

Then suddenly, early in 2016, the ISC announced there was funding for the project to proceed and the Army Corps of Engineers began a re-survey for the pipeline. Lopez himself had to find out from the state and the Corps what exactly the project would entail so he could inform the parciantes, which he did at a meeting on August 28: the Corps planned to place a 42 inch plastic pipe in the ditch for 1.3 miles to be covered by two feet of dirt, which would cost approximately $2.7 million. The portion of the cost share program for the acequia is 7. 5 percent, which would come to $203,625, amounting to individual payments of $182 if paid per water right or $1,339 if paid per parciante. The parciantes were of course taken by surprise and wanted to again vote on the project.

To his credit, Lopez, who in his interview with Cultural Energy said he saw the need for the project, tabled the August 28 meeting and scheduled a September 25 meeting with an agenda item to allow a vote. But before that vote took place, Lopez dropped a bombshell: an e-mail from the ISC on the previous Friday ordered that all ISC funded projects for which contracts hadn't been signed prior to September 6 be terminated because of state budget shortfalls. The ISC's portion of the Acequias Chamisal y Ojito cost would be $575,000 (17.5 percent). The former commissioners who backed the pipeline project immediately called for Lopez to cancel the meeting, but he told them that the Army Corps of Engineers wanted a definitive decision from the acequia regarding the project.

While the meeting progressed to the vote more quickly than the one in Llano San Juan—a little over an hour compared to three—the vote was less overwhelming: 21 to 20 to stop the project. Several parciantes were unable to vote because they weren't caught up with their dues and others didn't come prepared with signed proxies for those who couldn't attend. Commissioner Lopez ended up voting against the project but admonished the parciantes that this was a lesson to pay their ditch fees and remain active in both the governance and physical labor needed to maintain their community acequias.

We all recognize that we can benefit from the cost share programs provided by the ISC, Taos Soil and Water Conservation District, and other government agencies. But we need to be cognizant of limits, both financial and physical. These are our acequias, after all.

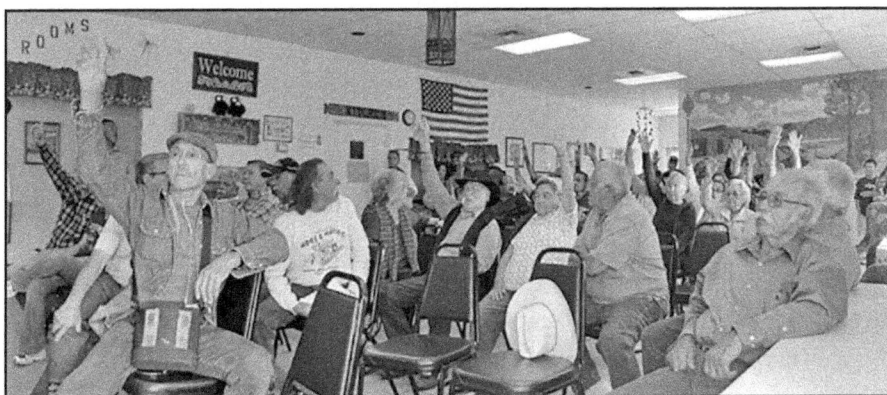

Parciantes of the Acequias Chamisal y Ojitos vote to kill the project.   *Photo by Robin Collier*

Thirty-eight

TOW Water Transfer Goes to a Hearing

The hearing process on the Top of the World (TOW) water transfer protest didn't pick up speed until March of 2016 when protestants submitted their witness lists to the Office of the State Engineer (OSE) hearing officer. Water transfer protests notoriously take a long time to wend their way through the bureaucratic process, and the actual hearing on this case didn't take place until October.

All of the protestants to the TOW transfer based their arguments on public welfare. To briefly recap, the TOW transfer proposed to move 1,752 acre feet (afy) of underground water rights from the Sunshine Valley area near Questa to the Pojoaque Valley as part of the Aamodt Adjudication Settlement. Two-thirds of these rights, 1,141 afy, are slated for the pueblos in the adjudication—Pojoaque, Tesuque, Nambe, and San Ildefonso—while 611 afy are earmarked for the non-pueblo water delivery system. Two-thirds of the 1,752 afy were being leased to the town of Questa, and the other third were being used to farm at the TOW location. The TOW application was one of three before the OSE that propose to move a combined consumptive use of 4,000 afy into the Pojoaque water system: 2,500 afy for the pueblos and 1,500 afy for the non-Pueblo users.

The county's initial witness list included a number of experts: Peter Vigil, director of the Taos Soil and Water Conservation District; administrative officials of Questa and Taos County; members of the Taos County Public Welfare Advisory Committee (full disclosure: I'm the former chair of the Committee and was included on the witness list); and Dr. José Rivera, former professor of community and regional planning at the University of New Mexico.

The other protestants to the transfer were three landowners who live in the move-to area of the Pojoaque Valley and are members of Northern New Mexicans Protecting Land, Water, and Rights (NNMProtects) as well as defendants in the Aamodt adjudication (David Neal, Tim Cash, and Beverly Duran-Cash, all *pro se* protestants). The group raised many public welfare questions regarding the settlement that they believed needed to be answered before any water should be transferred to a water delivery system: will enough residents choose to hook up to the system to make it viable; why were some communities excluded from the system; will there be sufficient water long term to supply the system; will the proposed water storage system be adequate; are the system cost estimates valid; and will the quality of the river water be assured.

The three NNMProtects protestants hoped to get some answers to these questions from the witnesses on the list they submitted to the OSE. They included: a representative of the Bureau of Reclamation, which is responsible for the Environmental Impact Statement being promulgated for the water system; the Santa Fe County manager, utility director, and district commissioner (Santa Fe County will operate the water system); Aamodt defendants who are members of the Pojoaque Basin Water Alliance and objectors to the settlement; hydrogeologists who could testify about the water supply at TOW Farm and its flow rate to the Rio Grande; and the governors of the four pueblos that are part of the Aamodt Settlement.

As we've often pointed out in *La Jicarita*, and others have argued as well, these kinds of transfers are paper transfers: there is no guarantee that unused groundwater in the TOW area will migrate to the Rio Grande and flow downriver to the move-to area as surface water in the Pojoaque Valley in a timely fashion. In order for a transfer to involve "real" water there needs to be a proven hydrological connection between the move-from and move-to area. In the case of the TOW water there are conflicting claims as to how much and how fast the underground water will migrate to the move-to areas. In a conversation with David Neal, one of the NNMProtects protestants, he expressed his frustration over what he calls the "inconsistencies" in managing the Rio Grande; in real time we don't know how many straws are sucking up how much water, the amount of conveyance losses that deplete the overall flow, and how climate change and drought will affect both native and San Juan/Chama supply. This is what was hoped would be part of a public welfare discussion.

Unfortunately, but not surprisingly, all the protestants who were participating in the hearing *pro se* were dismissed by the OSE for not meeting the requirements necessary to proceed with a protest under state statute. That left Taos County as the only protestant. After witness lists were submitted to the OSE in March, and prior to the hearing before an appointed OSE hearing examiner in October, applicants sought to get one of the attorneys who represented Taos County dismissed. Santa Fe water attorneys Peter Shoenfeld and Jennifer McCabe were hired by Taos County in June to represent its interests in the TOW water transfer protest. Attorneys for the pueblos claimed that because Shoenfeld had previously represented clients in the Aamodt Adjudication Settlement and signed a confidentiality agreement he should be disqualified from the hearing. Once it was established that a confidentiality agreement didn't preclude him from representing Taos County, a different client, they attempted to have him dismissed on the grounds of conflict of interest. The hearing examiner ruled against them and Shoenfeld continued to represent Taos County in the protest.

At the October 6 and 7 OSE hearings the attorney for the Water Rights Division (WRD), which represents the OSE in water transfer protest cases, objected to Taos County's expert witness on public welfare, Dr. José Rivera, a retired UNM professor of architecture and planning, who has testified previously in water transfer cases and published papers on the issue of public welfare. Ironically, the WRD attorney Kris Knutson claimed that because there is no official definition of public welfare Dr. Rivera couldn't be an expert. As I've discussed previously, for many years the only basis for protesting a water transfer was the impairment of someone else's water right. In 1985 the state legislature finally added the criteria of public welfare and conservation to the state statute that governs water transfer protests. But the OSE has avoided like the plague making any decision based on public welfare because it's seen as a Pandora's Box: to define what is the public welfare when it comes to the movement of water would demand a broader scrutiny of transactions that are seen only through an economics lens, or what is the "highest and best" use of the water. Public welfare has never actually been legally defined in case law in a water transfer decision and the OSE would like to keep it that way. The Taos County attorneys fought for Dr. Rivera's right to testify and although he ended up being classified as an expert on acequia culture and "public administration" his testimony on public welfare is now on record.

Rivera focused on the importance of determining what constitutes the public welfare of the state in water transfers such as Top of the World. To rely on an economic interest, or the idea of the highest and best use, infers that one area of New Mexico—and it's usually urban— is more important than another, which fails to acknowledge New Mexico's diverse population that includes pueblo and acequia communities. Inter-basin transfers could destroy this diverse fabric of the state. (At a 2016 Water and Natural Resources legislative committee hearing State Senator Peter Wirth noted that inter-basin transfers might not be welcome in New Mexico: "We really need to look at this.")

Rivera also pointed out that the New Mexico State Water Plan mandated regional water planning and a component of that planning was to determine what constitutes the public welfare of each region, which could best be developed by local stakeholders and could work to protect water resources from outside interests looking for water. All the regional water plans include public welfare criteria, such as cultural protection, agrarian character, watershed health, recreational opportunity, etc. As I've discussed previously, the Taos County Regional Water Plan tried to set up an advisory committee that would review all transfers both from and within Taos County to determine if they met the public welfare criteria of Taos County. When Attorney Knutson raised the objection that the OSE couldn't hear a public welfare argument because it hasn't been defined, he was right only in that the OSE has no business trying to define what the state's regional water plans have already defined. The applicants didn't call anyone as a witness on public welfare.

Ron Gardiner was also on the Taos County's expert witness list; tragically, Ron died unexpectedly on September 25 before the hearing took place. Ron was a repository of information regarding Taos County watershed health and forest restoration and shared his knowledge on numerous county committees including subdivision regulation and land use planning. He and I also worked together on the Taos Regional Water Plan to develop a Public Welfare Statement and later served on the Taos County Public Welfare Advisory Committee, which was set up by county ordinance after it was excluded from the Taos Regional Water Plan. His testimony would have been an invaluable asset to the County's arguments regarding public welfare. As a substitute for Ron, Taos County Planner Nathan Sanchez submitted the county documents that pertain to the issue of public welfare.

The other substantive issue at the hearing involved the hydrological implications of moving 1,752 afy from Top of the World to the Pojoaque Valley. The applicants claim that once the wells at TOW are retired, the groundwater will migrate to the Rio Grande, where it will travel downstream to the takeout at San Ildefonso Pueblo and be diverted, according to the Pojoaque Basin Regional Water System Environmental Impact Statement, "either by diverting surface water into a side intake structure or by collecting groundwater that is hydrologically connected to the river through the use of horizontal collector wells."

The applicants' witness Neil Deeds addressed three components of the supposed hydrologic connection between TOW and the Pojoaque Valley: the timing and accrual of water at the move from area at TOW; the transmission or carriage losses from TOW to San Ildefonso; and potential impacts of the diversion at San Ildefonso Pueblo. The Taos County attorneys challenged his testimony that relied on Bureau of Reclamation data without an onsite inspection and specifically challenged his claim that there would be no evaporative or seepage losses in the transmission of the water between Top of the World and the Pojoaque Valley. They also questioned his information regarding agricultural uses, his chosen Consumptive Irrigation Requirement figures, and the certainty his report provides.

While questions remain regarding the hydrology of the transfer—for instance, how long it will take for water at TOW to migrate to the Rio Grande—the case would be decided on the criteria of public welfare. The hearing examiner set a due date of December 6 for "findings of facts," or an interpretation of the conflicting views on the facts presented in the hearing. If this were a regular court of law that would be a jury or judge. In hearings before the OSE it is the hearing examiner who resolves the conflict and issues a recommendation to the State Engineer, who will then issue his decision. It seemed very likely in this critically important case that whichever party lost at the hearing would appeal the decision to District Court.

Thirty-nine

Deadline Looms: Will the Aamodt Settlement
Meet the Terms?

Four months after Taos County protested the proposed transfer of 1,752 acre feet of water rights from the Top of the World Farm (TOW) to the Pojoaque Valley as part of the Aamodt Adjudication Settlement in October of 2016 no decision had been rendered by the OSE. All water transfers and funding for the Settlement had to be in place by September 15 of 2017, (construction of the Regional Water System has until 2024 to be completed) or the Settlement would be scuttled, and all the parties to the adjudication would have to devise a new settlement (this one has taken over 10 years) or go to court. Whichever party was on the losing end of the decision—Taos County, the area of origin, or Santa Fe County, where the water is supposed to go—would no doubt appeal that decision. Any such appeal would never make it through the court system by September of 2017.

Much to my surprise, when in April of 2017 I asked John Utton, Santa Fe County attorney, how the powers that be could let this decision linger long enough to jeopardize the entire settlement, he told me that "The Aamodt deadlines do not require that all appeals be exhausted, only that the State Engineer approve the transfer prior to September—so if that happens as expected there won't be a deadline issue." He sent me the pertinent section in the Settlement Act that says that in order to meet the terms of the settlement the water rights have to have been "acquired and entered into appropriate contracts" and "permits have been issued by the New Mexico State Engineer to the Regional Water Authority" and that "the permits shall be free of any condition that materially adversely affects the ability of the Pueblos or the Regional Water Authority to divert or use the Pueblo water supply . . . ."

What Utton was saying, then—aside from his assumption that the transfer would be approved—was that the State Engineer could issue a permit for the TOW water rights even if that transfer was under an appeal in District Court. This brought up several immediate questions: 1) Isn't an appeal a "condition that materially adversely affects" the decision approving the transfer; and 2) If a transfer that is under appeal can be considered permitted under the terms of the Aamodt Settlement doesn't that negate the entire process of a water transfer hearing? I asked Utton this question and he responded that "The material condition provision applies to any condition that the State Engineer might place on the permit. It has nothing to do with an appeal."

The opportunity for appeal to district court is part of the water transfer protest process, guaranteed by the New Mexico Constitution, Article XVI, Section 5 and New Mexico State Statutes Annotated, Chapter 72, Article 7, Appeals From State Engineer 72-7-1. The Hearing Unit Procedures lay out steps the Hearing Examiner and State Engineer must follow in a transfer protest. Under 19.25.2.29 FINAL DECISION: D. FINALITY, it states: "A decision of the state engineer is final after 30 days, unless an appeal has been timely filed in accordance with NMSA 1978, Sections 72-2-16 and 72-7-1. The state engineer shall not seek enforcement of a compliance order until it is final, except where an emergency exists or the public health or safety necessitates."

Utton's interpretation of the terms of the settlement seemed to abrogate the New Mexico Constitution, state statute, and OSE regulations. I asked Taos County for a response, but it declined to comment. When I asked several New Mexico water law attorneys for their opinion the consensus was that a permit to the Regional Water Authority based on the State Engineer's decision could not be issued until the appeal process has been exhausted or completed. Utton told me he expected the State Engineer to render a decision during the summer of 2017.

Around the same time it appeared that the Regional Water System could also be in trouble. The state is committed to providing $72.5 million to the construction cost; $15 million was set aside in 2014, but the 2017 legislature voted against setting aside an additional $9.1 million. The Settlement Act stipulates that the funding for the Pojoaque Basin Regional Water System must be appropriated by the September 2017 deadline. A Settlement provision also stipulates that if the Regional Water System is not completed by 2024 a final decree would not be issued and the adjudication could be taken back to court. The County of Santa Fe passed a resolution in 2015 stating that it would not appropriate its share of the $261 necessary to fund the Regional Water System "until the legal status of County Roads running through the Settling Pueblos has been resolved." San Ildefonso Pueblo was claiming that county roads that cross through its "external boundaries" belong to the pueblo and was seeking easement payments. The county claimed that it has rights of way on all the roads in question.

New Mexico District Court Judge William Johnson signed the Aamodt Decree on July 14, 2017, and Interior Secretary Ryan Zinke signed it into law on September 15. The powers that be behind this 51 year old adjudication pushed this controversial project through the legal process with little regard for fairness, cost, burdensome bureaucracy, the abrogation of the transfer protest process, the cumulative impacts of moving paper water from basin to basin, dipping one more straw into the Rio Grande, and most importantly, the changing nature of our environment and climate that could easily render water supply inadequate or even nonexistent.

The legal process allows for a challenge to the Final Decree in the appellate court. Attorneys for more than 300 Pojoaque Valley objectors to the Aamodt Settlement filed an appeal of the Final Judgment and Decree on October 30, 2017 in the 10th Circuit Court of Appeals. The appeal is based on several basic arguments: 1) That the New Mexico state executive branch officials who signed the Settlement Agreement are not authorized to approve settlements of water rights, only the legislature is; 2) The settlement subverts the rights of junior water rights users based on whether they went along with the United States settlement demands; and 3) Lack of due process.

This is the concluding statement of the appeal that addresses the first argument:

"The District Court erred in entering the Partial Final Judgment and Decree on the Water Rights of the Pueblos of Nambe, Pojoaque, San Ildefonso and Tesuque (incorporated into the Final Decree and Judgment) on the basis of approving the Settlement Agreement (compact) thereby creating and/or improperly extending New Mexico law, creating state financial appropriation obligations and agreeing to Mutual-Benefit projects, based solely on State Executive branch approval. The District Court erred in failing to recognize that settlement of this type is properly vested in the New Mexico Legislature per the State Constitution and should not have entered final judgment absent a valid legal and binding settlement agreement. This court should remand the matter back to the District Court with instructions to require the New Mexico executive branch officers to obtain the required state legislative approval of the Settlement Agreement and require any settlement agreement fully comply with all provisions of relevant law including both the US and NM Constitutions before final decree and judgment may be entered."

This is an interesting argument in light of a lawsuit that that was filed back in 2014 by three New Mexico State lawmakers—Republicans Paul Bandy and Steve Neville of Aztec and Democrat Carl Trujillo of Nambe—against the New Mexico State Engineer and Interstate Stream Commission over the Navajo Water Rights Settlement claiming that former Governor Bill Richardson pushed the settlement through his office in 2010 without getting authorization from the legislature to fund the state's part of the $800 million total price tag. Until defeated in the 2018 primary, Trujillo represented the constituents of the Pojoaque Valley who are parties to the Aamodt Adjudication. According to Trujillo, the Supreme Court declined to hear their case until all the appeals of the Navajo Settlement have been heard. While the New Mexico Appeals Court issued the final decree in 2013, appeals were filed by non-Native ditch associations, conservancy districts, and numerous acequia parciantes in January of 2016.

The second argument, that junior water rights users are subverted in the settlement, is based on the fact that their rights have been "tiered" according to whether they accepted or objected to the settlement. The deadline for objecting to the settlement was April 7, 2014; 792 objections were filed in court by that time. On March 3, 2016 the District Court entered an order overruling all the objections and approving the Settlement Agreement. The appellants claim that the Settlement punishes those junior water rights owners who objected to the settlement by forcing them to accept the curtailment of future priority calls by the pueblos while owners who signed the settlement but own water rights that may be junior to those of the objectors' will be exempt from priority calls. According to the appeal, because such an exception to priority administration doesn't exist in the law, the executive branch of the government is in essence creating a new law, which under the New Mexico Constitution (New Mexico Constitution Article XVI Sec. 2) is only within the purview of the legislature.

The third argument is that the settlement is an abrogation of due process in that it provides no protection for those who objected to its terms. The appeal cites a previous court case that "the policy of our law is to favor amicable settlement of claims without litigation when the agreements are fairly secured, are without fraud, misrepresentation, or overreaching, and when they are supported by consideration." The appellants point out that in the Aamodt Settlement not all parties agreed to enter into a settlement in which they gave up their rights, in which they received "no/unacceptable compensation or benefit," and in a settlement "that can result in disparate access to water and/or costs for water access (flowing from operations and maintenance of systems) in which they have no voice per the settlement terms."

When I spoke with Representative Trujillo about the lawsuit against the Aamodt, I asked him if he felt the appeal by the objectors had any chance of success. He thought not, but went on to hold out hope that the Settlement would be derailed because of the ongoing conflict between Santa Fe County and the pueblos over easement rights. As I reported in *La Jicarita* in 2017, the county has been at odds with the pueblos over access and easement rights on county roads that fall within the exterior boundaries of the four pueblos involved in the Aamodt Settlement—Tesuque, Nambe, Pojoaque, and San Ildefonso—and in 2015 passed Resolution 2015-25, which requires that the legal status of the county roads be resolved before the county commission appropriates funding for the regional water system. The water system must be initiated by 2018 and completed by 2024 under the terms of the Settlement or the Decree will be null and void.

The Santa Fe County Commission and representatives of federal agencies and the pueblos met to discuss the road easement controversy several times over the last few months of 2017 but prevented Trujillo, whose district covers part of northern Santa Fe County, from attending these closed door meetings. Trujillo was skeptical the county and pueblos would reach an agreement because of the pueblos' unwillingness to issue rights of way. If the county and state failed to meet their fiduciary obligations and the deadlines for the regional water system were not met, would this signal the end of this long (50 plus years), hotly debated, and burdensome adjudication?

Forty

The Abeyta Settlement Gets Even More Contentious

The Abeyta, or Taos Pueblo Settlement, was having some problems as well. In a unanimous vote at their annual March 2017 meeting, the parciantes of the Acequia Madre del Rio Lucero y del Arroyo Seco voted to reject the Aquifer Storage and Recovery (ASR) wells that are part of the Settlement Agreement. This project would move water rights from the Llano Community Ditch in Questa to the Acequia Madre in a scheme that calls for diverting the water from the Rio Lucero in the winter, storing it in ASR wells, and then pumping it from the wells during the irrigation season to augment the acequia system. To formalize this decision the Acequia Madre Commission laid out its objections in a second letter to the Office of the State Engineer (OSE), the Bureau of Reclamation (BOR) (responsible for building the ASR system), and the Interstate Stream Commission (ISC): the costs of maintenance, permitting, and labor would exceed the acequia's annual budget; the well water would be treated with chemicals the parciantes find objectionable; the historic Rio Lucero ditch would be compromised; and deep water mining could potentially lower the water table and threaten domestic wells. The Acequia Madre Commission also stated in the letter, "we do not give authority to anyone to make decisions on behalf of our Acequia regarding the ASR well, pipeline, retention ponds, reservoirs, without discussion and consent from our membership."

I spoke with Acequia Madre commissioner Chris Pieper about the acequia's decision to reject the ASR wells. Because the water rights are junior rights that can only be used in the winter, the acequia's rejection of any reconstruction of the acequia would also preclude a retention pond as that would require that the water be piped from the Rio Lucero to the pond.

The Acequia Madre del Rio Lucero y del Arroyo Seco parciantes were not the only ones concerned about deep wells. The commissioners of the Madre del Llano Acequia of the Rio Hondo also sent a letter to the agencies outlining their similar concerns: cost and maintenance of mitigation wells slated for their area; the unknown chemical composition of the deep well water on the river; and the potential drawdown on the aquifer and domestic wells. According to the Settlement, the mitigation wells, which reach a 1,000 feet or more into the deep aquifer, will be used by the town of Taos, El Prado Water and Sanitation District, and the mutual domestics to offset at least 50 percent of any Taos Valley tributary surface water depletions resulting from future groundwater pumping. They are responsible for the cost and maintenance of the wells.

The end of the Madre del Llano Acequia letter reads:

"We would like to see far more effort made in conservation and other alternatives to these ASR and mitigation wells. We believe the decision to use this extremely expensive and potentially destructive solution was not made in the spirit of promoting long term health to our environment, nor the well being of general population living in Taos County.

"As per Article 13.3 in the Abeyta Settlement, we would like to reconvene and negotiate a more sustainable solution, and forgo the mitigation wells."

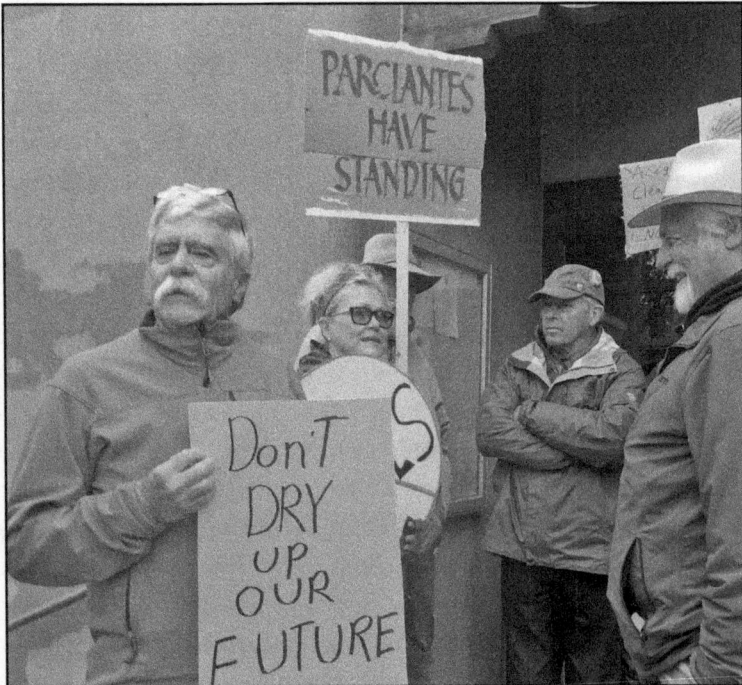

A group of parciantes from the Arroyo Hondo acequias showed up with signs on April 27 at an Abeyta "Taos Settlement Implementation Planning Meeting" to let the bureaucrats know that they didn't like the terms of the Settlement that would most directly affect their acequias—deep mitigation wells and Aquifer Storage and Recovery wells. Representatives of the Bureau of Reclamation, which is the agency responsible for the implementation of these wells, first told the protesters that the meeting was not open to the public and they were stuck out on the porch in the rain. After the press arrived—the *Taos News* and *La Jicarita*—and some of the attorneys representing the parties to the Settlement raised an objection, the acequia commissioners were allowed to enter the meeting "to express their concerns" and then leave. Then John Painter, a member of the El Prado Water and Sanitation District, proposed that the commissioners from the acequias be allowed to stay throughout the meeting, as the lawyers and agencies would be discussing the very wells they're concerned about. So only the press was asked to leave.

We did get to hear from several of the commissioners and parciantes before our departure, however. As I've discussed previously, much of their concern stems from what they believe is a lack of transparency and communication from those who negotiated the Settlement agreement. The Settlement negotiations were held behind closed doors by representatives of the designated parties: the Town of Taos; Taos Pueblo; El Prado Water and Sanitation District; the mutual domestic associations; and the Taos Valley Acequia Association (TVAA), representing 54 acequias in the Taos Valley. Even though the Abeyta Settlement was signed in 2010, many of affected parciantes claim they were largely left out of the information loop.

The Arroyo Hondo parciantes I spoke with before the meeting expressed the same lack of communication between those who negotiated the Settlement and the rank and file. Pam Harris, of the Arroyo Hondo Mutual Domestic Association, told me that the association had spent years and money getting the uranium out of their well system and were concerned about what chemicals the mitigation wells might contain. A representative of the Acequia Monte de Rio Chiquito questioned the BOR as to whether the financing of the mitigation wells would be for perpetuity, as his acequia, like that of Arroyo Hondo and Acequia Madre, cannot cover the costs. Bill Woodall, of the Acequia Madre del Rio Lucero y del Arroyo Seco, stated that he had attempted to conduct a feasibility study of the ASR wells on his own (the BOR will have to conduct either an environmental assessment or an environmental impact statement before the well system is built) and concluded that the maintenance costs are well beyond the capacity of the acequia. He also accused the government agencies of "leading people into a cycle of water use and growth that is unsustainable" with a massive spending of funds that encourages people to "grow more grass" [i.e., hay and alfalfa]. How can they sell this to people who can't afford it?" When I spoke with Woodall the next day he also told me that the acequia doesn't want the transferred water rights from Questa: "Give them back or sell them. We have our water allotment from the Settlement that will maintain our traditional usage."

Several months later the BOR scheduled another Taos Settlement Implementation Planning Meeting that demonstrated even less finesse. The parties to the Abetya Settlement all sat at a table with their backs to the audience, which largely consisted of parciantes who own water rights on the acequias within the Taos Valley that are part of the Settlement. After introductions, the lawyers, bureaucrats, and Taos Pueblo representatives left the room for an "executive session." They came back a few minutes later, declared there was nothing to report on the list of substantial agenda items dealing with the particulars of the Abeyta implementation. Less than half an hour after the meeting began they vacated the meeting room.

Why? Because Mike Tilley of the local community radio station KCEI was there to record the meeting (I was also there, along with Bill Whaley of *Taos Friction*) and Nelson Cordova and Gilbert Suazo of Taos Pueblo refused to participate in a recorded session. So instead of asking Mike Tilley to leave this "not open to the public" meeting, which is how the attorney Bradley Bridgewater of the Department of the Interior classified it, they essentially cancelled the meeting by claiming there was nothing to report. Just before they left the room, one of the many parciantes who had come to observe the proceedings, asked if any future implementation meetings would be open to the public. Bridgewater again declared, "These aren't public meetings." The parciante responded, "Don't we, as water rights owners, who will be impacted by the decisions made in this settlement, have any say in its implementation?"

After the meeting I spoke again with Chris Pieper, commissioner on the Acequia Madre del Rio Lucero y del Arroyo Seco, who told me of a recent conversation with a New Mexico Environment Department official who confirmed his fears. According to this official, treatment costs of water from these 1,000-foot deep aquifer wells will be prohibitive: the only way to meet state standards is through reverse osmosis, a multi-million dollar expenditure. Chris believes that the meeting was also cancelled because the technical team that was supposed to address agenda item #1, "Follow-up on OSE [Office of the State Engineer] model 'update' discussion," had no follow-up to report. Would newer, more informed hydrologic models also confirm parciantes' doubts about the efficacy of these mitigation wells?

At the implementation meeting there was a handout provided that showed the status of all the projects included in the Settlement. The mitigation wells range in depth from 800 to 1,000 feet, the Town of Taos and El Prado Water and Sanitation District wells range in depth from 800 to 2,500 feet, and the two Aquifer Storage and Recovery Wells are 1,000 feet deep. The wells will be located in communities on each of the valley stream systems:

• Rio Hondo mitigation well of Upper Rio Hondo (acequias are opposed to well);

• Rio Lucero/Rio Pueblo de Taos mitigation well of Upper Ranchitos (the lawyer Mary Humphrey who has represented the mutual domestic associations in the Settlement withdrew her representation because she was unable to make contact with the commission);

• Rio Fernando de Taos mitigation well in the Town of Taos (working on location and financial assistance application);

• Rio Grande del Rancho mitigation well of Llano Quemado (working on relocation of well and financial assistance);

• Rio Chiquito mitigation well of Acequia Madre del Rio Chiquito and Acequia del Monte (acequias not interested in constructing the project);

• Arroyo Seco Arriba Project, Aquifer Storage and Recovery Option of Acequia Madre del Rio Lucero y del Arroyo Seco (undetermined whether they want to move forward with the project);

All of the mitigation wells have a price tag of over a million dollars.

The costs assigned to these wells has been questioned over and over again by parciantes, and at a TVAA meeting in March of 2018 Bill Woodall again accused the BOR of failing to provide any information as to how they came up with these cost estmates. Kyle Harwood, the TVAA lawyer who replaced Rebecca Dempsey, told the group that they were refining the mitigation well operation agreement to specify who would pay for the well construction and maintenance costs. They would also be reviewing the Acequia Storage and Recovery Agreement with the Acequia Madre del Rio Lucero y Arroyo Seco at the behest of the acequia.

But the more "startling" (not to those of us who have long raised this issue) announcement Harwood made was that a 2016 New Mexico Tech report on the hydrogeology of a portion of Taos County that lies within the Settlement parameters has revealed it is much more complex than the hydrology model upon which the Settlement is based. Kyle Harwood told the group that they were now "integrating these findings into the Settlement."

As of this writing, the Abeyta Partial Final Decree has been listed in the Federal Register. A Final Decree won't be issued until the OSE completes the adjudication of domestic wells within the Settlement area.

Conclusion

A number of years ago I ran a quote in *La Jicarita*, taken from a study called "Climate Change and Its Implications for New Mexico's Water Resources and Economic Opportunities," by NMSU Agricultural Economics Professor Brian Hurd and UNM Civil Engineering Professor Julie Coonrod: "Under current climate there is virtually no spare water in New Mexico. Imagine a very plausible future, as this study attempts, of significantly less water and at the same time significantly more people." They warn us that water transfers from agriculture to urban use will hugely impact not only our ability to grow food in the future but our "environment, our identity, and the character of New Mexico. . . . Irrigated lands support more than crops. They provide habitat for wildlife, open space and scenic vistas for the backdrop to New Mexico's thriving art, tourist and recreation economies."

All of us who've been involved in the regional water planning process as non-governmental stakeholders trying to address critical water issues within both the planning and implementation processes have bumped up against the Interstate Stream Commission (ISC), an agency that has never heeded the advice given in that report. (In 2017 the ISC won the Society of Professional Journalists' Black Hole Award for its "outright contempt of the public's right to know."[54]) A member of the Middle Rio Grande Water Assembly, the all volunteer organization whose purpose is to "assure effective implementation of the Middle Rio Grande Regional Water Plan through an open, inclusive, and participatory process . . . for a sustainable water future that balances water use with renewable supply . . . " told me, when push comes to shove, state agencies still stick to "top down" as opposed to "bottom up" planning when it comes to decision making.

The Middle Rio Grande Water Assembly, which drafted its regional water plan in 2004, has seen considerable strife and controversy over the years as plan implementation slowed to a crawl and numerous changes to the water situation occurred. While some positive steps have been taken to conserve water, initiate the San Juan/Chama drinking water diversion plan (some folks would challenge that that's a success), and restore the Rio

Grande bosque, this plan experienced the same division between the stakeholders and the decision makers as in the Taos Regional Water Plan. Once the ISC had initiated a process to update all the regional water plans, the Council of Governments took over the organization of the Middle Rio Grande Assembly steering committee assigned to guide the update and the Assembly was denied membership on that committee. The Assembly represents the diverse community of stakeholders, not the governmental interests that are now guiding the process.

As I discussed previously, when the Taos Regional Water Plan was presented to the ISC for approval in 2007 the commission voted to delay approval until the "parties could reach consensus." The "parties" they referred to were the stakeholders, who represented unincorporated communities, environmental organizations, acequias, mutual domestics, and other water users who met for over two years, as volunteers, to draft the plan, and who came to public meetings across the region to help devise critical strategies, which included a priority of keeping water in its area of origin. The "consensus" that was trying to be reached was the creation of a public welfare oversight committee to look at all water transfers both within and from the region, and based on the public welfare criteria that had been developed (cultural protection, agrarian character, watershed health, and long-term economic development), make an informed recommendation to the Office of the State Engineer (OSE) as to whether the transfer was in the public interest.

Did we come to consensus? Hell no. With the backing of the ISC, the "decision makers"—Taos region municipalities and water district officials, along with Abeyta Adjudication parties who had objected to the public welfare component of the regional water plan—informed the stakeholders that their job was done and were no longer part of the process. It was time for the decision makers to draft a final plan and that would not include a public welfare statement with a public welfare committee to review water transfers.

The process to update the regional plans appears to lie squarely in the hands of the decision makers, not the stakeholders. Water policies that were developed by the stakeholders to address public welfare and conservation are subsumed in the rush to fund infrastructure projects that require the movement of water out of its area of origin. The ISC decision makers approved the Gila River diversion, just as the regional water plan decision makers are approving updated regional water plans without the scrutiny of the stakeholders.

In Chapter Thirteen I quoted from the interview Mark and I did with Estevan López, who had just been appointed director of the ISC: "Let's have a discussion about growth, then. Is that something we ought to be trying to control? Frame it in terms of the available resources." As I've reported over the years, we've tried to have a discussion about "growth" and "efficiency in urban environments" and "water planning to overcome the momentum of our current growth" in the context of regional water planning, but either Lopez didn't represent ISC policy or he was just mouthing platitudes. The ISC was complicit in the high-jacking of several regional water plans and now is preparing to implement the ill-conceived Gila River diversion dam that will cost taxpayers millions of dollars. Whenever there's been a choice of less costly, conservation based water projects or big projects to move lots of water around, the ISC is usually on the side of the latter. It's thinking is very similar to the that of the United States Forest Service over many decades: if we don't approve big timber projects, even beyond a sustainable yield, we won't get the big federal bucks. If the ISC doesn't approve the big diversion and water delivery projects, they don't get the bucks from the legislature. They're certainly not getting it for planning.

A number of years ago an article in *Colorado Central Magazine*, based in Salida, referenced the water planning situation in that state and raised a scenario that provides at least a modicum of hope that water planners there may do things a little differently. This monthly magazine was started by Ed and Martha Quillen (Ed was a longtime columnist for the *Denver Post*) and continued after Ed's death under the editorship of Mike Rosso. One of its longtime contributors is George Sibley, who writes about water issues from the Upper Gunnison Basin. Sibley's article is titled "Are We Part of a City-State,"[55] which references the divide between Denver and the cities along the Front Range of the Rocky Mountains and the rest of the rural state, similar to our New Mexico divide along the Rio Grande Corridor. Sibley asks the question, why should the rest of the state, that probably has as much water as it needs, be engaged in water planning with the metropolitan areas that will need a lot more water to handle the projected 80 percent increase in growth by mid century: "The Front Range has a problem and needs for those of us in the rest of the state to see this as our problem too, hence a statewide water plan."

And within that statewide water plan, plans for every water basin in the state could potentially create a "post-urban" culture, or "basin-centric cultures capable of watering and feeding themselves." That means keeping water in its area of origin to underwrite agricultural production, provide energy resources from that water (along with the sun), "finally grow[ing] up to fit the land rather than just subdividing it into more real estate." In this more "locally efficient society," Sibley envisions sustainability extending to even greater economic and cultural independence, reducing the urban/rural dichotomy.

Many of us involved in New Mexico regional water planning envisioned the same kind of thing for our state. Instead, we got hugely expensive water rights adjudication settlements that depend upon the movement of thousands of acres of feet of water across the state and from basin to basin; buyouts of agricultural water rights to fulfill our compact obligations; transfers of agricultural water rights to compensate for groundwater pumping in our cities; and unrestrained "subdividing real estate" that Sibley warns against. As I've emphasized throughout this book, allowing natural resources to help determine sustainable growth and development patterns is not the way things work in a market economy.

Many issues involved in the adjudication settlements hang in the balance. On July 14, 2017, when the parties to the Aamodt Adjudication signed the Final Judgment and Decree—the city and county of Santa Fe, the state of New Mexico, the Bureau of the Interior, the pueblos of San Ildefonso, Pojoaque, Nambe, and Tesuque, and the U.S District Judge—they ignored the outstanding protest of the Top of the World water transfer. The New Mexico State Engineer denied Taos County's protest of the TOW water rights four days dater, on July 18.

Taos County filed a notice of appeal of that decision, which was also ignored when the adjudication's implementation deadline rolled around on September 15, 2017. As I talked about in a previous chapter, the Settlement attorneys claimed the Aamodt deadlines didn't require that all appeals be exhausted, only that the State Engineer approve the transfer prior to September. It certainly seems that these actions and claims are an abrogation of the process of a water rights transfer protest. Taos County never stood a chance. One might also question why Santa Fe County is involved in the Aamodt Settlement in the first place, pitting the two counties against each other. The TOW water rights were initially acquired and designated for use by the city and county of Santa Fe at the Buckman Well Field, their main water source, below Otowi Gauge. When that elicited an outcry of opposition (Otowi has always functioned as a de facto barrier to norteño water moving south to the cities), and when the judge in the adjudication issued a decision that limited the pueblos water supply, the politicos got involved and the TOW water was redirected to the adjudication parties. In order for that water to reach the pueblo and non-pueblo residents of the Pojoaque Valley it had to be piped, which meant a water delivery system that most of the non-pueblo residents didn't want. Santa Fe County will be the administrator of that system.

The Final Decree was appealed by 375 water rights owners in the Pojoaque Valley shortly before the September 15 deadline. If the Aamodt regional water system never comes to fruition the adjudication could also end up back in court. Santa Fe County, faced with the likelihood that not enough non-pueblo residents plan to hook up to the water delivery system, is floating the idea of giving residents another option: hook into the water utility for indoor use while keeping wells for outdoor use. Under this proposed option, residents who have rights to 0.5 acre-feet of water a year would have the option of transferring 0.3 acre-feet to the county to cover their household consumption while drawing 0.2 acre-feet annually from a well for outdoor use. Then, in an even more surprising turn of events, as I finished up this book, Santa Fe County announced it wouldn't be transferring the 600 afy of Top of the World water rights quite yet, and would instead lease them to Ed and Trudy Healy, who bought the TOW land from which the water rights were separated.

The county did, however, resolve the easement issue with the pueblos, at least for now. They signed an agreement on January 30th of 2018 that's good for 99 years and then automatically renewed for the next 99.

Under the agreements, all roads in question will become public roads and access issues will be resolved for 90 percent of non-Indian property owners, according to the county attorney. The county agreed to construct new roads within San Ildefonso to connect with existing roads within five years. Compensation payments will be made to the other pueblos: Tesuque will receive $185,000, Nambé $1 million and Pojoaque $1.7 million now, and payments of $500,000 on the 25th and 50th anniversaries of the agreement.

The past two years in el norte have demonstrated what everyone refers to as our "new normal," or wildly fluctuating conditions. The 2016-2017 winter snowpack was at 103 percentage, which was a blessing, although not so much in El Valle. Here the winter storms left much less snow than usual; the snowline that used to provide us with storms of a foot or eighteen inches receded to above 8,000 feet. The highest accumulation we had that year was six inches. What we did get melted quickly in the warmer temperatures. I cross-country skied much less than I usually do as conditions near my house were marginal and higher elevation trails I often frequent quickly melted to that sub-freezing slush that clings to your skis, turning a glide into a stomp.

Spring took a different course, however, dumping several feet of snow in El Valle over the course of several storms. All the fruit trees were in bloom, of course, and I lost all my apricots, cherries, pears, and most of my peaches and apples. I had to replant my garden three times to get germination. Up in the high country the snows destroyed the nut and berry crops upon which the bears and other wildlife depend.

Then came the non-winter of 2017-2018. Measured snowpack in the high Sangre de Cristo peaks in my region was at 18 percent of median measures from 1981 to 2010. All the other basin measurements were below 50 percent. There was less snow on the mountains than I've ever witnessed in my entire time in New Mexico. Winter almost escaped El Valle entirely. I don't remember a snowstorm that deposited more than four inches, and that happened only several times over the course of the entire season. The ski areas stayed closed throughout the holidays and only opened at all with massive snow making efforts. Unlike 2017, we weren't saved by spring storms. As I write this, in June of 2018, I'm faced with a water famine. I'm guessing the run-off in the Rio de Las Trampas will not last much longer than the end of this month. I'm scaling back my garden to save what water I may have for my orchard. I'm not growing a hay crop. Most of the villages have made orchards and gardens a priority so whatever hay is grown will cost a fortune.

Heirs of the Las Trampas land grant first settled El Valle in the mid-1700s. For almost three hundred years folks have been living here, vulnerable to changing weather patterns, world wars, economics, and migrations. Their lives were never easy, but despite harsh conditions and numerous vicissitudes, they retained their land-based culture, whether the crops were wheat or hay. Conditions today—climate change, continual war, a recession, and changing demographics—create a situation just as dire but more global in concept. We can only hope that once again the children who grew up here but had to leave for work and those who value what these villages have to offer will find their way back and the acequia waters will continue to flow.

Notes

1. Nichols, John, "The Writing and Filming of The Milagro Beanfield War,"*One Hundred Years of Water Wars in New Mexico*. Santa Fe: Sunstone Press, 2012.

2. Rivera, José, *Acequia Culture, Water, Land & Community in the Southwest*. Albuquerque: University of New Mexico Press, 1998.

3. Kay Matthews. "Avoiding Priority calls for the rights and wrong reasons," *La Jicarita*, April 2013, https://lajicarita.wordpress.com/2013/04/23/avoiding-priority-calls-for-the-right-and-wrong-reasons/.

4. Suzy Kane, "Water is Complicated," *La Jicarita*, December 2012, https://lajicarita.wordpress.com/2012/12/18/water-is-complicated/.

5. J.R. Logan, "Settlement water rights a liquid asset," *The Taos News*, April 2015, http://taosacequias.org/pressroom/2015/TaosNews_150416a.pdf.

6. Reclamation: Managing Water in the West, http://www.usbr.gov/lc/region/g4000/24mo/2015/MAY15.pdf.

7. Matt Jenkins, "The water czar who reshaped Colorado River politics," *High Country News*, March 2, 2015, http://www.hcn.org/issues/47.4/the-water-czar-who-reshaped-colorado-river-politics.

8. White, Richard, *The Organic Machine: The Remaking of the Columbia River*. New York: Hill and Wang, 1995.

9. DeBuys, William. *River of Traps: Life in a Mountain Village*. Albuquerque: University of New Mexico Press.

10. Kay Matthews and Mark Schiller, "Peñasco Area Acequia Federation," *La Jicarita News*, January 1997, http://www.lajicarita.org/97jan.htm#paaf.

11. Kay Matthews, "Taos County Citizens Weigh in on the Abeyta Settlement: Will the Commission Listen," *La Jicarita*, January 2015, https://lajicarita.wordpress.com/2015/01/29/taos-county-citizens-weigh-in-on-the-abeyta-settlement-will-the-commission-listen/.

12. J.R. Logan, "From Taos County Farm to Santa Fe Faucets," *The Taos News*, March 27, 2015, http://taosnews.com/stories/from-taos-county-farm-to-santa-fe-faucets,33148.

13. Ferry, Barbara, *The New Mexican*, December 10, 1997, B-5.

14. John Brown, "Puntos de Vista: Environmentalists, Economists and Instream Flow 'Rights,'" *La Jicarita News*, June 1998, http://www.lajicarita.org/98jun.htm#puntos.

15. Owen, David, *Where the Water Goes: Life and Death Along the Colorado River.* New York: Riverhead Books, 2017.

16. Kay Matthews, "Acequia Parciantes Assert Pre-existing Right on Federal Land," *La Jicarita News*, January 2001, http://www.lajicarita.org/01jul.htm#pre-existingrights.

17. Mark Schiller, "Editorial," *La Jicarita News*, December 1998, http://www.lajicarita.org/98dec.htm#editorial.

18. Kay Matthews, "Editorial: Water Transfer Protests, *La Jicarita News*, September 2003, http://lajicarita.org/03sep.htm#editorial.

19. "American Indian Water Rights Settlements," http://uttoncenter.unm.edu/pdfs/American_Indian_Water_Right_Settlements.pdf.

20. Kay Matthews and Mark Schiller, "Aamodt Water Rights Litigation: 35 Years of Controversy," *La Jicarita News*, April 2001, http://www.lajicarita.org/01apr.htm#aamodt.

21. Brown, F. Lee and Ingram, Helen, *Water and Poverty in the Southwest.* Tucson: The University of Arizona Press: 1987.

22. Peter White, "Puntos de Vista, *La Jicarita News*, January 1999, http://www.lajicarita.org/99jan.htm#puntos.

23. Kay Matthews and Mark Schiller, "Interview with Estevan López, Newly Appointed Interstate Stream Commission Engineer," *La Jicarita News*, February 2003, http://www.lajicarita.org/03feb.htm#interview.

24. Barlow, Maude and Clarke, Tony, *Blue Gold: The Fight to Stop the Corporate Theft of the World's Water.* New Press: 2005.

25. Kay Matthews, "Editorial: State Engineer's 'Proposed Active Resource Water Management Regulations," *La Jicarita News*, August/September 2004, http://www.lajicarita.org/04augsep.htm#editorial.

26. Brown, F. Lee and Ingram, Helen. *Water and Poverty in the Southwest.* Tucson: The University of Arizona Press: 1987, p. 99.

27. Kay Matthews, "It's Time to Define Just What Exactly Public Welfare Means," *La Jicarita News*, July/August 2006, http://www.lajicarita.org/06julaug.htm.

28. Kay Matthews, "Taos Regional Water Plan: Nearing Finalization," *La*

Jicarita News, November 2006, http://www.lajicarita.org/06nov.htm.

29. Kay Matthews, "Editorial: Taos Regional Water Plan Hijacked by the Powers That Be," *La Jicarita News*, March 2008, http://www.lajicarita.org/08mar.htm#editorial.

30. Taos County Document Center, Committee on Public Welfare Impacts of Water Appropriations and Changes in Point of Diversion, http://www.taoscounty.org/index.php/government/document-center/file/220-committee-on-public-welfare.

31. Kay Matthews and Mark Schiller, "Acequias Confront Forest Service Over Access Rights," *La Jicarita News,* April 2009, http://www.lajicarita.org/09apr.htm#acequias.

32. Arellano, Anselmo, "Acequias de las Sierras and Early Agriculture in the Mora Valley," *Center for Land Grant Studies*, http://southwestbooks.org/unpublished.htm.

33. Ebright, Malcolm. "Making Water Run Uphill," *New Mexico Historical Review*. Volume 92, Number 2, Spring 2017.

34. Matthews, Kay, *Culture Clash: Environmental Politics in New Mexico Forest Communities*. Santa Fe: Sunstone Press, 2016.

35. Kay Matthews, "Water Updates," *La Jicarita News,* August 2008, http://www.lajicarita.org/08aug.htm#waterupdates.

36. Allen Best, "Are Some Strings Being Pulled to Develop Wolf Creek Village?" *La Jicarita News* (reprinted from *Colorado Central*), May 2006, http://www.lajicarita.org/06may.htm#wolfcreek.

37. Cecile Rohwedder, "Louis Bacon Tries to Turn Around Taos Ski Valley," *Wall Street Journal*, April 2014, http://www.wsj.com/articles/SB10001424052702304311204579507651771533522.

38. Andy Stiny, "The new king of the mountain: Taos Ski Valley's new owner is mega-rich and an advanced skier," *Albuquerque Journal*, February 2014,http://www.abqjournal.com/349429/the-new-king-of-the-mountain-taos-ski-valleys-new-owner-is-mega-rich-and-an-advanced-skier.html.

39. Jason Blevins, "Billionaire Louis Bacon Battles ranch from big utilities solar power plans," *The Denver Post*, July 2017, http://www.denverpost.com/2010/11/26/billionaire-louis-bacon-battles-to-protect-his-ranch-from-big-utilities-solar-power-plans/.

40.https://lrgadjudication.nmcourts.gov/index.php/admin/unpublished-docs/reports/1896-april-amended-2016-monthly-adjudication-report/img0097.pdf).

41. Lynn Montgomery, "Water Crisis Demands a Better Balance," *Sandoval Signpost*, February 2013, http://www.sandovalsignpost.com/feb13/html/eco-beat.html#d.

42. Hall, Em, *High and Dry: The Texas-New Mexico Struggle for the Pecos River.* Albuquerque: University of New Mexico Press, 2002.

43. Correia, David, "The Future of the Commons: Imagining a Future New Mexico Without the Forest Service, *La Jicarita*, August 2012, https://lajicarita.wordpress.com/2012/08/17/the-future-of-the-commons-imagining-a-future-new-mexico-without-the-forest-service/.

44. Mark Schiller, "State Legislature Considers Strengthening Acequia Autonomy, *La Jicarita News*, March 2003, http://www.lajicarita.org/03mar.htm.

45. Kay Matthews, "San Miguel County Ready to Regulate Oil and Gas Development," *La Jicarita*, September 2013, https://lajicarita.wordpress.com/2013/09/17/san-miguel-county-ready-to-regulate-oil-and-gas-development/.

46. Bill Whaley, *Taos Friction*, www.taosfriction.com.

47. Norman Gaume, April 2014, http://www.gilaconservation.org/wp/wp-content/uploads/2014/06/2014-04-30-Gaume-testimony-c.pdf.

48. Southwestern New Mexico Audubon and Gila Native Plant Society Position Paper on Protection of the Gila River, http://protectthegila.org/wp-content/uploads/2014/01/SWNMAudubon-GNPS-Position-Paper_2.pdf.

49. Staci Matlock, "Water deal could ease tensions between counties," *Santa Fe New Mexican*, March 2015, http://www.santafenewmexican.com/news/local_news/water-deal-could-ease-tensions-between-counties/article_2ae94021-88d0-5931-ab3b-20f840356224.html.

50. Augustin Plains Ranch, LLC, http://sanaugustinwater.com/.

51. Kay Matthews, "The Political Economy of Acequias From Democratic Communalism to Business as Usual," *La Jicarita*, May 2015, https://lajicarita.wordpress.com/2012/05/20/the-political-economy-of-acequias-from-democratic-communalism-to-business-as-usual/.

52. Kay Matthews, "New Mexico Farming & Gardening Expo: A Cele-

bration of Growing Food," *La Jicarita News*, March 2004, http://www.lajicarita.org/04mar.htm#expo.

53. Cultural Energy, Samuel Lopez, September 23, 2016http://www.culturalenergy.org/listenlinks.htm.

54. *Society of Professional Journalists, Black Hole Award*, http://www.spj.org/blackhole.asp.

55. George Sibley, "On the Ground—Are We Part of a City-State," *Colorado Central Magazine*, July 2014, http://cozine.com/2014-july/ground-part-city-state/.

www.ingramcontent.com/pod-product-compliance
Lightning Source LLC
Chambersburg PA
CBHW032122020426
42334CB00016B/1043